OUT OF THE SHADOWS

OUT OF THE SHADOWS

Portugal from Revolution to the Present Day

NEILL LOCHERY

BLOOMSBURY
LONDON · OXFORD · NEW YORK · NEW DELHI · SYDNEY

Bloomsbury Continuum
An imprint of Bloomsbury Publishing Plc

50 Bedford Square   1385 Broadway
London   New York
WC1B 3DP   NY 10018
UK   USA

www.bloomsbury.com

Bloomsbury, Continuum and the Diana logo are trademarks of Bloomsbury Publishing Plc

First published 2017

British Library Cataloguing-in-Publication Data
A catalogue record for this book is available from the British Library.

Library of Congress Cataloguing-in-Publication data has been applied for.

ISBN: HB: 978-1-4729-3420-8
EPDF: 978-1-4729-3418-5
EPUB: 978-1-4729-3421-5

2 4 6 8 10 9 7 5 3 1

Printed and bound in Great Britain by CPI Group (UK) Ltd, Croydon CR0 4YY

To find out more about our authors and books visit www.bloomsbury.com.
Here you will find extracts, author interviews, details of forthcoming
events and the option to sign up for our newsletters.

For Emma, Benjamin and Hélèna with love

Contents

Introduction

'Lisbon and Portugal's best days are behind them' is a common theme put forward by writers who focus their attentions on the golden eras of the Portuguese discoverers, the Empire and the role of Lisbon as a major Atlantic power. In writing this book about the first 40 years of post-authoritarian democratic Portugal, following the 25 April Revolution in 1974, I have tried to keep an open mind about the political and economic difficulties that have blighted the country's development since 1974.

In doing this, I do not accept that the country is suffering from an inevitable decline, or that its current status as the poor man of Europe is permanent. Instead, I have tried to focus on the themes that run throughout the four decades of democracy that help explain why the present-day Portugal is struggling to find its place in Europe, the wider world and the global economy. Many of the mistakes that have been made since 1974 have been repeated over and over again by political leaders from both the major parties, with their preference for short-term fix over long-term meaningful reform.

From the outset, it was clear to me that this was not simply going to be a book about Portugal. One of the major failings in understanding the post-Revolution era has been the over-concentration on domestic over international factors in helping shape its story.

Even during the period of the authoritarian Estado Novo from 1933 to 1974, when Portugal was largely cut off from the outside world, relations with the United States, Great Britain and the rest of Europe were important in shaping the domestic narrative. International wars have also been central to the development of Portugal: the First World War, the Second World War and the Cold War all had implications, good and bad, for the country.

The Portuguese Revolution, and the resulting fight to establish a democratic state, did not take place in isolation from the international world. The reasons for the Revolution might very well have been domestically motivated, but the consequences of its outcome most certainly did not stop at Portugal's borders. The Revolution took place at the height of the Cold War, less than a year after the 1973 Arab-Israeli War, and at the same time that the United States was slowly losing a war in Vietnam.

It also came in an era when the United States and the Soviet Union sat at the top of a bipolar international system in which they competed for clients and influence. Neither the United States nor the Soviet Union were going to stand idly by and watch the post-Revolution struggle in Portugal simply as bystanders.

The United States, in particular, viewed the Revolution as a strategic threat to its interests in Europe, both in terms of the risk of losing Portugal to the Soviet Union, and in the potential domino effect of this on the rest of Southern and Western Europe. So a central theme in my book highlights foreign influences on the Portuguese story, starting with the response of the United States and the Western powers to the Revolution and the struggle between democracy and communism that defined the first stage of the post-Revolution era.

In outlining the events of 25 April 1974 from an international perspective, I have been lucky enough to make use of papers recently declassified in the National Archives of the United States and Great Britain. By piecing together the material it has been possible to create a narrative that illustrates the initially confused nature of the responses to developments in Lisbon. It highlights the deep divisions in the administration of President Richard Nixon over the best course of action to take to ensure that 'Portugal did not turn red'.

The rest of the book follows a similar pattern, by using documentary sources to portray the development of Portugal in an international context from the Revolution, to European Community (EC) membership, to the bailout, and beyond. Portugal's long and winding road to EC membership served as another key example of the role of external powers in shaping the Portuguese narrative. Many European leaders were initially, at best, nervous at letting Portugal, and the two other poor states of Europe (Greece and Spain), join what was known as the 'rich club' of Europe.

It was only after thorny, protracted negotiations that the three were allowed to join. Portuguese proposed entry was tied up for a long time in debates about EU enlargement and the complex Spanish-EU negotiations. In other words, the story of Portugal's accession was not a stand-alone narrative. The intention has been to avoid producing a book that merely revisits old ground in modern Portuguese history: rather it tries to add something new, and more three-dimensional, to contemporary Portuguese history.

The writing of modern history produces unique challenges for the historian. Most democratic countries have what is known as the '30-year rule'. During this period documents are locked away from the public, and this makes it difficult to obtain the information needed to produce a meaningful account of events that took place from 30 years ago to the present day. This problem often prevents historians from attempting to write major historical works until at least 30 years have passed, and the documents have been declassified and released in the respective national archives.

In writing this book, however, I navigated around this problem by requesting specific British diplomatic papers under the Freedom of Information Act (FIA). I was fortunate enough to be able to obtain the release of the documents that I requested, and it is those documents that are used in this book. The quality of these papers, and the new light they cast on key events, personalities and economic issues, have made this book a great pleasure to write. For me, it was akin to learning a new story that, at times, ran parallel to the one I knew, and at other points took the narrative off into completely new and previously uncharted territory.

Two points of caution need to be noted here: first, there are still more documents that need to be released in order to obtain a complete picture of some of the key events. For example, when the United States Secretary of State, Henry Kissinger, promised to turn Portugal into the next Chile (where the CIA had effectively plotted the overthrow of the government), how serious was his intent? Was he merely having a temper tantrum, as he often did while under great stress, or was he deadly serious? Or did other members of the Nixon administration, and the US intelligence service, talk Kissinger out of following a 'regime change' strategy for Portugal? Key CIA files on this area remain locked away, with only a selective range of documents being released.

Secondly, there is always the possibility that documents from foreign sources that make assessments about Portugal might turn out to be inaccurate in their analysis, or simply misinformed. Having spent a great deal of time perusing the documents from the United States and Great Britain on the period immediately preceding the 25 April Revolution, I see that neither country had any real understanding of the political temperature in Lisbon.

The US Embassy in Lisbon's assessment of the political situation in Lisbon during the winter and spring months of 1973 and 1974 turned out to be very wide of the mark. A low-level ambassador in the twilight of his diplomatic career, poor-quality junior diplomats and minimal intelligence staff represented a toxic mixture, which led to the Americans being effectively blind to developments in Lisbon during this crucial period.

That said, for the most part, in the preceding 40 years the British documentary sources, in particular, have been accurate, well informed and beautifully written. To this extent, they have been an enormous help in piecing together the narrative of Portugal and its interaction with the outside world.

One or two lines in each of the documents released have had the famous black marker pen of the Foreign Office run through them. This has been done in order to avoid publishing information that might embarrass a third party (a Portuguese leader). For the most part, the sentences that have been withheld from publication contain references to alleged financial, political and sexual scandals committed by unnamed individuals.

I have tried to avoid using the traditional intellectual crutch of the contemporary historian of conducting interviews with key leaders and other public figures. Given the sadly polemical nature of Portuguese politics, I felt that this would not achieve very much. Moreover, given that many of these public figures are still active in politics, or other related areas, I believed that there was too much danger of 'political colouring' in their responses to me (something I have experienced in some of my previous works related to other parts of the world).

Portugal is a small country, with a small elite (part of which has not really changed since the Estado Novo), and the interaction between this band of brothers is often difficult for an outsider to follow, or fully understand. I have lost count of the times that I have uttered 'Really?' or 'I didn't know that' when a Portuguese friend has told me that X is related to Y, or that A used to be married to B, who is the cousin of C. The impact of these closely intertwined relationships among the members of the political and economic elites is an important tool in comprehending some decisions, or events, that have no other logical explanation.

The writing of this book has been made all the more pleasurable for me by my own connection to Lisbon and to Portugal. My personal journey towards this book started back in 1985 when I arrived in Lisbon for the very first time, armed only with a pocket guidebook of the city and a hopelessly out-of-date history book, ironically entitled *A New History of Portugal*. The date, to be precise, was 27 September 1985, and my arrival in Lisbon coincided with an important historical event in the city, the opening of the Amoreiras Shopping Centre.

Young Lisboetas were rightly proud of the city's first shopping centre, explaining excitedly to me that it had everything I would need, including a cinema complex, which offered late-night showings of the latest Hollywood blockbusters. The opening of

Amoreiras, and the construction of luxury high-rise apartments in the same area, struck me as representing the birth of the new Lisbon, and I wondered about the seeming incompatibility of this 'new Lisbon' with the older parts of the city.

While I wandered around the shopping centre in the evenings, I spent the daytime exploring the areas that my guidebook referred to as downtown Lisbon. What hit me most about the centre of the city was the elegant beauty of the buildings, which were often obscured by layers of soot from pollution and by decades of poor upkeep. Perhaps the best example of what I saw back in 1985 was Rossio train station, the exterior of which was blackened and looked rather shabby.

On closer inspection, however, I could see that this was a building of great style, and its upper floor offered panoramic views of the city. From the various *miradouros*, or viewing areas, the city below resembled a film set from a bygone era of black-and-white movies. Above all I was struck by the fact that Lisbon was not only a very Portuguese city, but also a city that was poised to be transformed into something very different, as the opening of the city's first shopping centre appeared to confirm.

On 1 January 1986, Portugal joined the European Community, and parts of the city started to change, slowly at first but then with greater speed, as it hosted two important international events: Expo '98 and the Euro 2004 football championship. I had long since left the city for the choppy waters of the Middle East before these two events took place, but I had promised myself that I would return one day to write about the city, which had seduced me during the early years of my professional career.

Returning in 2007, and visiting frequently ever since, I have been a personal witness to many of the events that are described in this book. I watched the descent of the country into near economic liquidation, and could hear the demonstrations outside the National Assembly from an apartment at the top of the hill in the Lapa district of the city. I can recall the drama of the announcement on television that Portugal would require a bailout, and the endless blame games that followed the announcement.

When I began to write about Portugal, I chose to write first about the period of the Estado Novo, and my previous two books chronicle this era in modern political history. For me as a writer, it was important to have an understanding of what came before the democratic period that I personally experienced and witnessed during my time in the city. Having done that, I felt ready and able to write about what was, for me personally, living history.

Being a witness to history brings the potential problem of how this can cloud the judgement of the writer, as his own personal recollections can stand in the way of his objectivity. This is why, wherever possible, I have used documentary sources, as well as other people's accounts of the events described in this book. My own personal witness has been limited to adding background description to the narrative. In doing this, I hope to have avoided telling the story through my own eyes, expressing it rather through the lens of a more detached observer.

I hope that you, the reader, take from this book an understanding of the importance of Portugal to the recent past, its relevance to the present day and its future significance to the European continent. With importance, however, comes increased scrutiny. As I have written in the book, international scrutiny of this small country did not end when the officials of the Troika, responsible for monitoring Portugal's compliance with the terms of the bailout programme, departed from the country for the last time in 2014. Presently, the outside world is closely monitoring developments in Lisbon and the rest of Portugal.

In April 1974, however, it was a completely different story.

Prologue

On the evening of 24 April 1974, the outside world was not looking closely at mainland Europe's most westerly capital city. At twilight, as the light softened in the stormy skies above Lisbon and was replaced by the shadowy glow of street lamps, everything appeared normal in Portugal's city of light.

Despite difficulties caused by the economic crisis, and the ongoing wars in Portugal's colonies, there seemed to be little prospect of any immediate collapse of the authoritarian government led by Marcello José das Neves Alves Caetano. The rather dour and bureaucratic prime minister had ruled the country since ill health had forced his predecessor, the wily doctor, António de Oliveira Salazar, from office in 1968.

The Estado Novo had been in place since 1933, and despite its growing unpopularity with many Portuguese, it appeared to be so entrenched in power that it would take forces of considerable strength to dislodge it. True, there had already been an uprising of sorts when, between 15 and 16 March 1974, junior officers in the Fifth Infantry Regiment based at Caldas da Rainha had taken senior officers captive.

Under threat of bombing, however, they had eventually surrendered and some 200 junior officers were arrested. On 24 April, with the internal opposition deeply divided or imprisoned, foreign embassies in the city felt that there was little prospect of any political drama or upheaval in the foreseeable future.

In Lisbon, the noises of the evening rush-hour traffic could be heard throughout the city: the constant tooting of car horns, the bells of blocked trams and the screech of brakes as drivers performed emergency stops at junctions. With darkness came a slightly quieter city, as Lisboetas settled down to watch the news on RTP, which in 1974 was the lone television broadcaster in Portugal.

In the district of Lapa, home to most of the foreign embassies, all was quiet. A famously upmarket area, favoured by foreign embassies not only because of its proximity to the Parliament, but also because many of its buildings had stunning views down the steep hill to the River Tagus and beyond, to the dormitory towns and cities dotted along the southern bank of the river.

Locally, Lapa was also well known for the large amount of dog droppings that soiled its streets, and for the near impossibility of getting a parking spot on its overcrowded roads. The diplomatic community in Lapa was a small one, and most of the senior diplomats and staff knew one another from the usual round of social events. It was also a gossipy community and rumours, both false and genuine, were prone to spread like wildfire around Lapa when there was scandal or a major political development.

On the evening of 24 April, however, there appeared little to discuss or gossip about. Inside the British Embassy building on Rua de São Domingos several British officials were listening to the BBC radio commentary of the Atlético Madrid versus Glasgow Celtic European Cup semi-final.[1] Celtic went on to lose the game 2–0, and went out of the competition that was eventually won, for the first time, by Bayern Munich. The match marked the end of Celtic's time as a dominant power in European football, which had started when they won the European Cup in Lisbon in 1967.

Following the game, the diplomatic wires that were set up in the communications room were all quiet and the lights of the Embassy did not burn brightly late into the night. Embassy staff checked the wires one last time before informing the Ambassador, Sir Nigel Trench, that it was a 'full lid' – meaning that there would be no foreseeable major developments overnight.

A couple of blocks up the steep hill, which the number 25 trams climbed with difficulty at full throttle, was the residence of the United States Ambassador. That building was also quiet except for the presence of a couple of DGS (Direcção-Geral de Segurança) agents at the end of the street.[2] The Ambassador, Stuart Nash Scott, was in the twilight years of his diplomatic career. On the evening of 24 April 1974, Scott was not in his residence in Lisbon. Instead, he was visiting the US base in the Azores.[3] It was a routine visit for the Ambassador, and increasingly typical of his activities in Portugal.

Back in Washington DC, the Secretary of State was focusing on the Vietnam War, which the Americans were slowly and painfully losing, and on efforts for pushing US interests in the other theatres of the Cold War. Following the crisis surrounding the use of the Azores air base by US Air Force planes as part of the resupply route for US equipment bound for Israel during the 1973 Yom Kippur War, Kissinger had felt vindicated in taking a strong line towards Lisbon. The impact of the US military airlift to Israel on the eventual outcome of the war remains hotly debated by scholars of the Arab-Israeli conflict.[4] From Kissinger's perspective, 'little Portugal' was the only European country that complied with American requests for help.

In Washington, there was a feeling within the State Department that the eventual capitulation of the Portuguese government, led by Marcello Caetano, to the demands made by President Richard Nixon over the use of the Azores base in 1973 was an illustration of the influence that the Americans exerted over the Portuguese. Put simply, Lisbon had very little choice but to follow the lead of the United States in the bipolar international political system that characterized the Cold War era.

The outbreak of the Yom Kippur War took Israel completely by surprise, owing to the systematic failings of its intelligence services to provide a clear assessment of the military and political situation in Egypt and Syria. In the case of the Portuguese Revolution both the British and US intelligence services failed to foresee the events that came to be known as the Carnation Revolution of 25 April 1974.

Put simply, the US and British intelligence agencies were oblivious to the quiet winds of change that swept through Portugal during the first part of 1974. One of the main reasons for this failure appeared to be the deeply held belief that Portugal was a hugely hierarchical society, and that any change would come from individuals or groups within the existing elites in Lisbon.

Britain, Portugal's oldest ally, kept a close annual watch and record of the leading personalities in Portuguese society. The report was written by Embassy officials and was passed on to the Foreign Office, and from Whitehall it was circulated to the British intelligence agencies. The report was a little eccentric, a mix of local gossip together with a dose of where the political and international allegiances of its list of key Portuguese characters lay.

The list included profiles of the leading members of the opposition forces, the major economic families, and key military and political leaders. Naturally, the British assessment was that any major political or military moves to end the Estado Novo would originate from one or more individuals who were on the British list of key personalities.

The Americans adopted a similar elite approach. Diplomats, and the few CIA agents who were left at the Embassy, wined and dined the elite of Portuguese society at official functions such as the annual Fourth of July Independence Day party at the Ambassador's residence, or more informally at smaller events held in Lisbon's famous five-star haunts such as the Ritz and Tivoli hotels.

International journalists who visited the city during the early 1970s adopted a similar approach, rarely venturing beyond the bars and restaurants of the centre of Lisbon. Interviews were conducted with both official members of the government and the leading members of the elite of the Estado Novo.

Even those journalists who used Lisbon as a stepping-stone to longer trips to cover the wars in Portugal's colonies did not really interact with anyone else other than the local elite. Naturally, the coverage in the US and British media, particularly in the newspapers, reflected this. Put simply, nobody really understood the grievances, the debates and the struggles that were under way in Portugal during the long winter and early spring of 1973–4.

Equally importantly, the British and the Americans failed to identify or understand who the key players were to be in the Revolution. So strong was the American belief that nothing was amiss in Portugal in the first part of 1974, that the CIA gave serious consideration to closing down its station in Portugal altogether.[5]

One man who did appear on the radar of both the Americans and the British was General António Sebastião Ribeiro de Spínola, 'a vain autocratic officer of the old school, but with considerable charm', according to the British.[6] Although Spínola spoke no English, the publication of his book *Portugal and the Future* in February 1974, advocating a political solution to Portugal's colonial wars, was seen as the best prospect for political change in both Lisbon and the Portuguese colonies.[7]

The influence of the book within Portuguese society was profound in offering an alternative vision to the status quo of continued war and lack of meaningful political reform at home. The book rapidly elevated Spínola to the leading internal dissenter, and as a result of opposition from far-right-wing members of the government he was removed from his post in March 1974 as Vice-Chief of the Defence Staff to which he had been appointed in January 1974.

At the time of the publication of Spínola's book, the Americans were in the process of once again negotiating continued access to the air base in the Azores. In Washington, State Department officials were curious to understand how the book would impact upon Portuguese society. Would it really lead to major changes in Portugal's policies towards its colonies? And how would any negotiated solution to the colonial wars leave the Estado Novo and calls for a speedier pace of political reform in Lisbon?

Nobody appeared to have the answer to either of these questions, but the publication of Spínola's book appeared to give credence to the belief that there was a possibility that political change in Portugal and the colonies might just originate from within the established order in Lisbon.

The outside world, as a result, devoted a significant amount of time to watching and listening to Spínola. He was viewed as the litmus test for potential for political upheaval in the country. This, of course, fitted well with the belief that there was little sign of any political upheaval having its origins away from the established elites in the urban centres of the country.

The events of 25 April 1974, as a result, came as a surprise not only to most Portuguese but to the outside world as well. The fact that the outside world was not prepared for 25 April, and did not have plans in place to respond to the events, explains much of the muddled response to the Revolution and to the political mess that followed the historic day. Or, as the British put it, 'the corporate state [Estado Novo] gave way to an unstable free for all'.[8]

So on the night of 24 April, as the lights of the Embassies were turned off in Lapa and Restelo and diplomatic staff made their way to their residences, none of the diplomatic corps had an inkling of the events that were to unfold the following day.

Meanwhile, further up the River Tagus, a group of disaffected junior officers were plucking up the courage to drive to Lisbon to topple the government and bring to an end the Estado Novo. Their actions would transform not only Portugal, but the Portuguese colonies as well. Within a short period of time the Portuguese Empire would be lost for ever and the country would face a difficult search to find a place among the nations of the world.

The story of Lisbon's shift into the modern world started on 25 April 1974, but the transformation to a democratic nation with a healthy civil and political society would prove harder to achieve than removing the old authoritarian system. The outside world, especially the Europeans, offered Lisbon enormous support in trying to achieve the lofty aims of pushing the country into the modern world. At times, however, this help became more of a hindrance, and prevented democratic Portugal from maturing into a modern state.

PART ONE

Children of the Revolution

I

Revolution

It was nearly all over before breakfast. As revolutions go, this was a most un-dramatic, and near bloodless one. The plotters sneaked into Lisbon under the cover of the foggy dawn light, and experiencing only minimal opposition, moved quickly to seize the key points in the city. The Salazar Bridge over the River Tagus was cut off at both ends, TV and radio channels were taken over and Lisbon airport was closed. The only tangible opposition came from the secret police headquarters where shots were exchanged.

By April 1974, there was not much strong support left for Caetano. Most of the support that the regime had enjoyed was based on the strong patronage networks that existed in the country after four decades of authoritarian rule. The refusal of other parts of the armed forces to take up arms against the plotters ensured that Caetano could do little other than offer an orderly surrender of himself and his government to the revolutionary forces. As in most successful coups, success depends largely on achieving tactical and operational surprise over the existing regime and their supporters. The plotters clearly achieved both of these requirements.

Given the centrality of Lisbon to the political life of Portugal, once the city was taken over the rest of the country followed. As the foreign ambassadors in Lisbon awoke and headed for their embassies in Lapa, the city was already largely under the control of the plotters. It was not only the Caetano regime that was taken by surprise by the events of 25 April; the British and US Embassies had no information that a coup was about to happen.

Later, when American and British diplomats wrote their exhaustive accounts of the events leading up to the coup, and the day itself, they shifted the focus of these narratives to indicate that they had foreseen the events of 25 April. They had not.[1] Moreover, they had no idea of the identities of most of the leaders of the Revolution, nor any intelligence information about them.

An additional complication for the Americans was that its Ambassador, Stuart Nash Scott, was visiting the Azores, and with Lisbon airport closed, he was unable to return to Portugal. Instead, in a curious move, he decided to continue with his original plan to attend a reunion at Harvard University.[2] This decision, as well as the lack of reliable intelligence material coming out of the Embassy in Lisbon, did not endear him to the US Secretary of State, Henry Kissinger.

Rarely in modern political history has it appeared to be so easy to remove a regime that had ruled a country for over 40 years. The revolutionaries mixed good organization and planning with a healthy dose of amateurs' luck. With the benefit of hindsight it is not difficult to understand how the outside world misunderstood Portuguese politics in 1974. The army officers who were known as the Armed Forces Movement (MFA – Movimento das Forças Armadas) acted partly out of 'democratic idealism and partly as a result of professional grievances'.[3]

General Spínola had proven to be an important catalyst in the fall of the Caetano regime, but his role in the actual events of 25 April was largely restricted to accepting the surrender of Caetano, who was holed up in the police station at the Largo do Carmo, surrounded by large crowds. Caetano was subsequently secretly escorted away from the building and eventually settled in Brazil.

The coup went like clockwork and was greeted with a sense of euphoria by the vast majority of the Portuguese population. Lisboetas poured out on to the streets, with children playing next to the soldiers who continued to guard the city's main thoroughfares. On the surface, there appeared to be an almost carnival atmosphere.

There were, however, instances of score settling, usually against people suspected of being informants of the secret police.

The threat of intimidation and violence was never far away, particularly in the city's working-class suburbs. No revolution is ever completely free of these factors, and the Portuguese Revolution certainly contained more than its fair share of threats. Fearing the worst, several members of the city's super-wealthy families fled, either on the day of the Revolution, or immediately afterwards.

In the aftermath of the coup all political prisoners were released. Exiled political leaders such as Mário Soares (leader of the Portuguese Socialist Party) and Álvaro Cunhal (leader of the Portuguese Communist Party) returned to Portugal. Crucially, censorship was abolished and there was an explosion of political activity from all sides of the political spectrum.[4] Despite his complete lack of any meaningful political experience, General Spínola was installed as the provisional President.

His appointment was initially a popular one for many Portuguese, and also for the NATO powers. At first, in the heady days following the Revolution, there appeared to be real prospects for a successful and smooth political transition to the post-Revolution era. Sadly, this did not happen, and the Revolution eventually tore the country apart and came close to plunging it into what would have proved a disastrous and bloody civil war.

Traditionally, it is the winners, and not the losers, who get to write the official narrative of wars and revolutions, and the Portuguese Revolution of 25 April 1974 was no exception to the rule. There are two major myths surrounding the Revolution that have grown in the 40 years since what were described by the British as the 'cataclysmic' events of April 1974.[5] The first surrounds the assumption that the Revolution was a solely Portuguese affair – it was not. The international implications of the Revolution for the western flank of NATO meant that there was a large international dimension to events before, during and immediately following the Revolution.

The second myth was that it was a dramatic and swift break with the past achieved against the odds, and that the Revolution was a one-day affair – it was not. In reality, the revolutionary period lasted for nearly two years. As in most revolutions, getting rid of the old system was the easy part, but planning what came next turned out to be much harder. As Nigel Trench put it, 'the shock of the release was great'. He went on to warn, however, 'there was virtually no violence; but after half a century of submission to an authoritarian system, few of the new rulers had any clear idea of how to operate the democratic system which they had advocated so enthusiastically.'[6]

The organization of the new state was made all the more complicated by the deep divisions within the ranks of the winners of the Revolution. It would be superficial to suggest that this was merely a classic case of a confrontation between socialism and communism. There were major disagreements within the two camps over both ideology and tactics for achieving and retaining power in the post-Revolution state.

Nor is it possible to use classic civil–military explanations to highlight the divisions. The military did not make a serious bid for political power in the post-Revolution period, and most of the brave junior officers who overthrew the Estado Novo were soon pushed into the political wilderness.

To make matters worse, the Revolution weakened the Portuguese economy, which was already in deep crisis. After the coup, and after nearly 50 years of strict control of industrial relations, things rapidly got out of hand. There was a wave of strikes and demonstrations in the early summer of 1974, which centred upon unrealistic wage claims. Many companies, fearful of the new power of the workers, simply gave in to these claims and subsequently went bankrupt.[7]

A loss of confidence in the economy led to heavy withdrawals from bank accounts as people looked to protect their assets. The political uncertainty, and the lack of any coherent and clear economic policy on the part of the post-Revolution rulers, led to further macro-economic difficulties.[8] Put simply, the Revolution weakened the Portuguese economy and this added fire to the political crisis.

The change of regime in Portugal was, at first, almost universally welcomed abroad and led to a swift end to the country's diplomatic isolation that had existed since the start of the colonial wars. As the British suggested, it also provided Portugal with new foreign policy options. Writing at the end of 1974, the Ambassador put it:

> In the context of East-West relations, Portugal moved away
> from a position of implacable anti-Communism and quickly
> established diplomatic relations with the Soviet bloc. By the
> end of the year, trade, cultural and transport agreements had
> been concluded with a number of these countries. The govern-
> ment continued, however, to assert their loyalty to the Atlantic
> Alliance. This was no longer a source of embarrassment to other
> members of NATO, but it was clear among the new rulers in
> Lisbon there were differences of opinion about the value of
> membership.[9]

This viewpoint put forward by the British did not tell the full story. In the new post-Revolution Portuguese government there were Communists, and this caused widespread dismay among the Western European powers. Given that the Portuguese Communist Party was quite open about its strong political and economic ties with the Soviet Union, it was seen as a bridge too far by many Europeans.

For the United States, allowing Communists into the Portuguese government was simply something that should not be accepted, and Henry Kissinger's strategy was to try to force them out of government – and once out, to exclude them permanently from holding power. The Nixon administration, as a result, devoted a great deal of attention and resources towards achieving this aim in Lisbon.

With superpower involvement in the politics of post-Revolution Portugal, it proved to be hugely difficult for moderate Portuguese leaders, such as General Spínola, to navigate the tricky line of trying to develop a national political consensus that could produce a government capable of running the country. According to British scholar Kenneth Maxwell, 'Spínola's attempt to buy peace at home succeeded only in buying him hostility abroad from friends whose support he would need if he were to survive.'[10]

Both European and American leaders were so fearful of having Communist members of the government that they overlooked what Spínola personally represented, which was moderation and gradual change in the key areas of the economy and the colonies. In truth, given the deck of cards that Portugal's first post-Revolution leader was dealt, it would have taken a politician of great experience and skill to be able to manage the seemingly divergent interests of internal Portuguese politics and the demands of the outside world.

For all his importance as a catalyst and a symbolic figure of the Revolution, Spínola was not a wily politician, nor was he worldly wise. A more experienced and internationally astute leader would not have misunderstood and underestimated the reaction of Kissinger and what he saw as the communist threat to NATO's western flank.

A wiser leader would have noted the Nixon administration's reaction to the election of Salvador Allende in Chile in 1970 and the US-supported coup in 1973, which removed him from power. During this period, the Nixon administration worked to cut off US aid and to help finance and support Chilean opposition groups. At no time did Kissinger reconcile himself to the legitimacy or even the existence of the Allende government.

Heavily distracted by his attempts to find consensus at home, Spínola failed to develop a worldview. Surrounded by advisors who emphasized the special Portuguese nature of the Revolution, he failed to see how the Americans plotted to put Portugal on the defensive. Kissinger highlighted the importance of the base on the Azores and the fear of a European domino effect, particularly in the Southern European countries of Italy and Greece.

Kissinger made it clear that he had little time for the Socialist Party leader, Mário Soares, who he consistently argued would be outflanked by the Communists. In a meeting with European leaders, Kissinger gave a blunt assessment of Soares:

I am just not impressed by Soares. He is the classical socio-logical type of victim. He won't win. He will always be a day

too late or make a speech in the wrong place. Our aid won't
help Soares. You have said that the real decisions will be made
in the next few months, but I ask: what sort of decisions?
Existing parties will be suppressed. The Communists will win
or some left-wing dictator who will follow the Communist
line.[11]

America's emphasis on Portugal's role in global politics mysteri-
ously shifted from it being termed as an Atlantic Power to being
seen as part of the Mediterranean bloc. The US military made it
clear that, given that Portugal was no longer a trusted member of
NATO, key security documents were no longer shared with Lisbon.
The Portuguese responded to all of this by adopting a more 'hard-
headed than before' stance over negotiations on the continuation
of American access to the Azores.[12]

As the summer heat in Lisbon gave way to the cooler autumn air
there was still no let-up in the political intrigues and infighting that
characterized the post-Revolution period. With the end of censorship, Lisboetas were treated to a much wider variety of opinions
and information published in the daily newspapers.

Much of the speculation that swirled round the city concerned
the future of General Spínola and his attempts to provide leadership
to the country. His efforts appeared more and more to be doomed,
with opposition to his position becoming ever more vocal. In truth,
it came as little surprise to the outside world when Spínola resigned
from office on 30 September 1974.

By this point, it was fairly clear that Spínola was out of step
with the trends of government policy, especially towards the colonies. He had flirted with the conservative 'silent majority' with the
intention of trying to reassert his diminishing authority over
the government.[13] The Communists calculated, correctly, that if
this move succeeded, their own position would be greatly weakened, and they mobilized all their resources against any show of
popular support for General Spínola.[14]

Lacking the full support of the military, and keen to avoid a
potential slide into civil war, Spínola resigned from office. His

supporters in the government followed him out of office. What came after, to the horror of the Nixon administration, was, as the British described: 'Most of the newly resurgent right-wing parties were then banned on the pretext of a highly unconvincing "counter revolutionary plot" and a number of prominent conservatives were arrested and held without trial for a time.'[15]

It soon transpired, however, that most of those arrested were quickly released without publicity.[16] In the meantime, General Costa Gomes had replaced Spínola as the new President. General Gomes was regarded as being more in tune with the sentiments of the revolutionary movement.[17]

As the internal political divisions in Lisbon deepened over the latter part of 1974 and into early 1975, US concerns over Portugal's direction continued to grow. The resignation of President Nixon on 9 August 1974 over the Watergate scandal, and his replacement by Vice-President Gerald Ford, did not lead to any immediate change in US policy towards Lisbon. The administration in Washington was becoming ever more alarmed that Portugal might be lost to the Communists.

At a breakfast meeting, starting at 7.45 a.m. at the Pentagon on 22 January 1975, between Henry Kissinger and Secretary of Defence, James Schlesinger, the situation in Portugal was top of their agenda. Kissinger started off the conversation, 'We should have a programme in Portugal. There is a fifty per cent chance of losing it.'

Without any pause, Schlesinger replied, 'We have a contingency plan to take over the Azores – that would be stimulating Azores independence.'[18]

The Secretaries did not discuss any further the details of the plan to effectively occupy the Azores, and shifted the conversation on to developments in the Middle East.[19] The existence of a plan to instigate a takeover of Portuguese sovereign territory was a sign of how seriously Washington took the Portuguese internal political situation. According to Kissinger, the negotiations over the continued American use of the base in the Azores had never really got under way, owing to the political situation in Portugal.

The Portuguese did allow the United States continued access to the islands for as long as it took to reach a new deal over the base.

In subsequent meetings with the CIA heads, Kissinger was told that the chances of 'stimulating Azores independence were minimal'. The majority of the population on the islands were loyal to Portugal and the military garrison was equally loyal to the forces of the Revolution back in Lisbon. At one stage, the CIA did, however, assess the potential for using Portuguese exiled groups in Spain as a means to starting a process in which these groups would seize both the Azores and the Madeira Islands. But little came of the plan, which was quickly dismissed as dangerous and unworkable.[20]

The CIA was keen to explore other means to influence Portuguese internal politics, using its action in Chile as a model and framework. There was a fear articulated by some CIA leaders that any CIA help to the non-Communist forces in Lisbon might turn out to be counter-productive. The fear was that US aid would be leaked. On several occasions Kissinger demanded answers, and more plans, from the CIA as to how they were going to stop Portugal being lost to the Communists and their allies.[21]

Kissinger's patience with Lisbon was clearly fast running out. In a meeting with the Portuguese Foreign Minister, Ernesto Augusto de Melo Antunes, in Bonn in the spring of 1975, Kissinger took great offence at comments he attributed to Antunes that 'foreign governments (without exception) have no business making public comments – even favourable ones – about Portugal's internal politics'.[22] Kissinger's concern and irritation with the Portuguese came out in the meeting, after which he noted:

> I stated US interest in seeing an independent, democratic and prosperous Portugal, but I expressed very frankly our concern that events could lead to results that no one anticipated or wanted. I also expressed our concern over Portuguese foreign policy stating that it had become constantly anti-American and adopted a radical stance on the Third World – this had to be a problem for us.[23]

Portugal was living on borrowed time with a US Secretary of State who was famed for his ideological outlook towards the world, and also for his lack of patience with those individuals and countries that did not share his view of the world. Kissinger, however, was about to get a slap in the face from elements in Portugal who were more sympathetic to his anti-left-wing position.

2

Wish You Were Here

To complicate the situation for the Americans, a 'clumsy attempt' at a right-wing coup took place on 11 March 1975 and ended in fiasco, which led to the flight of General Spínola to Brazil and another wave of arrests of right-wing personalities.[1] The result of the coup was that the leftward trend of Portuguese politics was given a sudden shot in the arm with, much to Kissinger's annoyance, the Communists in the ascendant.

The Americans recognized that the abortive coup attempt of 11 March had discredited the parties of the centre-right and given the left the occasion for limiting the activities of centrist forces.[2] The British considered the coup something of a joke and wondered about the motives of those that took part. Nigel Trench reported back to London on the attempted coup:

> So inept was the planning and execution of the whole affair that the suspicion of PCP (communist) provocation was irresistible. Be that as it may, the result was to discredit General Spínola even in the eyes of his friends, and he and a group of followers were forced to flee the country.[3]

The failed coup was confirmation of the poor political judgement of General Spínola and vindication of Anglo-US opinion that he was not a man capable of giving Portugal the strong leadership that both countries felt was needed in Lisbon.

Portugal's first democratic election in 50 years brought better news for the members of NATO. The campaign for the Constituent Assembly elections had proved troublesome, with outbreaks of violence, which dominated the headlines and led to threat and counter-threat from one side towards the other. Election day itself on 25 April 1975 was more successful. In the eyes of the outside observers, an extremely high turnout, and the low number of spoilt ballot papers, gave a high degree of legitimacy to the result.[4]

The biggest winner in the ballot was the Socialist Party (PS), and the biggest losers were the Communists and their allies, who between them obtained only 17 per cent of the vote. The most important result, however, was that it was clear that the vast majority of the Portuguese electorate wanted a civilian government.[5] In retrospect, the election represented a crucial turning point in the conflict, but there were still many twists and turns before it was clear that Portugal was not to be governed by the Communists and the radical military.[6]

In Washington, the results were cautiously welcomed. The US Ambassador to Portugal, Frank Carlucci, who was appointed on 9 December 1974 and who had arrived in Lisbon in January 1975, entitled his report 'two cheers for democracy'.[7] He argued that while the results were a welcome boost to the anti-communist forces, they represented the start of a further period of uncertainty. He suggested: 'Two key questions now emerge from these election results: What conclusions will the AFM and the ruling Revolutionary Council draw from this moderate victory; how far and in what manner will the non-Communist winners press their victory.'[8]

This turned out to be a pretty astute assessment of the situation in Portugal. The appointment of such a senior man as Carlucci to the Embassy in Portugal had been an indication of just how seriously the United States was taking events in Lisbon. Even though the Secretary of State, Henry Kissinger, had effectively appointed him, the two men came to adopt critically different visions in dealing with the Portuguese situation.[9]

Kissinger placed Portugal well and truly within the global context of the American struggle against checking what he saw as communist global expansion. Given Portugal's membership of NATO, and the strategic value of Lisbon and the Azores Islands, he could not, and would not, accept the presence of any Communists in the Portuguese government. He saw no chance for compromise with the Communists and other far-left groups, whose agenda was clearly to turn Portugal into a non-democratic state. An ideologically driven conservative, Kissinger's low opinion of Mário Soares fitted with similar views he held on other European left-of-centre leaders.

Ambassador Carlucci, on the other hand, argued for a 'wait and see' policy. His gut feeling on the ground in Lisbon was that the forces of democracy would eventually triumph. The Americans, and in particular the CIA, should proceed with caution in trying to help foster this outcome.[10] He was in favour of small amounts of US aid to be given to pro-democratic parties and newspapers, but this was to be done through a third country.

What Carlucci feared most was that the Portuguese Communists would discover a trail that led back to the CIA. This, he believed, could damage US credibility beyond repair.[11] Clever and politically astute, Carlucci was a wily Ambassador who wasted little time in becoming well connected in Lisbon society. His, at times, heated discussions with Kissinger back in Washington centred upon tactics for achieving the result that both men wanted – the triumph of democracy over communism.

The year from 25 April 1974 to 25 April 1975 had been an historic one, with the transition from dictatorship to democracy still far from complete. Worryingly, the attitude of key members of the United States remained hostile to the Portuguese post-Revolution governments. Several Western socialist governments had provided funds to the Socialist Party (PS) in Portugal. This, they hoped, would help counter the influx of funds from the Soviet Union to the Portuguese Communist Party. Another issue was the effective communist takeover of the Portuguese media. The British estimated that in 1975 around 8 per cent of the daily press was under communist control as well as TV and radio.[12]

By the summer of 1975, the outcome of the political struggle in Portugal was still far from certain. The Revolution, which had originally been motivated by internal Portuguese conditions, now had a decidedly international feel to it, with the United States, the Western European powers and the Soviet Union all trying to influence the final outcome of the transition to a new political system.

It had been a turbulent year in Lisbon with two main unresolved issues: first, the struggle for power between the extreme left forces on the one hand, and those groups that favoured a pluralistic democracy on the other; secondly, and equally importantly, the search to define the role of the Portuguese armed forces in the new political system.[13]

With the outside world now watching Lisbon very closely, and with a new, more able US presence in the city based in the US Embassy, there was still much drama to come. There was also much suffering and tragedy to follow, as the full human cost of the Revolution started to become visible in Lisbon.

During 1975, Lisbon airport resembled an indoor Second World War transit camp. The smell of over-used and under-cleaned toilets was made all the worse by the near total lack of air conditioning in the airport. The air was thick with cigarette smoke that hung around the poorly ventilated building. The once white walls of the airport had turned grey and were in desperate need of attention. The litter bins were overflowing with half-consumed stale food that was now rotting.

Nobody seemed to know whose responsibility it was to empty the bins and to clean the mess around them where people had continued to stack rubbish. This could have been any airport in the Third World, but it wasn't. This was ugly Lisbon – in its worst post-Revolution free-for-all mess. Macho men whose overt confidence was fuelled by too much alcohol shouted instructions, while dazed airport workers did their best to make people, particularly the children, as comfortable as possible.

Both the arrival and departure lounges were crammed full of families who had left Portugal's colonies. Most carried only a carry-on case. Those that had managed to pack some possessions to put in the hold of the plane more often than not discovered that their belongings never arrived in Lisbon. Most had nowhere to go in Lisbon. With jobs lost, and financial assets seized in the colonies, their prospects were bleak. The British Embassy in Lisbon put the number of returnees at approximately 300,000 in 1975 alone.[14]

At the time of the 25 April Revolution in 1974, the population of Portugal was just under nine million, and the re-absorption of the returnees represented one of the biggest challenges of the post-Revolution era. Lisbon had not seen as many displaced persons since the flood of refugees into the city during the Second World War. In 1975, however, things were different. Unlike the war refugees, who were in temporary residence while they waited for passage out of Europe, the vast majority of the returnees were back in Lisbon – permanently.

It wasn't only the airport that was cramped to breaking point. Ships overflowing with returnees slowly chugged up the River Tagus to deposit their human cargo in the city. Not since the Second World War, when ocean liners had sailed down the river into the Atlantic Ocean carrying the refugees trying to escape the horrors of the Nazi occupation, had the Lisbon docks seen such activity. It all made for a sad picture, a snapshot that defined the brutal and sudden end of Portugal's empire and its once glorious era of seafaring discovery of the New World.

Over the summer of 1975, the piles of randomly stacked wooden crates grew around the docks area. It resembled a shanty town, a photograph of defeat for a once proud group of people. Frantic returnees searched for their crates amid the chaos, not helped by the 'could not care' attitude of the left-wing militant workers at the docks. Screams of delight could be heard from time to time as a family discovered a crate that contained some of their hastily packed possessions from their African homes.

These were the lucky ones. Many of the returnees who arrived back in Lisbon carried only photos and small mementos of their lives in the colonies. The look of bewilderment on many of their faces was an illustration of their sense of the loss of the old world, and the fear for their future in their new world back in Portugal.

The arrival of the returnees in Lisbon compounded an already difficult unemployment situation in the country, and placed further strains on Portugal's inadequate economic resources.[15] In trying to help solve the problem the Portuguese authorities sought the help of other countries, particularly in South America, to accept some of the returnees. As the British put it, their arrival added to the already 'confused political situation'.[16]

The returnees were not universally welcomed back by Portugal, which had undergone a massive political transformation. Many of them were viewed as belonging to the past and were seen as opportunists who had gone out to the colonies to work and receive salaries several times what they could earn in the motherland. In the heady days of 1975 many were accused of being fascists, and a few were even targeted by far-left gangs. In reality, the returnees were a pathetic bunch, setting up a tented village outside the National Assembly to protest against their plight.

In retrospect, the returnees represented the human cost of the Revolution. Forty years after the Revolution the scars and bitterness remain within this group. Many families did not survive the stress of effectively having to start again from scratch. Divorce rates were high. The lucky ones were able to stay with parents who had remained in Portugal. Many of the parents, however, lived in small apartments with only minimal spare space. No matter, the returned slept on sofa beds and in hallways.

The key to survival was finding a job. This proved to be no easy task for most of the returnees, who found themselves competing with hundreds of local Portuguese for a single position. Old family networks and contacts had long disappeared to be replaced by new corrupt Communist-led networks, in which party members were looked after first and given access to key positions.

The Revolution had not ended the Portuguese authorities' love affair with bureaucracy. Returnees who had worked as drivers in the colonies tried to become taxi drivers back in Lisbon, but soon found their pathways blocked by good old-fashioned red tape. Under pressure from the taxi drivers union, the government limited the number of taxi licences it issued.[17] There were long waiting lists, and the returnees were told they would have to wait their turn.

Desperate for work and tired of waiting, the cab-owning return-ees blocked access to the National Assembly and lived there in their cabs with their families.[18] With only newspapers on their windows for privacy they waited until the government backed down and agreed to issue some 650 new taxi licences, including 250 in Lisbon.[19] This represented a small victory for the returnees, but many others still struggled to find work, and several were forced to take positions that they were eminently over-qualified to fill.

There was not at this stage, however, a victim mentality among the returnees. In deliberations about potential US aid for the refu-gees (the Americans used this term) Kissinger informed President Ford, 'The refugees also have shown themselves a potent political force, willing to take political action to remedy what they see as government neglect of their needs.'[20] He went on to argue that: 'under these circumstances I believe we should increase our assis-tance to Portugal, both as a humanitarian gesture and to prevent the kind of refugee discontent which could further destabilize the new and struggling [Portuguese] government.'[21]

Kissinger also called for an increase in the air support that the Americans were offering in Angola to help get the Portuguese out of a country that was descending into near anarchy. During the autumn months of 1975, the United States increased its airlift capacity from 500 to 1,000 evacuees per day.[22] In a one-month period, US aircraft helped evacuate approximately 13,000 refugees from Angola to Portugal.[23]

In undertaking this seeming humanitarian operation, Kissinger believed that the United States was helping to politically strengthen the hand of what he termed 'the moderates' in Lisbon over the radi-cals. The US agreement to double its airlift was also predicated on assurances from Lisbon that the Portuguese military equipment in Angola would not fall into local hands.[24] As usual, Kissinger rarely gave humanitarian aid away for nothing, and Lisbon agreed to try to prevent such a scenario from occurring.

The chaos that surrounded Portuguese attempts at rapid decolo-nization was the catalyst for the human tragedy of the returnees. The British, who know a thing or two about messing up decolonization, offered its assessment of the problem. Writing back to the Foreign Office in London, Nigel Trench offered a withering assessment of the decolonization policies of the leaders in Lisbon. He wrote: 'Portuguese plans for the transition of their overseas territories to independence came disastrously to grief in 1975, and it is difficult to condone the combination of self-congratulatory incompetence and irresponsibility with which they treated the problem.'[25]

The negative economic impact of the returnees was all the greater given the extremely fragile state of the Portuguese economy and the near total absence of any coherent and fully implemented plan for dealing with the mess.[26]

Foreign economists were alarmed by the statistics coming out of Lisbon in 1975. The bottom line was that the country was said to be consuming around 30 per cent more than it was producing.[27] In short, wages rose sharply during 1975 and productivity fell sharply. Unemployment rose sharply too, reaching around half a million in the final part of the year. With nationalization of the banks and insurance companies taking place in March 1975, the state controlled around 70 per cent of the country's economic activity.[28] In 1975, however, the state lacked the administrative resources to successfully manage this large chunk of the economy.

Equally worrying was the failure of foreign companies to invest in Portugal. Foreign tourists also voted with their feet, with a number of tour companies choosing alternative destinations. Given the political uncertainty this was hardly a surprise, but they were accused by far-left members of the government of trying to sabotage the Revolution. During 1975 public works programmes came to a near standstill, with the state only investing in small civil works.[29]

Put simply, the Revolution had created one giant human and economic mess that would take a generation to, at best, partially resolve. Things were to get worse before they showed any sign of improvement.

3

SOS

Considering all the political intrigues, infighting and score-settling that dominated the headlines for much of 1975, there was a very real prospect that the country's economy could have gone bust. With the Americans guarded in offering aid, the Soviets only interested in the far-left, and Western Europe still in recession as a result of the oil embargo following the 1973 Arab-Israeli War, the chances of a major bailout were limited.

The member states of the EEC did supply some modest aid, but this was of limited economic benefit.[1] The Western European socialist parties were keen to offer more assistance in the hope that the economic aid would help strengthen the supporters of democracy in the country. In reality, most of the aid from Europe at this time represented a token offering, rather than having any real potential for helping resolve Portugal's economic crisis.

Portugal still had one card to play, but seemed reluctant to use it. As Nigel Trench noted, 'So far the large gold reserves which were the legacy of the Salazar regime have remained virtually untouched.'[2] The sale of the gold, which he estimated to be up to 400 tons, could have helped to stimulate the economy, reduced the social costs of unemployment and offered more help to the returnees. The decision not to use the gold was not commented upon directly by the Americans, but there was a sense that it was not being sold for unspecified political reasons. If ever Portugal needed to use the gold, then 1975 was the moment.

Instead, Portugal tried to diversify its trade relations in the hope that this would reduce its dependency upon any one market. In doing this, they looked eastwards towards the Soviet bloc.[3] Here Portugal encountered two problems. First, the Soviets were not interested in signing any big deals with the Portuguese, confining its trade with the country to relatively small-scale deals. Secondly, as the Portuguese soon discovered, Moscow was highly skilled at driving a hard bargain with these deals.[4]

It was also noticeable that the Soviet bloc traded with Portugal for economic and not ideological reasons. There were no cut-price or subsidized deals offered by the Soviets, or other inducements in the way that Moscow had courted President Abdul Gamal Nasser of Egypt in the 1950s. All of this became a source of resentment among many leaders of the far-left in Portugal. Slowly but surely Portugal's leaders took note and came to the realization that the country's future economic prosperity lay in developing ties with its traditional trading partners in Western Europe.[5]

Before this happened, there was a brief attempted economic flirtation with the Arab world. The Portuguese viewed the Middle East as a potential source of finance, new market opportunities for Portuguese exports, and most importantly, lower priced fuel.[6] According to the British, the Portuguese toyed with the idea of providing the Arabs with a formal guarantee that in the eventuality of a new round of Arab-Israeli fighting, Lisbon would deny the use of the Azores for any US military resupply of Israel.[7] Lisbon also looked at providing support for any anti-Zionism resolution at the United Nations.[8] The attempts came to little, but did further antagonize Kissinger in his attitude towards the country.

The Arab world in 1975 was already in a state of quiet transformation, with President Anwar Sadat of Egypt preparing to swap sides in the Cold War and join the US camp. Kissinger had been able to tame the threat of the radicals in the Arab oil-producing world, and in doing so, had largely averted the potential for a second Arab oil embargo of the West. Lisbon, as a result, would not receive many incentives from the Arabs. Instead, as the financial crisis worsened in Lisbon, it was clear to most Portuguese leaders that wooing back existing trade partners represented the most prudent economic approach.

Most Lisboetas simply did not understand the economic crisis, nor its root causes, or its potential short- and long-term impact on the life of the country. Instead, as the autumn nights drew in, and the city's population returned from its summer holidays, discussions and arguments centred upon what most people saw as the mounting conflict between the far-left and the democrats. Lisbon looked different in the fading autumn light. The middle classes parked their cars wherever they wanted, usually as close as possible to the café or shop they visited.

The feeling of rebellion was not confined to those classes that strongly supported the Revolution. Lisbon and Portugal remained in an administrative mess with the various police forces nervous about making arrests, and the judicial system not functioning properly. It might have only taken a few hours to kick out the leaders and the enforcers of the Estado Novo, but building new empowered democratic institutions and agencies was to take much longer. In the meantime, it was a free-for-all with many individual Portuguese pushing the boundaries of how far they could go in bending or breaking the law.

The city of Lisbon appeared a little more in need of attention. With only a limited public works budget, several of the main roads in Lisbon became riddled with deep potholes when the rainy season came. The posters, graffiti and banners of the Revolution gave the city a distinctly red political feel. On any given day, there appeared a demonstration – for more money, more rights or as a show of support for a particular political party. The CIA money that had been channelled into the country through third parties was put to use, trying to help the supporters of democracy take the streets back from the Communists, who had hitherto enjoyed a strong hold over demonstrations and strikes.

Unlike in pre-Revolution April 1974, in November 1975 the outside world watched Lisbon very closely. Foreign embassies in the city had been staffed up, both in terms of actual numbers and in the quality of the diplomats that had been dispatched to Lisbon to monitor the post-Revolution period. The diplomatic gossip at embassy social events was that the status quo could not continue much longer. There would be more political upheaval, and violence, before any semblance of calm could be restored. The European nations looked to the Americans for leadership, and wondered what Washington would do next.

Following a private conversation between Henry Kissinger and the Portuguese Foreign Minister Melo Antunes on 10 October 1975, Kissinger summarized the seriousness of the political situation in the memorandum of the meeting:

> The Secretary, prefacing his next question by mentioning his inclination to consider even highly unlikely events, inquired as to what the Foreign Minister thought the possibility might still be for civil war to break out in Portugal. The Foreign Minister replied that it seemed certain to him that this could still happen. Although he considered that the highly critical period had passed, conditions still existed in Portugal for possible serious confrontations between certain population groups and the Armed Forces. But such a danger did not seem imminent.[9]

Kissinger went on to underline that if fighting did break out in Portugal, he would make it clear which side the United States supported:

> The Secretary indicated that, in the event of a tragedy, we would be ready to support the Foreign Minister and his group. But the Foreign Minister would have to tell us when. At any event, we [the US] had preliminary plans for this purpose. The Foreign Minister expressed gratitude for the intended support, which he said would of course be very helpful in the event of need. He went on to stress that the position of his group was clear and had been made so from the start; namely, that they stood ready to hold out to the very end, both politically and

militarily, against any threat by the Communists to take over power in Portugal.[10]

Kissinger was a Secretary of State who believed in key moments and battles, and he felt that the US needed to make a stand to support its allies in Lisbon against what he saw as its ideological enemies in the city. The advice that Kissinger was getting in Washington appeared to confirm that Portugal was heading towards a second, and potentially more bloody, revolution. The day after his conversation with the Portuguese Foreign Minister, the National Security Council articulated its fears for the future in Lisbon:

1 Increasing politicization of the military with polarization between moderates and leftists, resulting in a serious breakdown in order and discipline. This is critical since stability in the military is necessary for stability in the government.
2 Subversive activities and demonstrations of the Portuguese Communist Party (PCP) and far-left groups. Ex-Premier Goncalves and his supporters are suspected to be behind much of this activity.
3 Worsening economic and social problems, which are exacerbated by the influx of Angolan refugees (now approximately 175,000), many of whom blame their troubles on the radical governments, which have dominated affairs over the past year.[11]

The report then went on to predict the various scenarios as to where this could all lead. This was the part of the memorandum that interested Kissinger the most. The findings were mildly reassuring for Kissinger.

The present volatile situation could lead in any of several directions:
1 Survivability of the present government, albeit in a very shaky condition.

2 Return of a more radical government, either pro-communist
   or far-left.
3 Large-scale civil disorder, with possible civil war, or at least a
   leftist government in Lisbon and widespread disorder in the
   rest of the nation.
4 Attempted rightist takeover.
The Agency believes that the first alternative listed above is the
most likely to pertain for at least the near term.[12]

The memorandum had a postscript, however, that suggested that
there was still a distinct possibility of a 'final showdown' – diplomatic language for a potential armed confrontation:

> The Portuguese talent for last-minute accommodation to avoid
> final showdowns may once again reassert itself, and head off
> any decisive resolution of these uncertainties at least for a time.
> The Azevedo government, and the moderate elements in the
> Armed Forces and political parties still have assets – includ-
> ing a majority of popular support. But the tendencies toward
> disintegration of institutions – especially the Armed Forces and
> the government's control over them – make the outlook more
> uncertain than ever.[13]

The explosion when it came was of a much more limited
nature than the United States and Western European countries had originally feared. The outcome of the confrontation
was extremely satisfactory for the Western powers. Events had
moved very fast from the middle of November. A two-day siege
of the Prime Minister by dissatisfied construction workers in
Lisbon led to the government suspending all its activities. This
was done in protest at the failure of the military to support
the government. As the British noted, partly in response to this
a 'moderate' was appointed as commander of the Lisbon area
military. Naturally, this was viewed as pure provocation by the
left-wing military units in Lisbon and the country waited for
the resulting conflict.[14]

On 25 November 1975, mutinous paratroopers moved to seize military installations in Lisbon and several other parts of the country. The government's response was both swift and robust. The commandos loyal to the government, who were dispatched to deal with the rebellion, made relatively short work of the largely undisciplined left-wing military units in the Lisbon area.

By the evening of 26 November, troops loyal to the government were fully in control of the city of Lisbon and nearly all of the remainder of the country.[15] On the other side of the River Tagus, Almada was the only city where the coup had not been quelled. Both the Portuguese Navy and the Air Force remained loyal to the government and Air Force planes flew over Lisbon on 26 November in a show of force and support for the government.[16]

As Nigel Trench noted in his report on the events, this helped prove 'the left-wing strength was largely illusory'.[17] Within three days the rebellions in bases in other parts of the country were put down with only a minimal number of casualties. In retrospect, the attempted coup mirrored the events that had taken place earlier in the year on 11 March.

This time, however, the coup represented a major setback for the Communists –regardless of whether or not they had actually been involved in the coup. Following the events of 25 November, the military was largely purged of its leftists, many of whom were arrested. The new military leadership swiftly set about 'depoliticising and professionalising the armed forces'.[18] Importantly, a similar process took place in the state-controlled media.[19]

In the US Embassy, Frank Carlucci wrote excitedly back to Washington on 26 November:

> Moderates have just about won a striking victory militarily.
> Pro-government forces, while stretched thin, are on top and
> have the momentum bred by success. Politically, we expect
> Popular Democrats, Socialists, and Prime Minister to take
> tougher stance on Communist role in government, and Costa
> Gomes to resist expulsion of Communists from position of

influence. Moderates will exploit victory, but lurch to right will not take Portugal back to pre-March 11, 1975 situation.[20]

To a certain extent, the outcome of the events of 25 November was a vindication of Carlucci's careful approach to the post-Revolution political situation in Portugal, over the more globalist and interventionist line adopted by his boss, Henry Kissinger. Back in the State Department, Kissinger read the Ambassador's account of events and his analysis of the continued rocky road ahead with at least a partial sense of relief. It was after all good news for the United States.[21] For all intents and purposes, to borrow Churchill's quote from the Second World War, the events of 25 November did not represent the end of the battle between the far-left and the democrats, but they did represent the beginning of the end.

As the year of 1975 came to an end, and the smoky sweet smells from roast chestnut stands took over the street corners in Lisbon, a degree of normality had been restored. The revolutionary period had lasted for a full nineteen months from 25 April 1974 until 25 November 1995. In downtown Lisbon, and across the country, the Communists and other far-left groups continued to be most expert at getting their people on the streets to protest and make political noise. They were still a force to be reckoned with, but a large measure of political stability and order had been restored following the upheavals of the previous nineteen months.

As Trench concluded in his end of the year dispatch from Lisbon, the government was based on a much more solid 'foundation of legitimacy' and crucially it enjoyed the backing of the Portuguese military that had been purged of its far-left elements.[22] The government set about preparing for the holding of elections in 1976 and, for the first time, appeared to be giving serious thought to dealing with the huge economic problems the country faced.[23]

There were still many problems ahead, but by the end of 1975, it looked more than likely that the 25 April Carnation Revolution would eventually lead to a democratic country that would be able to continue to play its part in NATO, and later within the EEC as well. The year of 1975, as a result, had been a historic one for the country. Lisbon, and the rest of Portugal, could look forward to 1976 with some sense of optimism, feeling that the worst of the political turmoil was over.

4

In the City

In 1976 Lisbon continued to be a vibrant Portuguese capital city. Green-and-cream-painted double-decker buses chugged their way along the city's major roads. The sound of the drivers cranking through the rusty old gears could be heard from afar. Tram routes circled the city centre, with dirty soot-covered fading yellow trams jangling over the shiny rails, packed with Lisboetas, rather than the tourists of the present day.

Almost everybody wore polyester flared trousers, which when caught by a gust of wind threatened to catapult their owners high into the Lisbon sky. Men wore their hair long, and usually unwashed to give it a proletarian look. Long bushy sideburns were the order of the day, topped off with poorly trimmed moustaches.

Women dressed not to look rich, even if they were wealthy. It was the era of baggy sweaters and ill-fitting jeans and little make-up. In 1976, while London was pogoing to the punk rock sounds of the Sex Pistols and the Clash, Lisbon appeared to be lost in a time capsule of tame music and lame fashion. Conformity, rather than new bold self-expression, remained the chosen path for most Lisboetas. The dictatorship was over, but 'the birth of the cool' in music, fashion and the arts was a long way from taking shape.

Motor cars in Lisbon all resembled one another, and their poorly maintained engines spewed a dirty grey smoke into the city's already highly polluted air. The city's buildings continue to suffer from years of neglect and many were in dire need of repair. Rossio train station, once a symbol of the beauty of the city centre, was covered in a layer of grimy black soot from the pollution.

Central Lisbon had become a ghost of its former glorious self. Added to this was the increase in the number of empty buildings with the shutters firmly closed, their owners having fled to exile in Spain, or further afield in Brazil. Soon the doorways of these houses would be bricked up to prevent vandalism or occupation by squatters. Most were soon covered in graffiti and election posters from the various political parties pasted across their fronts.

Importantly, Lisbon – the city with a great, and hugely influential past – was starting to look to the future. After the politically hot period of chaos of the previous two years, the intensity of the political struggle in Lisbon shifted focus in 1976, as the country started to build the democratic institutions that would form the post-Revolution state. During the first half of the year, a Constitution, a Parliament, a Presidency and a Government were all set up. This represented major progress and was widely welcomed by the watching Western powers.[1] Progress was also made in civil–military relations, with the armed forces continuing to try to define a new role for themselves.

Increasingly, the man Henry Kissinger had dismissed as being unimpressive and incapable of winning moved to the front of Portuguese politics. The year of 1976 witnessed Mário Soares win an election, and lead a minority Socialist government. Naturally this pleased the Europeans. The principal aim of Soares' foreign policy was the integration of Portugal into Western Europe, and this was supported by the European powers.[2] This was widely perceived by European leaders as being the most prudent way of ensuring that Portugal continued along the path of democracy.

The victory of the Socialist Party (PS) in the April elections was by no means comprehensive; it won 35 per cent of the popular vote, but the implications of the victory for Portuguese politics far outweighed the size of the victory. When, on 16 July 1976, Mário Soares was invited to form a government he took the decision to staff it solely from the ranks of his own party, and in doing so rejected any coalition with other parties from the left and the right.

The immediate concern for both the new government and the outside world remained the poor state of the Portuguese economy, which was characterized by 'diminishing foreign reserves, inflation and unemployment'.[3] On top of this, it should be remembered that Portugal was a small, poor country that was almost totally devoid of resources and was having to deal with the arrival, en masse, of the returnees from its former Empire. The process of decolonization, particularly in Angola, removed from Lisbon access to rich natural resources.

Perhaps the only economic upside was that Portugal no longer had to pay for the war it had fought to try to keep its Empire intact during the period prior to the 25 April Revolution. The downside was the question of unemployment, with soldiers returning from the wars in Africa seeking jobs. Along with more than half a million returnees, the prospects of getting work were bleak. Many Portuguese simply voted with their feet and headed away from the country to seek work. The majority chose France as a destination and sought work in Paris and the surrounding areas.

In 1976 Lisbon airport, which had witnessed the arrival back in the country of the returnees during the previous two years, now found itself the scene of tearful and emotional goodbyes. Hundreds of young Portuguese men and women walked through the departure gates in the hope of finding a better life abroad. Many families were divided along generational lines, with the parents remaining in Portugal while their children sought a brave new world. Of course this was nothing new.

During the darkest years of the Estado Novo, in the 1960s, hundreds of thousands of Portuguese had emigrated in the hope of finding work in the service industries of Europe. Moreover, the idea of seeking experiences and work outside the motherland was not unique to Portugal; it was true of many of the poorer European countries. The long-term aim of many of the emigrants was to secure enough money to be able to return to the motherland, where they would spend their retirements in their newly constructed homes.

Anybody who has driven around the Portuguese countryside can testify as to how many were successful in achieving this aim. Other emigrants, however, did not return, except for an annual visit for the August holidays. Throughout its rich history, the Portuguese have shown a willingness to search for new worlds, but in the post-Revolution era, however, the continuation of the trend of emigration represented a significant challenge for the new government.

In short, the challenges facing the Soares-led government in the foreign and domestic policy areas were both of a political and of an economic nature. The British thought of Mário Soares as an important and flawed leader, describing him thus:

> Over the years he has moved politically to the right. Originally a Marxist, in recent years he has moved closer to social democracy (he is sometimes described as a 'non-practising socialist'). Now strongly anti-Communist. Adroit politician and an attractive personality. Prefers broad-brush approach. The reverse of a technocrat and does not have much grasp of economics.[4]

Given that Portugal's economy in 1976 was in deep trouble, there was concern that the leader of its minority government did not have a detailed understanding of economics. Soares, however, put his personality to good use by convincing the outside powers to provide aid to Lisbon to help prevent the economy from a potential collapse. Soares' aim was for Portugal to join what he termed the 'club of the rich nations', more widely known as the EEC.[5] Moreover, he made it clear that he hoped to join ahead of the Spanish.

During the second part of 1976 planning for a formal application to the EEC was already under way, with Soares planning to tour European capitals during the first part of 1977 in order to seek support for Portugal's membership. The British, however, were apprehensive about a country as poor as Portugal with its huge economic problems being included in the EEC.

Outsiders sometimes have a tendency to over-focus their attentions on key figureheads at the expense of ideology and policy trends, and in looking at Portugal it appeared to the world that it was increasingly a struggle between Mário Soares, leader of the

Socialist Party, and Álvaro Cunhal, the Secretary-General of the Communist Party (PCP). Given his seeming iron grip over the PCP, outsiders were intrigued by the beliefs, personality and ideology of perhaps the most intellectual of the Portuguese leaders of the post-Revolution era. Cunhal the leader horrified the Western powers, but Cunhal the man was a little more intriguing to the same powers.

In reports to the Foreign Office in London, British diplomats who had watched him closely in Lisbon gave their impressions of him:

> A fine-looking man with great personal magnetism. Reported to be very able. He represents a Stalinist brand of hard-line Communism and has little time for Euro-Communism. He publicly supported the Soviet invasion of Czechoslovakia in 1968 and Afghanistan in 1980; sought to play down the Polish War in 1981, but kept to a pro-Soviet line. Although the Communist Party under his leadership suffered decisive setbacks in late 1975, his own position is secure; he has the public endorsement of the Soviet leadership and he stands head and shoulders above the rest of the Communist leadership in Portugal.[6]

Those diplomats who had met with him went on to describe their sense of frustration at discovering very little from their conversations: 'Talking to him is unrewarding. He is a practised conversationalist but he only tells you what he judges you ought to hear. Under his leadership the PCP discipline provides a favourable contrast to the unruliness of other political parties.'[7]

Most of the Western diplomats in Lisbon knew Cunhal's history off by heart from their background briefing papers. They understood that he had become a member of the Communist Party while studying law at the University of Lisbon in 1934. In 1936, he became a member of the Central Committee of the Communist Party and disappeared underground.[8] He had eventually been arrested in March 1949 and his trial had taken place in May 1950.

Convicted, he spent nearly a decade in prison, including eight years in solitary confinement.[9]

In January 1960, he had managed a daring escape from the fortress prison in Peniche, about an hour and a half's drive north of Lisbon.[10] He then spent fourteen years in exile in the Soviet Union and Czechoslovakia, before returning to Portugal after the 25 April Revolution.[11] His central political aim, to create a communist state post-Revolution, and the events of 1976 must have been a great disappointment to him, with political shifts towards democracy not only in the country, but crucially also in the armed forces.

Civil–military relations matured during 1976. General Ramalho Eanes, who was one of the main officers responsible for the defeat of the left-wing uprising on 25 November 1975, had been promoted to Chief of Army Staff on 27 November 1975. Much to his credit, even after his promotion Eanes continued to accept only a Lieutenant Colonel's salary, which helped to give him his nickname, 'the Incorruptible'.[12] General Eanes cleverly used his position to help maintain the chain of command in the hands of moderate officers. This did much to enable the holding of the country's Parliamentary Elections in April 1976.

Portugal went to the polls two months later, this time to choose a President of the Republic. In the end, the caretaker President General Costa Gomes did not put his name forward, but General Eanes, who enjoyed the support of the three main democratic parties, did run. The result was a clear victory for the democrats, with General Eanes winning nearly two-thirds (61.54 per cent) of the popular vote. To the outside world, and also to many Portuguese, in 1976 General Eanes remained something of an enigma. The British characterized him as best they could:

> He is a man of few words with an austere, rather wooden public image whose speech is clipped and rapid and often difficult to follow. He does not appear to enjoy ceremonial occasions; he is a serious and somewhat mysterious man, but a human one with a (carefully disciplined) sense of humour.[13]

General Eanes' central professional objective, however, was clear for all to see. He wanted to depoliticize the armed forces, restore discipline and professionalize the services.[14] Naturally the election of Eanes as President of the Republic, along with his modernization agenda, was viewed favourably by the Western powers, who saw it as further evidence of the growing control of the moderates in the army over the far-left political interventionists. In reality, as the Soares-led minority government fully understood, there was still much work to be done in depoliticizing and modernizing the Portuguese armed forces.

To some extent, there was an attempt to institutionalize the role of the military in the Constitution with the recognition of the Council of the Revolution, which was a military body consisting of 18 members as a type of second chamber.[15] The Council comprised the President, who acted as chairman, the Chief of Staffs of the three branches of the armed services, and the main junior officers who had been central to the 25 April Revolution.

It came as little surprise when deep divisions soon appeared in the Council, which mainly, but not totally, centred upon splits between those officers who had helped put down the rebellion of 25 November 1975 and the extreme left-wing officers.[16] That said, by the end of 1976 progress had been made in achieving the central objectives of President Eanes in regard to the armed services.[17]

Following the elections that saw the formation of the minority Socialist Government, and the election of the moderate General Eanes as President, Portugal was largely welcomed back into the NATO fold. In Washington, there was widespread relief that the Communists had been repelled from the government, and Portugal, as a result, was brought back into some of the more sensitive parts of the organization. For his part, Soares' determination for Lisbon to play a more positive role in NATO was widely applauded by NATO leaders.

In the United States, the defeat of President Ford in the Presidential Election in November brought to an end a period of eight years of rule by the Republican Party. It also removed the major critic of Portugal's post-Revolution governments, Henry

Kissinger. The victory of Jimmy Carter brought changes of both substance and tone to US foreign policy over the following four years.

In Lisbon, the election of Jimmy Carter was greeted with some relief. Not since President John F. Kennedy's confrontation with Lisbon over the Portuguese colonies at the start of the 1960s had a US administration adopted such a strong ideological line towards the country as Nixon and Kissinger did in the post-Revolution period.

As democratic Portugal slowly started to be embraced by the Western powers, and looked forward to the process of further integration within Europe, there was still a sense of anger directed towards Lisbon over its handling of the decolonization process.[18] In 1976, relations between Lisbon and its former colonies remained highly problematic.

In February 1976, Portugal recognized the Movimento Popular de Libertação de Angola (MPLA) as the legitimate government of Angola, but in May of the same year Portuguese diplomats were forced to leave the country. Much work then went into resolving the diplomatic stand-off, and at the end of the year diplomatic relations between Lisbon and Luanda were established.[19]

Portugal continued to experience difficulties in its relations with Mozambique and Portuguese Timor, which was absorbed by Indonesia. In summing up the problems, the British diplomatic reports offered an appropriate summary: 'From Portugal's point of view, the best that could be said on her hasty decolonisation was that by the end of 1976 most of the problems concerned in this process had been shifted to others' shoulders.'[20]

Put simply, the outside world was left to unpick the mess and confusion from a decolonization policy that brought unseen political complications, continuous crisis and unnecessary misery to millions of people. The sense of frustration that was directed towards Lisbon from Washington was because in the rush to exit its former colonies, the Portuguese had left the door open to Soviet-backed groups gaining the upper hand in national and regional conflicts in the African continent.

The main architect of US policy towards the Cold War, Henry Kissinger, could never quite forgive the Portuguese for failing to accept their responsibilities to their former colonies. From an American perspective, the prolonged political mess and civil war in Angola would continue to require careful attention.

Back in Lisbon, as 1976 drew to a close and attention shifted to the holiday season, there was a sense that a corner had been turned and the people had spoken in favour of democracy. Much of the detail was still to be decided. The British opinion of Soares adopting 'a broad brush approach' seemed appropriate. Lisbon, however, at the end of 1976 was in much better shape than the previous December when the impact of the failed rebellion of 25 November was still strongly felt in both the leadership of the armed forces and the political elite.

The end of the Nixon/Ford/Kissinger era in the United States, and the transition to the Carter era, offered democratic Portugal the opportunity of a clean slate with Washington. For Mário Soares, the fundamental foreign policy challenge lay in Europe, and specifically in trying to convince the nations of the 'rich club' of EEC nations that it was in their interests to give a small, poor country like Portugal a place at the table. This, as it turned out, proved to be no easy task.

The far-left waited noisily in the background, with their highly motivated and disciplined party members ready to seize on any opportunity to exploit weakness or failure. Leaders such as Álvaro Cunhal had not given up hope of one day ruling Portugal. By the end of 1976, such a scenario appeared less likely than at any point since the heady days of April 1974. Lisbon, and the rest of Portugal, was slowly starting to move into the next chapter of its exciting narrative.

The Western powers watched developments closely and were keen to offer assistance wherever possible, provided that it did not damage their own national self-interest. This was the problem that faced Mário Soares, and proved to be one of the most important challenges of his political career. As the British duly noted, he might not have been the wisest of sages, but he was the only game in town.

In short, Soares needed to get himself up to speed quickly in diplomatic statecraft if he was to convince his fellow European leaders of the merits of the case for Portugal's entry into Europe. Until Soares could succeed, Lisbon was living on borrowed time, or rather borrowed money, from an outside world that was still reluctant to fully open its purse strings to Portugal.

PART TWO

Safe European Home

5

Trans-Europe Express

The date of 28 March 1977 was something of a slow news day across the globe. In the evening, the 49th Academy Awards took place in Los Angeles with *Rocky* winning the Best Picture award. The rags-to-riches story of the small-time boxer Rocky Balboa centred on the tale of a poor underdog heavyweight fighter and his quest against the established rich elite of the boxing world.

For Portugal, the date was one of the most important days in its modern history. On this day, Portugal lodged its formal application to join the European Economic Community (EEC), also sometimes known as the Common Market.[1] Earlier in the year, Portugal's very own Rocky Balboa, Mário Soares, had visited the heads of each of the EEC governments to explain his reasons for wanting to join.

In the meetings, European leaders assured Soares of their desire to help solidify Portuguese democracy and recognized Portugal's 'European vocation'.[2] In London, and in Lisbon, Soares tried to convince Portugal's oldest ally of the merits of its case for membership, and why it was essential for Portugal to make this move. Speaking to the British Ambassador he said:

Portugal has lost her African colonies and after two years of turmoil has by the skin of her teeth avoided a takeover by the totalitarian Communists. She has made great strides in establishing a democratic structure, but now she faces formidable

economic difficulties that demand privations and sacrifices
from her people. These will only be accepted if the country
is engaged in a great enterprise. This must be her integration
into Western Europe, which can only be achieved through full
membership of the EEC.[3]

This was essentially the message that the energetic and charismatic
Soares took to all the European capitals. The British and the West
Germans offered him and his agenda a warm public welcome.
Other countries were more cautious, and reminded the Portuguese
leader about the scale of his country's economic problems and the
huge disparity in wealth between Portugal and the nine members
of the EEC.[4]

Nobody wanted to be seen to be closing the door on Portuguese
membership, but, at the same time, leaders felt that it was fool-
hardy to downplay the obstacles to full Portuguese membership.[5]
The EEC had undertaken careful preparation for Soares and his
European tour. In essence, it wanted all its member states to give
the Portuguese leader the same response.

The final draft for use by those hosting Soares was approved by
the Council at its meeting on 8 February 1977, and stated:

The Council of the European Communities and the
Representatives of the governments of the Member States
meeting within the Council:
1 Would draw attention to the fundamentally open nature of
   the Community, as asserted in the Treaty of Rome, and to
   Portugal's European Vocation and would welcome the political
   commitment to Europe of that democratic country, which can
   thus aspire to become a member of the Community.
2 Would express their concern over the problems which short
   term economic integration would entail for both Portugal,
   in view of its economic, financial, social and agricultural
   circumstances, and for the Community, whose patrimony
   and internal and external development prospects must be
   preserved.

3 Would recall all the joint actions already undertaken since Portugal's return to democracy and would emphasize all the progress, which can still be achieved in strengthening cooperation between the Community and Portugal.

4 Would reaffirm their will to continue the common search with Portugal for ways and means of aligning their economies more closely with the ultimate aim of leading to the full and complete accession of Portugal to the Community under conditions and on a timescale most favourable to all parties.

5 Would take note of the Portuguese government's intention to submit a request for accession to the Community on the basis of Article 237 of the Treaty of Rome.

6 Would recognize that the procedure provided for in the Treaties requires, before the opening of negotiations, the search for and the definition of satisfactory solutions to all the problems standing in the way of Portugal's economic integration into the Community.

7 Would restate their readiness to contribute to strengthening their co-operation with Portugal both in the political and economic spheres.[6]

As it transpired, the trickiest trip on the Soares European tour of 1977 turned out to be to Paris where he was greeted by President Valéry Giscard d'Estaing. During the meeting, the President made it clear to Soares the extent of French reservations to Portugal's membership of the EEC. This did not come as a surprise to Soares. Prior to the meeting, the Portuguese government had calculated that the major risk to their application was the threat of a French veto.

Following the meeting with President Giscard d'Estaing, Soares was sent off to meet representatives of the French motor industry. Keen to please the French, the Portuguese Prime Minister understood the hint and agreed to a major and controversial deal for the manufacture of French cars in Portugal.[7]

In essence, the state-owned Renault car company was to set up a manufacturing plant in Portugal. The Portuguese government would help the plant for five or six years by agreeing to guarantee it a large share of the market in Portugal.[8] This was to be done at the expense of existing car assembly plants in Portugal, and as the British pointed out would lose it around £20 million a year in British car exports to the country.[9] 'As usual the French have reaped tangible benefits from being politically brutal,' wrote the frustrated British Ambassador to Lisbon.[10]

The European tour of Prime Minister Soares had proved to be something of a success. The measurement for this success was the simple fact that nobody, not even the French, after the Renault car deal, closed the door on Portuguese membership of the EEC. While no European leader underestimated the difficulties that lay ahead, there had been a small sea change in thinking. European leaders were looking for more ways to help facilitate Portuguese membership of the EEC rather than focusing solely on the economic difficulties of the application to join the 'rich club'.

Being a visionary is one thing, but the diplomatically inexperienced, and poorly connected, Soares discovered during his tour that his fellow leaders of Europe were themselves embarking on a journey to turn a far grander vision into a political reality. While the linkage between full Portuguese integration into Western Europe and the entrenchment of democracy in the country was widely accepted by European leaders, debates centred upon the extent of the integration and questions over the enlargement of the EEC.

The latter was seen as the most pressing issue, given the Greek and Spanish request for membership. At the heart of the issue was the belief that enlargement of the EEC would complicate efforts at stronger economic and political integration of the Community.

During 1977, the economic statistics did not make for pleasant reading for the Portuguese government trying to convince the outside world of the merits of its case for joining the 'rich club' of Europe. Inflation was running at around 30 per cent and the balance of payments deficit grew steadily worse. Exports covered only around 40 per cent of the cost of Portugal's imports with the country importing more than half of its food.[11]

It was oil, however, that did most to cripple the already weak economy. As a country that imported 100 per cent of its oil, Portugal was always vulnerable to international price fluctuations. In January 1977, Portuguese fuel prices were increased by 23 per cent, a move that made Portuguese petrol the most expensive in Europe.[12] Given the rural base of a large chunk of the population, and the poor state of public transport, this placed a further strain on expenditure. The only real upside was that with relative political calm restored, foreign tourists returned to the country in large numbers, bringing relief to the service industry in the Algarve and in Lisbon.

Just when it looked as if things couldn't get any worse economically, the weather broke during the harvesting season. The bad weather, together with continued chaos in agricultural areas caused by the Revolution, led to a disastrous harvest in 1977. This was right across the board, with wheat, rye, barley, oats, wine and olive crops the worst for years.[13] The outside world watched with concern as the government seemingly failed to make any real progress in tackling the 'backward and inefficient' agricultural sector and resolving questions of ownership of lands redistributed, or in dispute, following the Revolution.[14]

Given the importance of the agricultural sector to the economy, there was a pressing need for the introduction of modern farming techniques and diversification of products. The lack of capital available to aid this change meant that the donkey and the cart remained in use and the era of modern tractors and combine harvesters was still a long way off.

Under strong foreign pressure led by the International Monetary Fund (IMF) and the United States, the escudo was devalued by 15 per cent in February. In the same month the United States provided Lisbon with a $300 million loan to help tide it over. This represented the first major act of goodwill by the new Carter administration in Washington towards Lisbon, although the Portuguese complained that this amount fell far short of what Washington had promised. Europe also made contributions, with Britain granting £20 million in aid.[15]

With Portuguese democracy still in its infancy at three years old, dependency ties were already starting to be formed with the outside world. Over the following years and decades, the country would become increasingly dependent on gift capital from the European powers and international financial organizations such as the IMF. No gift capital comes without political and economic strings attached to it and more often than not results in a loss of sovereign power. Put simply, it was clear from early on that Portugal's quest for a stable democracy would have to be underwritten by an outside world ever keen to intervene in Portugal's own affairs.

For Mário Soares and the majority of the supporters of democracy in 1977, it was deemed to be a price worth paying. In reality, given the perilous state of the Portuguese economy, and the potential for resulting political unrest, Portugal's leaders had little choice but to accept outside help. Wherever they could, they tried to navigate around the strict conditions laid down by the providers of the gift capital, sometimes with success, and sometimes not.

On 10 October 1977, the IMF team arrived in Lisbon for talks about their requirements for helping to effectively bail out the Portuguese economy. As they arrived, most Lisboetas showed little interest in their mission expect for watching a brief report on the evening RTP news broadcast. Lisboetas simply didn't understand the purpose of the mission. Instead, as they sat drinking their *bicas* (espresso coffee) in the city's cafés, most people talked about the previous day's World Cup qualifying game in which Portugal had defeated the hosts, Denmark, by four goals to two.

As the nights drew in, and the first autumnal rains fell over the city, there were frequent demonstrations organized by the trade unions, most of which were firmly under Communist control. There was still a feeling of rebirth, and a focus on the motherland rather than on events taking place in the outside world. But the outside world was scrutinizing Portugal with an ever more critical eye. The IMF team was in Lisbon to play hardball with the Portuguese government. The price it demanded for IMF help was high. It looked for all intents and purposes as if it would prove to be impossible for the minority Socialist government to agree to the IMF demands. These demands were summarized by the British: 'A substantial reduction in the balance of payments deficit, to be achieved by strict limits on domestic credit expansion, which would impose financial discipline on the public sector and throttle demand, and by a further considerable devaluation [of the escudo]. The IMF also called for the dismantling of import controls.'[16]

As Lisboetas entered their third winter under democratically elected leadership, an agreement with the IMF had still not been reached. The negotiations were suspended on 10 November, the same day that Roy Jenkins, the President of the EEC, arrived in Lisbon for a two-day visit and talks with Portuguese leaders about its application to join the EEC. Jenkins met with Soares and members of the government in what were in reality negotiations about the future formal negotiations to enlarge the Community. Jenkins was an austere old-fashioned-looking President, who had something of the academic in the manner in which he spoke to everybody. In photographs of their meeting both men look slightly ill at ease. Nobody smiled, and the meetings focused on the detailed arguments and requirements for potential Portuguese membership of the 'rich club'.

Jenkins' impressions of Lisbon were favourable, but he was surprised by the lack of open support for the ancient alliance with Britain. In his diary, he noted, 'Lisbon as a whole was remarkably francophone and amongst the middle-aged and older generation almost equally non-anglophone.'[17] Jenkins would return to Lisbon in 1978, but his point about the francophone orientation of the city was interesting. French was taught as the second language in Portuguese schools and the majority of Portuguese spoke it relatively fluently. Knowledge of English was not so widespread away from the private and international schools in the city.

The presence of the IMF in Portugal, and its calls for adherence to a strict programme of austerity and economic reform, were a constant political destabilizing force. During the first week of December, Soares attempted to get the opposition parties to agree on a platform or general understanding, which would have led to sharing of the political fallout from, as the British put it, 'the bitter medicine prescribed by the IMF'.[18] Having failed to achieve this goal, Soares asked the National Assembly for a vote of confidence in the minority government.

The vote took place on 8 December with the Centre Democrats, Social Democrats, Communists and a few independent Socialists all voting against the government. The Soares-led Government, as a result, was defeated by 159 votes to 100.[19] It was a crushing blow for the Socialist Party (PS), and came at the end of a year during which Portugal had experienced a degree of political calm. Soares agreed to continue in office while a new government was formed and on 28 December, after consulting with the senior leaders, President Eanes asked Mário Soares to try to form a new government.

During the course of 1977, President Eanes attempted to contribute to the development of Portuguese democracy. His speech to the National Assembly on 25 April 1977, marking the third anniversary of the Revolution, was viewed by many Portuguese and foreign commentators as endorsing the PS government. This naturally led to resentment from Social Democrats who, by the end of the year, were starting to become openly critical of his leadership.

Among the more conservative elements of the armed forces there was also some dissent at his leadership; several senior officers felt that he needed to become more authoritarian.[20] His major goal remained upholding the Constitution and democracy. Eanes did not travel abroad as much as the Prime Minister, but did undertake two successful visits to Spain and West Germany. The relative calm within the armed forces and its continued withdrawal from political life was a testament to his leadership. Planned reforms of the military, however, were not implemented owing to disagreements between central staffs, army staff and regional commanders.

President Eanes didn't know it at the time, but he was about to move to the political centre stage. His role was to become ever more critical to the outcome of the search for a stable and democratic Portugal. As Lisboetas celebrated Christmas and visited downtown Lisbon to admire the lights and decorations, they did so with no new government in place.

Mário Soares was finding it ever more difficult to attract new partners to provide him and the PS with a working majority in order to deliver a stable government. With both the President of the EEC and the IMF due back in Lisbon early in the New Year, this was a worrying development for President Eanes, and for the country. In the meantime, had President Eanes wandered out of the Presidential Palace for a stroll around the Belém neighbourhood in which the palace is located, he would have seen the surreal sight of Belém being transformed into a Hollywood film set, complete with street signs in Spanish.

6

Picture This

In the opening scene of the Hollywood movie *The Boys from Brazil*, a sinister-looking long black Mercedes car waits at a level crossing in Belém while the Cascais to Lisbon train passes by. The car then heads for an esplanade café on the renamed Praça Afonso de Albuquerque, where a man drinking a beer is waiting. All, however, was not as it seemed. Parts of Belém, Lisbon and wider Portugal were transformed into Paraguay for the Hollywood film that starred Gregory Peck, Laurence Olivier, James Mason and a young Steve Guttenberg.

The film was the largest and most expensive Hollywood production to have been shot in the country, and represented a big shot in the arm for a country that was suffering from lots of negative international press attention at the time. The makers of the film explained their reasons for choosing the country to shoot a large part of the movie:

> Portugal was chosen, for it combined cheapness, sun, the ideal locations, and enormous enthusiasm from the authorities concerned. It is like the Spain of 10 years ago. We were a little nervous about coming here because Portugal is unsophisticated when it comes to filmmaking, and all our crazy needs and ways, but we couldn't have been more pleased. The government was extremely cooperative, from the highest to the lowest levels, and, best of all, everyone we took on for the film was so enthusiastic.[1]

The filming of the major movie, along with the presence of two leading film stars of Hollywood in the city, provided Lisbon with some much-needed international positive publicity. When the film was released in 1978, the international press were quick to pick up on the slightly exotic and 'off-the-beaten track' choice of Portugal as one of the main locations for the film. As the press pointed out:

> For Portugal, *The Boys From Brazil* represented the biggest movie ever made in the country and around $2 million in income; it was certainly a boost for the nation's depleted foreign currency coffers and the 300 jobs the film provided for three months to local workers gave some pre-Christmas help to many families, a bonus not to be scorned in a country, where unemployment is officially placed at more than 16 per cent.[2]

Old Hollywood buddies, Peck and Mason, were accompanied to Portugal by their families, who made the most of their time in Lisbon taking in the local culture and sightseeing. Mason had not originally been offered a part in the film, which focused on the story of a Nazi hunter in Paraguay discovering a sinister plot to try to rekindle the Third Reich. The main role of Dr Josef Mengele was given to Peck, but the producers and screenwriters soon discovered that in much of the original book, written by Ira Levin, Mengele did not speak to anybody about his thoughts and schemes. Consequently, a new role was created for Mason as a sounding block for Peck's character. Mason accepted the lesser role, and recounted later: 'It was convenient, it was acceptable, I could even make sense of the character, and besides, it was four weeks work in Portugal, where I'd never been before. When I arrived on the set in Lisbon, I asked if Paraguay had pine trees. "It does now," I was told.'[3]

A young and impressionable Steve Guttenberg also played a key role in the film and in his memoirs he describes the slightly surreal mixture of trying to make a movie in which political unrest was never far from the surface. He described his experience:

We arrived at sunrise, Lisbon time . . . We dropped Marty and
his producing partner Bobby Fryer at the Ritz. It was where
Gregory Peck and his family, and James and Pamela Mason
were staying. It looked every bit the best hotel I had ever seen.
That's not where I was staying. The production company put
me at the modest Hotel Tivoli on Avenida da Liberdade. The
window looked out onto the main thoroughfare where, the
day I arrived, they were preparing for an anti-Communist
demonstration . . .[4]

After a day shooting in Belém, Guttenberg recalled his strange
fascination in watching the political events of the day unfold in
front of his hotel room:

The van wound its way back to the Hotel Tivoli, which was
surrounded by demonstrators, both anti and pro-Communist. They were forcibly arguing in Portuguese, and there were
bottles and sticks being thrown. This was ten in the morning.
The whole day I didn't sleep, just watched the thousands march
down the street.[5]

The Hollywood production team finally departed Lisbon at the end
of 1977 to shoot in additional locations, and to prepare for the film's
release in the autumn of 1978. The film had mixed reviews; it was
nominated for three Oscars, including Laurence Olivier (but not
Peck in the best actor category), but it failed to win any of them.
The film had cost an estimated $12 million to shoot, but still made
over $7 million in profit.[6] The Portugal they left was still reeling
from an endless cycle of political and economic crisis that gave the
impression of regression. Things were to get a lot worse before there
was any hint of light at the end of the tunnel.

For Lisboetas, the year of 1978 was an especially expensive year.
The prices of gas, electricity, public transport and other utilities
were raised by up to 50 per cent.[7] Not only did Portugal have the
most expensive petrol in Europe, but also its utilities were in 1978
amongst the priciest on the continent.[8] Given that the country

also had one of the lowest average salary rates in Europe, the point appeared to be reached in the year where many people simply could not afford to cover their basic living costs.

Any thoughts that the transformation from authoritarianism to democracy would lead, in the short-term, to an increase in the standard of living of the majority of the population were put to rest in 1978. The Revolution that had promised so much, had in many ways changed few of the basic economic realities that dogged the country during the rule of the frugal doctor.

The city of Lisbon continued to creak, with its potholed roads and bricked-up decaying buildings creating an impression of the city leaving the First World and heading backwards to the Third World. The city of light was fast becoming the grey city. Not even the beautiful bright early morning rays of spring sunlight that rose over the city could alter this impression. Urgently needed public works programmes were put on hold as the cash-strapped city and country signed up to the harsh terms laid down by the IMF.

The once beautiful buildings in the banking centre of the Baixa area of downtown Lisbon had served as a barometer to Portugal's glorious golden era of Empire. In 1978, Baixa resembled a pale reflection of its former self. The buildings, like the city and the wider country, gave the impression of waiting to be saved by somebody or something.

Democratic politicians appeared hell-bent on prioritizing deal-making and coalition-building over any concerted attempt to deal with the problems of the day. At the centre of all this energy was the attempt to form a stable and viable government that would provide leadership to the country, and be able to sit down and negotiate with the EEC over the terms of Portuguese membership.

Increasingly, during 1978 membership of the 'rich club' became viewed as the country's 'golden ticket' – the only chance for it to escape its impoverished state once and for all. The diplomatic stakes could not have been higher, but first Portugal needed to find the elusive new and stable government. To make matters worse, at this key juncture in the country's history the outside world remained to be convinced that any of the key party leaders had what was needed to guide the country forward on a pathway towards integration with Europe.[9]

The year of 1978 proved to be a watershed for Portuguese politics in bringing to an end the short-lived dominance of the Soares-led Socialist Party (PS).[10] The British noted a seeming shift to the right in Portugal during the course of the year, and a growing tide of disillusionment with the political parties in general.[11] At this point President Eanes stepped forward to play a much more central and stronger role in the political processes.[12] Few, however, believed that Portugal was returning to a dictatorship or some form of 'military autocracy'.[13]

Over the year, there were four Portuguese governments, together with three Prime Ministers, and the political parties were divorced from direct participation in the government that came to be dominated by independents. On a more positive note, Portugal eventually reached an agreement with the IMF, which, in the short term, helped bring some much-needed stability to the economy. Both the political and economic developments were watched closely by the member states of the EEC, with whom formal negotiations were opened for Portugal's membership.[14]

The year started with Soares and his colleagues in the PS successfully forming a new coalition government. The PS formed a coalition with the conservative Centre Democrats, who as part of the deal received three Cabinet posts. For nearly six months the coalition appeared to work and gave the country 'a moderate and what appeared to be a stable government'.[15]

Internal squabbles and political posturing within the largest opposition party, the Social Democratic Party, added to the apparent chances of the government surviving. The issue of the different ideologies between the two parties, however, meant that strains soon appeared in their relations. Much of the tension was put down to the personal failings of Soares. Lord Moran, the British Ambassador to Lisbon at the time, summarized the problems:

> Dr. Soares took his partners too much for granted, allowed
> purely socialist policies on health and education to be

put forward, and let a hopelessly inadequate Minister of
Agriculture, Luis Saias, tolerate the infiltration of the agricultural bureaucracy by the Communists. He himself came
to a tacit understanding with the Communists to go slow on
the return of reserves to former owners under his own Land
Reform legislation while they ensured industrial peace.[16]

At the end of the day, this all proved too much for the membership
of the Centre Democrats, who effectively forced their leadership
to withdraw from the government on 24 July.[17] The apparent
'tacit agreement' between Soares and the Communists over the
implementation of the Land Reform legislation confused several
diplomats tasked with watching Portuguese affairs. The key questions asked centred upon the extent to which Soares would be
willing to work with the Communists on other areas, and the
extent of the continued support of the Communists in key rural
parts of the country.[18]

In the event of the Centre Democrats quitting the government, Soares had promised to resign, but he was persuaded by
his colleagues to try to continue, albeit, once more, in a minority
government. President Eanes, however, was having none of it and
duly fired Soares. The various parties in the National Assembly
then tried to find an alternative government that would command
a majority, but it soon became apparent that this was not going to
be possible.

Sulking, and in a state of political shock, Soares was left to lick his
wounds, and for some time afterwards his personal relationship with
the President deteriorated. Whispering of a return to a more authoritarian style of government did the rounds at diplomatic social functions
in Lisbon, but the rumours lacked real supporting evidence and were
soon dismissed. Soares was still very much a part of the diplomatic
circuit in the city. The best known of all of Portugal's democratic leaders, he continued to put the case for his vision of the country's future
to the eyes and ears of the outside world.

In truth, foreign diplomats in Lisbon were growing weary of
Soares' political style, which encompassed a curious mixture of

drama, vanity and moments of high tension. He would briefly return to the premiership during the 1980s, but in the summer and autumn of 1978 there appeared to be a real prospect that he would be consigned to the dustbin of political history.[19] Diplomats increasingly talked of Soares being a leader who was important in shaping the transition from authoritarianism to democracy, but who was not suited to the cut and thrust of daily governmental leadership.

Henry Kissinger's comments made after the Revolution that he didn't think that Soares was able 'to play hardball' took on a new meaning in 1978 with his failure to keep a viable working government in place in Lisbon.[20] Supporters of Soares argued that he remained extremely relevant to the political process. His, and the Socialists', declining fortunes were, according to this group, largely down to the poor state of the economy that the government had inherited. Whatever the merits of either of these arguments, it is clear that Soares did learn some hard political lessons from his difficulties during the summer and, according to Lord Moran, tried hard to 'repair his fences' during the latter part of the year.[21]

The political crisis during the summer of 1978 left President Eanes with few practical options. From the standpoint of the political parties, he chose perhaps the most confrontational one. President Eanes chose to appoint a government of independents and an engineer-businessman, Alfredo Nobre da Costa, as Prime Minister. In political terms, Costa was centre-left and was not well known as a wily political operator. In the National Assembly the parties refused to accept it and made it virtually impossible for Costa to succeed.

Eventually, amid much political bickering, raised voices and arguments that threatened to boil over into something nastier, the Assembly voted the government's programme down on 15 September.[22] After this, the political parties once more failed to find a formula that would have led to the formation of a stable coalition government. This failure moved President Eanes to appoint a second government of independents, this time to be led by Carlos Mota Pinto, and this government was able to win a vote of support in the National Assembly on 22 November.

The performance of President Eanes was widely applauded by the outside world as helping to ensure that the political process did not stall and that a government was in place to deal with Portugal's ongoing economic crisis.[23] During his overseas visits in 1978, leaders of Great Britain, Brazil, the United States, where he attended a NATO summit, and at the European Parliament warmly greeted him.

While Soares and the Socialists continued to feel that he had overstepped his constitutional role in dismissing their government, overseas, the President was seen more and more as the protector of democracy and stability. His political antennae appeared to accurately detect the changes in the general consensus of the Portuguese.

In truth, Portuguese opinion had become deeply disillusioned with the political parties and had shifted towards the right. The foreign press in Lisbon widely disseminated a Portuguese opinion poll that showed the majority of those questioned thought that the best government in recent years was that of the authoritarian leader, Marcello Caetano.[24] In a symbolic indication of the shifts in Portuguese politics, the last of the Presidents from the era of the Estado Novo, Américo Tomás, was allowed to return to Lisbon from his exile in Brazil.[25]

The return of the ex-President served as a reminder for many Portuguese of the Estado Novo and the diplomatic isolation that the country had faced for much of the 1960s and 1970s, up to April 1974. In censor votes at the United Nations against Portugal's actions in its African colonies, the country could count the votes opposing the motion on one hand. In a sign of how far the country had come in terms of international relations since the Revolution, in November 1978, Portugal was elected a member of the United Nations Security Council (to be taken up on 1 January 1979).[26] Lisbon made an effort to try to improve relations with its former colonies, with mixed results.[27]

In Washington, Portugal was welcomed once again as a trusted member of NATO, and the question of the use of the Azores base by the United States was not as emotive as it had been in the immediate aftermath of the Revolution. Of greatest importance in foreign affairs, however, was the formal opening of negotiations with the EEC over Portuguese membership. Lisbon was now well and truly on the road to greater integration into Europe, something which was met with concern by many Portuguese who shared Salazar's scepticism of such organizations.

For the President, and the new Government, dealing with the dire economic plight of the country remained the central aim and objective. Successfully addressing the economic crisis was needed for both the country, and its application for EEC membership. On 8 May, after months of wrangling, a deal had eventually been agreed between the previous government of Mário Soares and the IMF.

The government agreed to strict control of credit and the continued devaluation of the escudo (on the day of the agreement it was devalued by 6.1 per cent).[28] All of this helped reduce the critical problem of the balance of payments deficit with imports remaining at about the same rate as the previous year, but with exports rising by 13 per cent in volume in the third quarter.[29]

Additional good news came in the form of increased remittances from emigrants and from tourism. Economic growth picked up, but with the squeeze of credit a lot of large and small companies experienced financial difficulties. The worst-hit sector remained, however, agriculture, which was in a total mess. It was a similar story in the fishing industry, which was also in near-total disarray. Confirmation of this mess was illustrated by the simple fact that by the end of the year Portugal was importing two-thirds of its food.[30] By the end of 1978, bad old habits were starting to creep back into the management of the economy.

Most worrying was that Portugal seriously exceeded the credit limit that it had agreed with the IMF for the heavily bloated state sector.[31] With the political shift to the centre-right during the course of the year, the outside world was looking for a leader from that side of the spectrum to emerge as a dominant force, just as Soares was for the centre-left. By the end of the following year the identity of that leader would be clear.

London Calling

Portugal was not alone in turning to the right. On 3 May 1979, the leader of the Conservative Party in Great Britain, Margaret Thatcher, the 'Iron Lady', won the first of her three successive elections and would lead the country for over a decade. In total, the Conservatives would govern Great Britain for an unbroken period of 18 years. Thatcher's election ended the British post-war consensus, which was characterized by a general agreement between the major parties on key economic and welfare issues. The election of Thatcher had political repercussions for Lisbon as well.

Thatcher's personal attitude towards the EEC was highly critical of any move towards closer union within the member states of the Community. She believed that one of the ways of ensuring that attempts towards closer political and economic integration would be thwarted was through the enlargement of the Community. Thatcher, as a result, was supportive of Portugal's application for membership, along with those of Greece and Spain. All of this was based on the proviso that agreements could be reached on how best to incorporate the country, given the ongoing economic problems that Lisbon faced.

Politically speaking, Thatcher argued that all the Western European democracies needed to be part of the EEC. Giving the Churchill Memorial Lecture in Luxembourg, she outlined her future vision for the EEC. Thatcher was keen to illustrate what she viewed as the positive expansion of the Community and said, 'the life of the Community will become richer and still more varied when it is joined by the new democracies of Greece, Portugal and Spain. I look forward to their entry.'[1] British support for Portuguese membership, while strong, called for a transition period of ten years in some sectors to help protect the fragile Portuguese economy.[2] Similar periods of transition were also earmarked for parts of the Greek and Spanish economies.

On a personal level, Thatcher had something of a soft spot for Portugal. In 1951, she had spent her honeymoon in Lisbon, Estoril and Madeira. When as Prime Minister she made an official visit to the country in 1984, a journalist from ITN (Independent Television News) asked, 'Were there any particular memories that were brought back during your visit?'[3] Her reply was interesting:

> I looked around for some of the buildings and remembered some of the roads and some of the squares in Lisbon. Of course, I was married not long after the war and I remember when I came here we had been used to a world of great austerity and utility goods, and food rationing and clothes coupons and so on, and so we came into this world of Lisbon and saw many goods of a luxury which we had not seen and I had almost forgotten about until I came here again. But Lisbon has changed. Tall buildings have gone up, many factories have come and it is just not quite the same world, but there were some very happy memories.[4]

The austerity of post-Second World War Britain, when the rationing of food and clothes continued for years after the end of the war, made trips to cities such as Lisbon exotic and exciting for members of the British working and middle classes such as Margaret Thatcher. In terms of Anglo-Portuguese relations, Thatcher viewed Lisbon as a trusted ally and often highlighted its long membership of NATO as a sign of stability. With its population of less than ten million, she also viewed the potential entry of Portugal into the EEC (as well as that of Greece) as less complicated than that of its larger Iberian neighbour, Spain.[5]

At more or less the same historical juncture three other important world leaders emerged who would play fundamental political and economic roles in their respective nations, and in foreign policy that would help bring the Cold War to its climax and eventual ending. In the United States, the Republican, Ronald Reagan, was elected in November 1980 and took the oath of office on 20 January 1981. He would serve the maximum two full terms. In Germany, the conservative politician, Helmut Kohl, was elected in 1982 and would remain as Chancellor until 1998. Only France bucked the rightist trend by electing the socialist, François Mitterrand, as President and he would serve two full seven-year terms from 1981 until 1995. For four of Mitterrand's years in office he was forced into cohabitation governments, which were largely controlled by centre-right Prime Ministers.

These four key leaders in the Western world would dominate democratic politics for a generation and would bring at the very least a degree of political stability to the West during the crucial decade of the 1980s. Each of the leaders would prove to be important to Lisbon and its quest to find a place in Europe and in the wider democratic world.

In 1979, back in Lisbon, the political shift away from the centre-left towards the centre-right continued, but up until December, without any one centre-right candidate emerging as the dominant figure of the political bloc. Prior to that, the year saw the emergence, albeit briefly, of Portugal's first female Prime Minister, Maria de Lourdes Pintasilgo, and mounting problems (many of them self-made) for President Eanes.

In retrospect, it was a year of political transition that turned out to be important for the decade of the 1980s in Lisbon. It was also a period of maturation of Portuguese democracy with the country slowly, and, at times, with difficulty moving away from the symbolism of the Revolution and towards a modern democratic state.

Happening, as this did, within five years of the Revolution, it boded well for the future. There were, however, still key problems that needed to be addressed at both a political and an economic level before Portugal could sit at the high table of stable European democratic nations. Central to this was the pressing need to find a government that relinked the National Assembly to the Executive.

As the British noted, there was a fear that sometimes went unexpressed, or was quietly whispered in the corridors of power, that President Eanes was starting to become a tad dictatorial in his pronouncements and in his actions. The ghost of the wily old doctor from a seemingly past era continued to haunt and worry Portugal's new powerful elites.

The non-party government led by the conservative lawyer, Mota Pinto, tried during the first quarter of the year to continue with its agenda of speeding up the implementation of the agrarian reform law, to cut down the influence of the Communists in the media and to reform the labour laws. Its agenda proved unpopular with the parties of the left and right in the National Assembly, and in March its budget was rejected by the Assembly.[6] As a result of the vote, Mota Pinto tendered his resignation to the President on 28 March, but was asked to stay on to present a second budget.

The vote against the budget proved to be of great importance not only to the Pinto Government, but also for the Social Democratic Party (PSD) led by Francisco Sá Carneiro who had ordered its members to vote against the budget. Instead over 30 of its members stayed away from the Assembly and soon afterwards left the party, remaining in the Assembly as independents.[7] This split meant that the PSD became one of the smallest parties in the Assembly. Keen to remedy this situation as quickly as possible, Sá Carneiro stepped up his efforts to force elections at which he hoped to recoup the seats that the party had lost by the breakaway of 37 of its members.

The budget was eventually passed in a second vote in the Assembly, but with the loss of what Lord Moran, the British Ambassador, termed two of its most important measures.[8] The loss of a tax on the Christmas bonus and the 18 per cent ceiling on wage increases in due course led to the resignation of Mota Pinto on 6 June, throwing the country into yet another political crisis.

What followed was a series of political negotiations involving the Social Democrats and the Centre Democrats, who concluded an agreement to form the Democratic Alliance with the smaller

Monarchist Party on 9 June (the alliance was later also joined by a number of ex-Socialist reformers).[9] In retrospect, this merging of the right created a strong potential electoral force with which to take on the Socialist Party in elections.

The question of the timing of that election was duly considered by President Eanes who, according to the British, 'mistakenly believed that elections would change nothing, [but] decided nevertheless that there was no alternative to holding a special General Election'.[10] He did so despite the fact that there had to be, under the terms of the Constitution, a further election the following year in the autumn of 1980.[11] The special General Election was to take place on 2 December 1979, and in the meantime, on 13 July, President Eanes dissolved the Assembly and appointed a third non-party Government, which was meant to have a solely caretaker role and hold things together until the election in December.

Six days later, on 19 July, Maria de Lourdes Pintasilgo was appointed Prime Minister and she was sworn in on 1 August as leader of Portugal's fifth constitutional government.[12] President Eanes' choice was controversial and provoked much debate and argument among the foreign diplomatic corps based in Lisbon. Lord Moran described her as being a 'left-wing starry eyed progressive Catholic spinster who tried (unsuccessfully) to set the world to rights in five months'.[13]

Although her name had been touted in previous years as a possible caretaker Prime Minister, her appointment came as a surprise as it followed the more conservative-oriented leadership of Mota Pinto. The British suspected that President Eanes succumbed to pressure from the Council of the Revolution, where there was a small majority arguing that a leftist Prime Minister should be appointed to try to counterbalance the previous conservative-leaning administration.[14]

Once in power, Maria de Lourdes Pintasilgo made it clear from the start that she wanted to use her time in office to 'make some much needed changes in Portuguese society'.[15] In truth, despite these lofty aims she failed to come to terms with the complex machinery of government and her controversial social package of increases in pensions led to her own Finance Minister refusing to implement the changes.[16] In summary, her brief period in office could be viewed as being little more than an attempt at a political rebalance from the previous administration.

In Portugal, the political right had objected to her appointment and became vocal opponents of her government, particularly its financial policies.[17] As the Prime Minister toured the country and gave increasingly bizarre statements, it became clear that the real winners from her brief time in office would be the Democratic Alliance, the leaders of which were received by Margaret Thatcher and the British Foreign Secretary, Lord Carrington, in London on 8 November 1979.[18] During the visit, the Democratic Alliance leaders were given the opportunity to address the most prestigious foreign policy think-tank in London, Chatham House.

This visit gained the Alliance a much-needed international boost. Both the French and German leaders had refused to see Sá Carneiro during his overseas travels, and his visit to Washington was described by the US Embassy in Lisbon as 'a disaster'.[19] Margaret Thatcher and the Conservatives in Britain were widely regarded by the Democratic Alliance as its main international supporters.[20]

The focus of foreign government concern about Lisbon shifted during the second part of the year away from traditional fears about the perilous state of the economy (where there were some encouraging signs) and towards its foreign policy. There was a feeling among several foreign diplomats in Lisbon that in the second part of the year the Portuguese Ministry of Foreign Affairs lost control over foreign policy decision-making.[21]

The major authors of foreign policy during this time were President Eanes, along with key foreign policy advisors to him, and the Prime Minister, Maria de Lourdes Pintasilgo. The shift was towards the Third World and the non-aligned nations, which reflected the interests of the Prime Minister and the President. One of the most important areas where this could be seen was in the arena of the Israeli-Palestinian conflict, specifically in policy towards the Palestinian Liberation Organization (PLO) and its leader Yasser Arafat.[22]

At the time, the PLO was regarded as a terrorist organization by the European governments. The PLO had not renounced violence and refused to accept Israel's right to exist. Arafat's invitation to Lisbon was not an isolated one.[23] The PLO was in discussions with several European leaders over the potential changes in its attitude to the use of violence and an acceptance of a two-state solution as the basis for the resolution of the Israeli-Palestinian conflict. What was markedly different about Arafat's visit to Lisbon from his other overseas jaunts was the level and warmth of the welcome he was accorded. Indeed, Arafat could hardly contain his joy as he went from one high-level meeting to another with a knowing look on his face, aware that his visit effectively bestowed de facto Portuguese recognition of the PLO.[24]

The purpose of Arafat's visit was to attend an Arab and Palestinian Solidarity Conference between 2 and 6 November. The conference was one of the largest held in Europe, with over 600 delegates attending from over 100 countries and 36 organizations.[25] The conference came at a time when the PLO was trying to focus world attention back on the Palestinian issue following the signing of the Camp David Accords between Israel and Egypt, which Arafat rejected.

At the time of his visit to Lisbon, Arafat was calling for the Arab oil-producing states to cut off the supply of oil to the United States. Officials in Washington were so concerned about Arafat's hostility that they feared he might launch attacks against 'American installations'.[26] The State Department, as a result, increased security in all its embassies across the globe, including the US Embassy in Lisbon.

In Lisbon, however, Arafat was given the red carpet treatment. Greeted at the airport as if he was a head of state, he had meetings with President Eanes, the Prime Minister, the Minister of Foreign Affairs, the leaders of the PS and Álvaro Cunhal.[27] The local Jewish community in Lisbon protested about the visit, but its voice was drowned out by the wave of support for the Palestinian cause, and specifically the PLO, in the government and among the parties of the political left in Portugal.[28]

According to the Israeli scholar, Barry Rubin, one of the reasons that several European leaders were starting to open a dialogue with the PLO in 1979 was the hope that by doing so they would prevent PLO attacks taking place in their respective countries.[29] If the Portuguese motives for hosting Arafat had been, in part, to try to avoid an attack on its own soil, then the strategy failed spectacularly and very quickly.

One week after the end of the Arab and Palestinian Solidarity Conference, the violence from the Israeli-Palestinian conflict arrived on the streets of central Lisbon. On 13 November 1979, the Israeli Ambassador to Portugal, Ephraim Eldar, was shot and wounded as he arrived for work at the Israeli Embassy in the city. One of his local bodyguards was also shot, and died. Writing in 1980, the British Embassy in Lisbon argued that the link between the attack on the Israeli Ambassador and the Arab and Palestinian Solidarity Conference was not established.[30]

Regardless of the merits or otherwise of this argument, the attack represented a stark warning to Lisbon that the Israeli-Palestinian conflict was not confined to the borders of the Middle East. Three years later, the Israelis would use the attempted assassination of its Ambassador to London as the trigger for the launch of its invasion of Lebanon.

In Lisbon, the implications of the attempted assassination of the Israeli Ambassador were overshadowed by the political campaign for the General Election, which was held on 2 December. The result proved to be a triumph for the Democratic Alliance, which secured an absolute majority, albeit a narrow one.[31] Francisco Sá Carneiro, as a result, was invited to form the sixth constitutional government. The Democratic Alliance consolidated its victory at national level with a second triumph in the local elections, which were held on 16 December.[32] The results of both elections represented a huge setback for the Socialist Party that had dominated Portuguese political life since the 25 April Revolution in 1974.[33]

In reality, the results were a reflection of the unpopular austerity measures that the Socialist Party had implemented during its time in office. The major consequence of these measures for the voters was a steady reduction of wages in real terms (buying power). The temporary demise of the Socialist Party was typical of many political parties that attempted to implement austerity measures in democratic nations.

In Portugal, however, the results of the elections were all the more important in bringing Sá Carneiro to the fore and providing a seemingly strong mandate for the centre-right to run the country. On the surface, the period of political crisis that had dominated the preceding months appeared to be over.

The General Election, however, produced an additional result, which worried the Western powers. One million Portuguese (one-fifth of the electorate) voted for the Communists. Adding on the votes given to the other left-wing extreme groups it was clear that one in four of the Portuguese electorate had voted for some form of communism.[34] Rightly or wrongly, these statistics were seen as evidence that Portuguese democracy was far from secure, and in the era of Cold War politics this point was viewed with concern by the Western powers.[35]

The arrival in power of Sá Carneiro and the centre-right government he led went some of the way, but not all the way, in allaying these fears. President Eanes, who was widely regarded by the British as being the biggest political loser of the year, became a source of concern, with the view expressed in diplomatic circles in Lisbon that he only retained the support of the Communists in the National Assembly.[36]

As the year ended, Lisboetas continued to debate the merits of their political leaders, bemoaning the fact that with each passing year their salaries bought less, and arguing most passionately over the merits of Benfica or Sporting Lisbon football clubs. A new topic of conversation entered the bars and restaurants of the city, the *telenovela* (soap opera). In 1979 there were only two, state-run television channels in Portugal (RTP1 and RTP2). The lack of much channel choice gave populist programmes such as *telenovelas* enormous viewing figures and made the stars of the show major celebrities in the country. The rise of *telenovelas* was important not only from the perspective of RTP, but also as a way of exporting Brazilian culture into Portugal.

At the time, Brazilian production companies enjoyed a near-monopoly over the production of *telenovelas*, and for many Portuguese who couldn't afford to travel to Brazil they represented a very real connection with the outside Portuguese-speaking world. To some extent, the development of low-cost travel and the rise of Portugal's own *telenovela* industry changed this during the 1980s. The creation of two commercial channels, SIC and TVI, in 1992 and 1993 respectively, created more potential for locally produced *telenovelas*.

In 1979, the smash hit *telenovela* was *Dancing Days*, which had originally started to be broadcast in Brazil during the previous year. The star of this disco-influenced feast was the Brazilian actress, Sonia Braga, who for a time was perhaps the most famous Brazilian woman in Portugal. Exotic locations, dramatic sunsets and a script that was very tight by *telenovela* standards made for a hit programme that captivated a Portuguese audience, which started to pick up on some of the more Brazilian language colloquialisms used in the programme. The timing of the show could not have been better.

In 1979 disco music was at its global height and the bars, hotels and clubs of Lisbon were playing the hits of the year. It was a year in which the queen of disco, Donna Summer, sang about 'Bad Girls' and 'Hot Stuff' and the kings of disco, Village People, released the disco anthem, 'YMCA'. Gloria Gaynor sang 'I Will Survive', which was later to become a gay disco anthem, and the sophisticated New York group Chic put out their monster hit, 'Le Freak'.

While the political leadership was still grappling with the problems of the day, young Lisboetas were paying greater attention to the cultures that originated from outside the country. The Lisbon that had been so culturally isolated during the final decades of the Estado Novo was starting to reconnect with the world. This was beginning to have a significant impact on how the youth of the country perceived itself, and its own place, in a cultural world dominated by the United States.

8

The Eternal

During the course of 1980 the world said goodbye to two giants of popular music: the ex-Beatle, John Lennon, and Ian Curtis from Joy Division. The former represented an icon of the past and the latter an icon of the future. The murder of John Lennon in New York on 8 December made global headlines for the weeks following his death. The suicide of Ian Curtis on 18 May received less coverage in the media, but his legacy and music has lasted up to the present day.

Walk into a hip bar or club in Lisbon today and it will not be long until you hear the music of Joy Division played by DJs, most of whom were not even born when Curtis took his life. For all the tragedies of the year, however, one event came to dominate all others in Portugal: the death of the Prime Minister, Francisco Sá Carneiro, on 4 December 1980.

Sá Carneiro, along with Adelino Amaro da Costa (Minister of Defence) and five others, were killed when their light aircraft, en route to Porto, crashed shortly after take-off from Lisbon airport. Ever since his death there has been speculation, and investigations and parliamentary inquiries, to try to determine the cause of the crash. The key question has centred upon whether the crash was caused by sabotage. If so, who was responsible? Who was the intended target? And what was the motive?

It goes beyond the realm of this book to examine the evidence for the case of alleged foul play in the death of Sá Carneiro.

It is sufficient to say that the various theories and the apparent evidence have been recorded and published in the media in both Portugal and overseas. To date, however, even as the Prime Minister of Portugal in 2011, Pedro Passos Coelho, noted, no categorical conclusion has been reached on the cause of the accident.[1]

The death of Sá Carneiro robbed Portugal of arguably its most charismatic post-Revolution leader, and the one that the outside world had placed great hope in to implement reforms to the Portuguese economy. Paying tribute to Sá Carneiro, Lord Moran, the British Ambassador to Portugal, wrote: 'He was a vigorous and effective Prime Minister for eleven months . . . Sá Carneiro took from the first a tough line in favour of free enterprise and against Communist influence both nationally and internationally and sought to dismantle the last vestiges of the 1974 revolution.'[2]

The challenges that the Sá Carneiro government faced during its brief period in office were determined from the start by the knowledge that he would have to face the regular legislative elections in October 1980, followed by a Presidential Election in December of the same year. Put simply, he needed to demonstrate to the electorate that his economic policies were effective. Here his government was able to achieve some quick wins: inflation fell to under 20 per cent, some of the tax burden was reduced and the real value of wages did not decrease.[3] Foreign investment, moreover, increased and growth was at around 3.6 per cent.[4]

Some of the old problems remained in place or worsened. Unemployment remained high and agriculture still remained in need of radical reform. In 1980, Portugal continued, as a result, to import between 50 and 75 per cent of its food, an unbelievable statistic given the size of the agricultural sector in the country.[5] Labour disputes increased, fuelled by militant trade unions with strong political grievances against the centre-right government.[6]

During the Sá Carneiro era, a youthful Minister of Finance, Aníbal António Cavaco Silva, a strong advocate of economic liberalization, ran the economy. Bright, self-made and with a PhD in Economic Theory from the University of York, Cavaco Silva set out to reform the socialist economy that had been put in place since the Revolution. Back in 1980, few could have foreseen his development into arguably one of the two most important post-Revolution leaders.

He became Portugal's right eye, to the left eye of Mário Soares. He was to serve for a decade as Prime Minister, and two five-year terms as President of the Republic. For nearly 50 per cent of Portugal's 40-year plus history since the Revolution, he occupied one or other of the two most important leadership roles in the country. He also became the first Portuguese leader to secure an absolute majority in elections for the legislature.

The process of economic reforms implemented by Sá Carneiro and Cavaco Silva proved to be popular with the centre-ground constituency of the electorate. In the General Election held on 5 October 1980, the Democratic Alliance increased its majority, securing a total of 47.1 per cent of the vote.[7] This meant that the government's working majority in the National Assembly increased from six representatives to eighteen.[8] The achievement of a stable working majority in the National Assembly represented only a part of Sá Carneiro's electoral objectives for 1980.

The final part of the jigsaw was to secure the election of a President who was sympathetic to the aims of the Democratic Alliance in Presidential Elections that were scheduled for December of the same year.[9] Only after the election of a new centre-right President did Sá Carneiro believe that he would be fully able to chart a new course for Portugal from 1981 onwards.

In short, he believed that it was not possible to work with President Eanes, who he viewed as being untrustworthy and a prisoner of the left in Portugal.[10] Sá Carneiro, as a result, devoted considerable energies to trying to find an alternative centre-right political or military leader with the credibility to defeat President Eanes at the polls. This proved to be no easy task, and the Democratic Alliance eventually had to settle on an able centre-right candidate, General Soares Carneiro (not related to the Prime Minister).

Though popular in the armed forces, General Carneiro was relatively unknown by the electorate, ineffective in the campaign, and was soundly beaten by President Eanes in the Presidential Election.

The re-election of President Eanes, which came only two days after the death of the Prime Minister, would have thrown Portugal into a political crisis given the repeated promise of Sá Carneiro to resign in such circumstances.[11]

The fact that the Prime Minister rejected potential habitation with President Eanes revealed the divisions that still characterized post-Revolution politics in Portugal. The country had been spared the ravages of civil war that had scarred Spanish and Greek society for generations, but even in the absence of such a conflict, Portugal and the Portuguese remained bitterly divided in 1980, largely along a left-right split.

The boarded-up, rapidly decaying houses in central Lisbon, Estoril and Cascais, abandoned in a hurry by affluent and aristocratic families soon after the Revolution, were visual testament to the political divides. The losers from the Revolution chose, by and large, not to fight, but rather to put their children in the back seat of their cars and head for the border to Spain, and further afield to Brazil – to rebuild broken lives and set up new financial enterprises.

Had more opponents of the Revolution remained in Portugal, held firm and fought, then the prospects of a civil war would have been all the greater. If the Nixon administration, moreover, had not backed Ambassador Carlucci's plans and opted for the more interventionist ideas of Secretary of State Henry Kissinger, then the prospects for civil war would again have been much enhanced.

Kissinger's goal of using the 'Chile model' of steady de-legitimization of the left, together with funding (and arming) right-wing groups, could have led to a wave of violence not seen in Lisbon since the demise of the Republican era. Instead, Portugal was allowed to turn to the left, and efforts to rebuild the centre-left and right became the policy of the Western powers.

At the end of 1980, as the British Ambassador, Lord Moran, left Lisbon, he made a number of observations about the Portuguese and the state of the country as he saw it at a critical juncture in its history. Lord Moran's comments centred upon the underlying reasons why he believed that cohabitation between President Eanes and a government led by Sá Carneiro would, regrettably, not work.

The lack of a coherent political culture meant that the political struggle for the control of the Portuguese state was far from over. Although Moran believed that Sá Carneiro was wrong to rule out working with President Eanes, he viewed the Revolution as creating largely unfinished business between the forces of the left and the forces of the right in Portugal, which would not be reconciled in the immediate future.

The premature and untimely demise of Sá Carneiro elevated Francisco Pinto Balsemão to be his successor as Prime Minister. This made it more possible for the Democratic Alliance to work with President Eanes, who Sá Carneiro had always considered to be a member of the left-wing camp. Balsemão was a very different type of character to his predecessor.[12]

According to Moran, Balsemão was more moderate and flexible, but lacked Sá Carneiro's cutting edge.[13] Put simply, he represented a good choice for both the party and the country, which remained deeply divided over the orientation of its post-Revolution political direction. It is difficult not to wonder, however, just how different Portugal might have developed during the early eighties if Sá Carneiro had not died in the plane crash. As it turned out, the natural heir to Sá Carneiro was to be Cavaco Silva and not Balsemão, who only lasted a mere two and a half years in office.

The rise of the right in Portugal and the absolute majorities it obtained in the two General Elections held in 1980 brought to an end the first part of the post-Revolution era in Portugal. In democratic nations, the management of shifts in power from left to right (and vice versa) reveal the depth and security of political society. The year of 1980, as a result, although steeped in tragedy, remains one of the most important in the post-Revolution history of the nation. Lord Moran noted the changes during his four and a half years in Lisbon, from 1976 until 1981, in his end-of-posting report to the Foreign Office in London. Moran summarized events in Lisbon during this period into two columns.

As he stated, on the credit side there was no Communist takeover or breakdown; no attempt at military takeover; refugees from Africa were absorbed; finances were in better order and inflation was halved.[14] Put simply, the country was fundamentally stable. On the debit side, there was a left-of-centre President and a right-of-centre government, which was a recipe for frustration; the loss of Sá Carneiro in 1980; no improvement in agriculture; restrictive labour laws were still in place; and continued swollen public services and nationalized industries made huge losses.[15]

It was fairly typical for ambassadors to use their end-of-posting report to comment in colourful language on their experiences and personal views about their hosts to their superiors back in London. On this score, Lord Moran did not disappoint. He described the characteristics of the Portuguese people as being the opposite of the Germans. Here, it wasn't clear if he meant this as a compliment, or not. On a more specific note, Moran noted the changes in Lisbon from when he first arrived in the city in 1976. As he wrote:

> In 1976 Portuguese life was heavily influenced by left-wing thought. The country was still in the aftermath of what had been a profound social revolution. One reason why I got rid of our large Daimler [car] was that people in the street were apt to bang on the doors and cry out 'fascists'.
>   This sort of thing is no longer common. In 1976, the 'Captains of April' ensconced in the Council of the Revolution still loomed large on the Lisbon scene, and the Communists still called the tune in the Alentejo. Those who had lived through the Revolution were astonished when a military parade was held and the troops actually obeyed orders from their officers.[16]

Comparing 1976 to the start of the decade of the 1980s, Moran added his take on the state of the nation in 1980:

> The Revolution of 1974 seems far away. The Armed Forces are disciplined and comparatively free from politics. The Captains of the Council of the Revolution are now mostly irrelevant, former landowners have received back a portion of their former estates and Communist efforts to frustrate this have been ineffective.

There has been a slow but significant economic recovery helped
by the revival of tourism and a steady flow of remittances from
emigrants in France, Luxembourg and Germany.[17]

Moran chose then to comment on what remained the major
Portuguese foreign policy issue of the day, the Portuguese application to join the EEC. During the course of 1980 there had
been slow but steady progress towards establishing a date and the
economic terms for Portugal's entry into the club.

On 6 and 7 March 1980, the President of the European
Community, Roy Jenkins, had visited Lisbon to give some impetus
to EEC entry negotiations.[18] As ever, Jenkins was engaging and a
visionary about the enlargement of the club. He was a frequent visitor to Lisbon, with his main role being to try to reassure Portugal's
new leaders (and members of the opposition) that Europe wanted
Portugal to become a full member of the EEC. He also attempted
to allay Lisbon's fears that Portugal's entry into the EEC might be
delayed due to any linkage with the problems of Spanish entry into
the Community.[19]

While Jenkins was strongly supportive of Portugal's application
for entry, according to Moran, he appeared to overlook the difficult
question of who would foot the bill for the country's entry into
Europe. Indeed, without consulting the member states that had to
foot the bill for Portugal's entry he encouraged Lisbon to request
a substantial amount of pre-accession help in the form of an aid
package.[20] The Portuguese government, as a result, applied for a
very large package of aid, and after lengthy negotiations the EEC
agreed to grants and loans amounting to around £165 million, to
be spent on development projects in Portugal.[21]

In short, Lisbon was already in debt to the EEC prior to joining it and the dependency ties between the country and Europe
were established. What was also clear from the outset was that the
priority for using these funds was the development of new infrastructure, and in particular the opening up of the interior of the
country and the development of its transport links to the coastal
areas.[22]

Moran had become a convert to Portugal's entry into the EEC during his posting in Lisbon. Prior to taking up the post he had listened to the critics of Portuguese entry, who argued that membership would wipe out Portuguese industry.[23] Some British officials had suggested to the Ambassador that 'for Portugal the economic price of membership would be formidable, even disastrous'.[24] Moran came to view Portuguese membership, however, as being motivated and driven by political and not economic reasons.[25] In Lisbon, he argued, there was a strong belief that the aspects of the latter would take care of themselves.

In reality, the EEC's decision to agree to the aid package to Portugal in October 1980 helped create the illusion that this would indeed be the case.[26] The Portuguese leadership, moreover, believed that membership of the EEC would bring financial advantages and that these gains would outweigh any losses that the country incurred in joining the Community.[27] With the passage of time, it is clear that Portuguese thinking on the financial advantages of membership in the form of loans and aid from the EEC has remained an important factor in determining its continued support for the Community throughout the history of its membership.

In the final part of his farewell dispatch, Moran paid tribute to Portugal and the Portuguese. His sentiments reflected the continued close relationship between London and Lisbon, and though written with a hint of nostalgia, made for interesting reading: 'Portugal is an attractive land of surprising variety, full of pleasing old buildings, cobbled streets, cork oaks, and trees on which "hang in shades the orange bright, like golden lamps in a green night," though the new buildings are as displeasing as those elsewhere.'[28]

On the Portuguese people, Moran was full of praise, albeit with a warning about their political leadership. As he put it:

> I have found the Portuguese agreeable to live among. In an increasingly violent and lawless world they are notably civilised, gentle people though they have the faults that go with these virtues for they are frequently disorganised and feckless. Their politicians go in for clouds of meaningless verbiage, and in

Portugal everything is done very slowly . . . The Portuguese do not plan ahead: they improvise. But, in their sleepy, southern, but often surprisingly effective way they will, I think, manage, as they have done in the past four years.[29]

On the subject of the city of Lisbon, Moran summed up the state of Portugal's capital in the following way: 'Lisbon, once spotlessly clean, is now shabby and disfigured by political posters and slogans. But it is still an attractive city, relatively un-ravaged by development.'[30]

Lord Moran's generally positive comments about his posting in Lisbon were an accurate barometer of the state of Anglo-Portuguese relations at the time. Portugal's oldest ally remained a close observer and supporter of the new democratic nation. In summing up the ties that bound Lisbon and London, Moran wrote:

> Our own relationship with Portugal, based on our historical ties, on geographical realities (we are both maritime, ex-imperial countries on the periphery of continental Europe) and on our strong continental links, continues to be a fundamentally friendly one, reinforced by President Eanes's successful State Visit to London of November 1978 and by Princess Anne's equally successful visit to Portugal in May 1979. It helped too, that while a Labour Government was in power in Britain, Portugal had a Socialist Prime Minister, but when a Conservative Government came to power [in Britain] a likeminded government took over in Portugal.[31]

While Anglo-Portuguese relations remained close, Portugal's relationship with the United States had been less close. To some extent, Lisbon's relationship with Washington warmed as it became clear that there was not an imminent danger of a Communist takeover. The other factor that helped was the election of President Jimmy Carter in 1976, and the implementation of a less ideologically driven US foreign policy under his leadership than was the case during the Republican era.

During the course of 1980 both President Carter and the ex-Secretary of State, Henry Kissinger, visited Lisbon. On 26 June, President Carter made a flying visit to Lisbon and held meetings with President Eanes, Sá Carneiro and Mário Soares. Speaking during his one-day visit, President Carter was keen to articulate US support for Portuguese democracy. Speaking upon his arrival in Lisbon, he paid tribute to Portugal's transition to democracy.

> Over the past 6 years Americans have watched and supported
> Portugal's successful struggle to build a democracy. That strug-
> gle has given hope to believers in democratic liberty throughout
> the entire world. For all these reasons, I am grateful for the
> opportunity to visit Portugal and of being able to meet with
> your country's leaders.[32]

Underneath all the diplomatic niceties of President Carter's comments lay an American sense of gratitude towards the Sá Carneiro government for its strong opposition to the invasion of Afghanistan by the Soviet Union earlier in the year. As soon as the Sá Carneiro government had taken office it had strongly condemned the Soviet invasion and had recalled the Portuguese Ambassador to Moscow.[33]

The former Secretary of State, Henry Kissinger, arrived in Lisbon on 13 November and remained in the city until 15 November. During his stay, Kissinger met the same three leaders that President Carter had during his visit. There remains a degree of mystery and speculation over the exact nature of Kissinger's visit to Lisbon. It came at a time immediately following Ronald Reagan's victory over Carter in the US Presidential Election of 4 November 1980.

US sources have suggested that Kissinger was attempting to reboot private foreign policy initiatives in the hope that Reagan would subsequently appoint him as his Secretary of State when he took office in January 1981. Kissinger and Reagan were not close and Reagan's transition team detested him.[34] Whatever the political and personal motives for his visit, the topics for discussion with the Portuguese government centred upon Africa. Kissinger was acutely aware of Portugal's continued importance on the African continent as one of the major ex-colonial powers.

Speaking after his meeting with Sá Carneiro, Kissinger told the domestic and international press corps that Portugal's long experience as a colonial power in Africa meant its opinion would always carry weight.[35] Part of the talks involving Kissinger, President Eanes and Sá Carneiro also concentrated on issues relating to the Middle East, specifically the ongoing problem of US hostages being held in Iran and the Israeli-Palestinian conflict.

The Americans were pleased with Lisbon's response to events in Tehran. On 10 April, the Portuguese government had mirrored the EEC in calling for the release of the US hostages, and on 17 April, the Portuguese government formally ordered sanctions against Iran.[36] In retaliation, two days later, Iran cut oil supplies to Portugal.[37] But there was still concern over President Eanes' policy towards the PLO.

From 2 April until 8 April, PLO representatives had been in Lisbon carrying a message from Yasser Arafat for President Eanes. US policy (from both the Carter and Reagan administrations) towards the PLO was clear: no contacts or negotiations until Arafat renounced violence and accepted Israel's right to exist. US policy was also to oppose an independent Palestinian state. Following his meeting with Sá Carneiro, Kissinger reminded the gathered press corps:

> My own personal view, which I've also expressed frequently, and I'm now speaking of my personal view not necessarily Governor Reagan's, is that the one thing the Middle East does not need is another radical state tied to the Soviet Union. And therefore I have always believed that the West Bank negotiations are to be primarily between Jordan and Israel and are to be conducted in that framework.[38]

If Kissinger's motives for visiting Lisbon and other European capitals had been to remind the incoming Reagan administration of his continued stature as a diplomat, then the plan failed. The Reagan transition team announced that Alexander Haig was to be its nomination for the post of Secretary of State. His visit to Lisbon did, however, confirm just how much Portugal was back in the NATO camp with its foreign policy interests in line with those of the European states it hoped to join in the Community.

During the post-Revolution era, Kissinger had shown his ruthless and ideological side in preparing a harsh American response to a potential Communist takeover in Lisbon. By 1980 this all appeared to be forgotten, as was his assessment of Mário Soares not being able enough as a politician and leader to save the country from this threat. In another sign that Portugal's past was being forgotten by the outside world, the death of Marcello Caetano in Brazil on 26 October was hardly noticed outside of Portugal.

The death of Salazar's successor brought a symbolic ending to Portugal's authoritarian era and the first phase of its transformation into a modern European democracy. The more practical realization of the entrenchment of Portuguese democracy, however, lay in the relatively orderly transition of government from centre-left to centre-right by way of the two Presidential-appointed, functionary-led governments. In this respect, the death of Sá Carneiro came at a critical time for Portuguese democracy.

The challenges that came to dominate the 1980s centred on how best to build upon the development of democratic institutions in the state, and how to alleviate Portugal's endless cycle of economic crisis. All of this needed to take place amid Portugal's imminent membership of the EEC and a severe global economic recession that characterized the first part of the decade.

PART THREE

Mad World

9

Ghost Town

As the global economic recession deepened in 1981, there was major social unrest in parts of Europe. In the United Kingdom, the social costs of the economic reforms implemented by the Thatcher-led government were felt throughout the country. Violence, as a result, erupted across Britain in the poor inner-city neighbourhoods and developed into major outbreaks of rioting against the police.

Burnt out cars lay scattered across city-centre thorough-fares, blocking access to new no-go zones as policemen banged their truncheons on riot shields before charging at the groups of stone-throwing youths. It was the era when cities resembled – as the ska music group, The Specials, sang – a 'Ghost Town'. It was a time of youthful rebellion, racial and ethnic tension. Grubby, grey, polluted and decaying, Europe's inner cities were in need of rejuvenation.

In Lisbon, however, all remained quiet. Lisboetas watched events unfold overseas with a sense of curious detachment. Thatcherite economic liberalization reforms would arrive in Portugal only later in the decade. While Lisbon remained physically disfigured by years of neglect and by political posters and graffiti, the city was, at least, free from major social unrest. Politically, Francisco Pinto Balsemão brought a new, more moderate and conciliatory tone to the office of Prime Minister.[1] Internationally, Balsemão was well liked as a man. The British summed up their opinion of him in a diplomatic cable sent from Lisbon to London:

Balsemão speaks fluent English and is well disposed towards
the [British] Embassy. He has visited Britain often . . . and
held talks with Mrs Thatcher in London in December 1980.
Wealthy and well travelled. Rather vain and finds it difficult
to distinguish between friends and appropriate advisors. As a
young man very much a playboy and a womaniser, but settled
down and has grown in the job of Prime Minister.[2]

The problem that Balsemão had faced since coming to power was
that he had to learn how to run the national government at the
same time as learning to control the party he led.[3] This proved to
be no easy task for a man whose party political skills were limited,
and who faced strong opposition to his leadership from within his
own party and ruling coalition.[4] Several members of the party were
afraid that, with the untimely loss of Sá Carneiro, the party would
slip into decline under the less charismatic leadership of Balsemão.[5]
To complicate matters, not all parts of the Democratic Alliance had
approved of his elevation to the leadership of the party, in particular the CDS (Centre Democrats), but no other candidate was in a
position to unify the party.

Aware of his growing difficulties, Balsemão invited his close
confidant, Marcelo Rebelo de Sousa, to enter the government as
a Secretary of State with special responsibility for the coordination
and marketing of policies. Previously, Rebelo de Sousa had taken
over as editor of *Expresso* newspaper when Balsemão had joined
the Sá Carneiro government. Writing in 1982, the British viewed
Rebelo de Sousa as the closest advisor to Balsemão and a man to
watch. As they put it: 'He enjoys outwitting friends and foes alike
and often . . . [he] has a brilliant mind and is unrivalled in Portugal
as a political analyst. Possesses a keen sense of humour and manages
to keep many social engagements despite a heavy workload.'[6]

While the arrival of Rebelo de Sousa led to an improvement in
the performance of the government, it continued to be dogged by
difficulties more often than not of its own making.

The essence of the national political problem remained the
two conflicting election results from 1980 that saw a centre-right

government win an overall majority in the National Assembly and the left-leaning President Eanes retaining power following the Presidential Election. In 1981, while the government and political parties concentrated on internal squabbles, President Eanes used the opportunity to consolidate his appeal to the electorate.[7] His prestige increased as a result, but a formal revision of the Constitution in 1982, which was aimed at preventing him from seeking a third term as President, threatened his political future.[8]

Put simply, at a time when the country needed coherent, strong and disciplined leadership, the political elite appeared more concerned with settling old scores, dealing with personality clashes and manoeuvring for position for the apparent inevitable collapse of the Balsemão-led government.[9] Concerns from the European powers centred upon the volatility and unusual unpredictability of Portuguese politics at a time of economic crisis and at a key juncture in the negotiations for the country's entry into the EEC.[10]

The catalyst for the eventual demise of the Balsemão-led government was the local elections held on 12 December 1982. The results were viewed with heightened importance as they represented the first test of political opinion in the country for over two years.[11] The elections were also seen as a test of opinion on Balsemão's leadership. As a result, while the campaign was largely fought on local issues and personalities in most areas, conclusions were quickly drawn about their consequences at a national level.[12] The Democratic Alliance ran as an alliance in around 40 per cent of the municipalities, and as separate parties in the rest of the areas.

In a sign of the continued enthusiasm of the Portuguese population for the democratic process, voter turnout was over 72 per cent, which was made all the more impressive by the bad weather that led to flooding in the northern part of the country.[13] The results were in effect a mid-term reflection of the electorate's view on the government, and the Democratic Alliance performed poorly – although not terribly.

When all the votes were added up for the component parties the Democratic Alliance dipped under 43 per cent of the total vote and lost control of the university city of Coimbra, as well as losing its

absolute majorities in Lisbon and Porto.[14] Although the Democratic
Alliance did not do too badly, as the British suggested, when set
against Balsemão's fragile position in the party it proved to be
enough to deepen the sense of political crisis in the government.[15]
As the British noted:

> [The] results for the Democratic Alliance are not unexpected
> given Portugal's difficult economic situation and a govern-
> ment at mid-term. 43 per cent would still give the Democratic
> Alliance an overall majority on a national basis. The main
> embarrassment for Balsemão as both Prime Minister and
> President of the Social Democrats (PSD) is the rise in support
> for the Socialist Party (now the biggest single party in terms of
> votes cast) and the growing strength of his coalition partner, the
> Centre Democrats (CDS).[16]

In the wake of the election results, Balsemão finally decided that he
had had enough and informed his party of his intention to resign at
a meeting of the PSD National Congress held on 18–19 December
to discuss the election results. He informed President Eanes of
his decision the next day on 20 December.[17] Balsemão agreed to
remain as a caretaker Prime Minister, but with key potential leaders turning down the opportunity, there was little alternative other
than to have early elections for the National Assembly.[18]

While the trials and tribulations of the Balsemão-led government
dominated the political headlines during 1982, the visit of Pope
John Paul II to Portugal in May of the same year grabbed the atten-
tion of much of the population of the devotedly Catholic country.
The Pope visited Portugal from 12 to 15 May 1982, largely to see
Our Lady of Fátima. At the time, the visit was viewed as hugely
successful with vast crowds greeting the Pope from his arrival at
Lisbon airport to his departure from Porto. Over a quarter of a
century later, however, full details emerged of the threat to the
Pope's life that had occurred during his stay in Portugal.[19]

According to news agency Reuters, on 13 May 1982, the
Pope visited the shrine of Fátima to give thanks for surviving an

assassination attempt a year earlier on 13 May 1981, when he been shot in St Peter's Square by Turkish gunman Mehmet Ali Ağca.[20] During his visit to Fátima, a crazed ultra-conservative priest, Juan Fernández Krohn, lunged at the Pope with a dagger. Krohn was subsequently wrestled to the ground by bodyguards and arrested.[21]

The fact that the knife actually reached the Pope and cut him did not become public knowledge until October 2008 when a close aide discussed it in a documentary film about John Paul II.[22] As he put it, 'I can now reveal that the Holy Father was wounded. When we got back to the room (in the Fatima sanctuary complex) there was blood . . .' At the time, the Pope continued with his visit to Portugal, without disclosing the details of the incident or the wound he sustained.[23]

Towards the end of his trip, on 15 May, the Pope visited the University of Coimbra (one of the oldest universities in Europe) to address the representatives of Portugal's intellectual circles. During the course of his remarks, he paid tribute to the historical importance of Portuguese culture to the world:

> The Portuguese culture occupies a place of honour among the various cultures. It is a centuries-old culture, rich in very precise characteristics, which clearly distinguish it from other peoples. It expresses the personal way of the Portuguese of 'being in the world', their own conception of life and their religious meaning of existence. It is a culture forged with the passage of eight centuries as a nation, and enriched by the multiple and prolonged contacts which Portugal had during its history with the most diverse peoples of the various continents.[24]

He continued:

> It pleases me to recall at this moment that admirable work of civilization, along with that evangelization, that the Portuguese achieved throughout the centuries in all those parts of the world which they reached. In this area of contacts with new worlds and on this level of culture, how can we not recall Luis

de Camoes and his 'Os Lusíadas', rightly considered one of
the principal works of world literature. I wish also to recall the
noteworthy contribution that your country, with its discoveries,
has made to the development of science.[25]

The Pope's public tribute to Portuguese culture did not hide the
fact that modern Portugal still faced many problems. Earlier, in
a private address to the foreign diplomats based in Lisbon on 13
May 1982, the Pope highlighted the continued efforts in Portugal
to integrate the returnees into society. As he put it:

> Portugal, on its part, has had to, and has been able to, welcome
> a very great number of Portuguese citizens who had left the
> overseas territories during the era of the independence of those
> territories, and it is easy to imagine the precarious position
> of these people and the enormous burden which this fact
> represented for the country which, with great effort, strove to
> integrate them and offer them a new place in the life of the
> Nation.[26]

During his address the Pope also highlighted the issue of Portuguese
emigration to European countries, reflecting that it was a sign of the
continued divide in the wealth of nations between Northern and
Southern Europe.[27] The Pope's comments highlighted an important fact: democracy had not resolved the issue of the emigration
of Portuguese workers to European countries. While many of the
emigrants had little, or only low-level education, some were highly
qualified and the loss of this group was an important element for
the development of the country. In many respects, the economy of
post-Revolution Portugal was just as dependent upon the remittances of Portuguese workers based in France and Germany as the
authoritarian economy of the Estado Novo had been.

The Pope's visit was a reminder of the continued importance of
the Catholic Church in Portugal to the population. It also highlighted that the shrine at Fátima remained a central feature for
many Portuguese, particularly for those from rural areas and for

those who made the annual pilgrimage to the shrine. Fátima was one of the three Fs that were said to be the dominant character features of the Portuguese nation, the others being football and fado music. Although the tradition of the three Fs was strong in the era of the Estado Novo, they had remained central to the democratic Portuguese society. Rightly or wrongly, to many outsiders, the three Fs summarize Portugal and its importance to the outside world.

In footballing terms, Portugal's three top clubs, Benfica, Sporting and Porto, have been international brands for decades. Their names are well known from the first golden era of Portuguese football during the 1960s. In 1982, however, it was a vintage year to be a Sporting fan. It was the season when 'The Lions' celebrated twice – winning both the league and the cup. At the time, an Englishman, Malcolm Allison, coached Sporting. Allison was a colourful figure whose vivacious personality overshadowed the widely acknowledged fact that he was a brilliant coach.

His time in Lisbon represented something of a rejuvenation in the fortunes of Allison, who had previously coached and had a largely unsuccessful second spell in charge of Manchester City. What was important about Allison was that he was the torchbearer for a whole list of English coaches who came to ply their trade in Portugal. Allison's coaching theory also made him unique, and his methods were viewed by many as being decades ahead of their time. The use of physical preparation training was largely unheard of in European football at the time, and Allison's teams were among the fittest to grace the Portuguese football field.

For his part, Allison – or 'mister', as the fans called him – enjoyed the more scientific attitude towards football that the Portuguese embraced, as well as the centrality of the game to all aspects of Portuguese life. His teams always played with an attacking flair, often conceding several goals but winning by simply scoring more goals than their opponents could muster.

Allison felt at home in Portugal, where he was away from the British tabloid newspapers touting stories about his private life. He regarded his years in Portugal (he also coached Vitória de Setúbal and Farense) as some of the most fulfilling of his professional life.[28] Later another English coach, Bobby Robson, made a similar big impression in Portugal, leading both Sporting and FC Porto to success. Like Allison before him, Robson came to love Portugal and its football. Unknowingly at the time, Robson's major contribution to Portuguese football was probably giving a young José Mourinho his big break, by appointing him to act as his translator.

The centrality of football in Portuguese society remained undiminished amid the political transformation of the country. Café bars in Lisbon and across the rest of the country continued to show games on their TVs, and bus and tram drivers listened to the commentary on their radios as they navigated their way around the city. Given the importance of football to Portuguese society and to big business it was inevitable that sooner or later the game would be dogged by scandals.

Some of the allegations proved to be pure speculation, but others stuck. From the 1980s onwards charges of match fixing and bribes being offered to referees of both national and European games were commonplace. In a changing political world, however, football represented an ever-present sideshow of entertainment, gossip and speculation for the masses in the country.

During the summer of 1982, Portugal's Iberian neighbour, Spain, hosted the 12th FIFA World Cup. The competition, in truth, did little to advance Spain's economy, but did serve as an international calling card to highlight the successful transition of Spain from the era of Franco's authoritarian rule to democracy. In 1982, while Spain hosted football's biggest party, Portugal still appeared remote and less developed. The contrast was not lost, and Lisbon started to look towards international events that it could host that would send a similar message to the outside world. It would be 22 years before the country hosted the Euro 2004 football tournament, beating Spain in the bidding process.

The third F, for fado, never left the Portuguese soul during the years of political transition in the country. In 1982, fado music was as popular as ever. The queen of fado, Amália Rodrigues, released another successful album simply entitled *Fado*. Amália's career spanned both the era of the Estado Novo and democratic Portugal until her death, at the age of 79, in October 1999.

For decades, she was perhaps the most internationally recognized face, and voice, of Portugal, enjoying success in both the United States and Europe. Her most notable achievement was in putting fado into the international music scene. Today, the music of fado is a central feature in the international marketing of Portugal. Fado clubs in Lisbon offer tourists a taster of the 'authentic' music, and a new generation of Portuguese singers have carried the torch forward.

The centrality of Fátima, football and fado to the Portuguese nation and culture provided a reassuring continuity to many Portuguese as the political upheavals and ongoing economic problems dominated everyday life. For all its desire for political change and a removal of all the baggage related to the era of the Estado Novo, many Portuguese continue to be nostalgic, with values steeped in tradition and suspicion of the new and of the outside world. By the end of 1982, as the country limped from political crisis to crisis, and with the heavy footsteps of the International Monetary Fund (IMF) echoing in the background, it was clear that the country was struggling to move forward.

This is the Day

As the winter rains of early 1983 poured down and off the roofs of Lisbon's crumbling gutter-free buildings on to the streets below, the city looked at its most abjectly dirty, grey and jaded, and the whole country appeared to be stuck in neutral. Portugal was unable, and unsure, of how best, and at what speed, to move forward. The incessant rain added to the sense of melancholy, which could be felt right across the city.

The country was at a vital crossroads in its modern history, when its leaders would choose a path that would set the direction of the country for decades and possibly centuries. As was the case in several other European countries, political and economic leaders appeared to be way ahead of the population in driving a vision of a united and unified continent of Europe, a concept which large sections of the population found it difficult to comprehend, sign up to and support.

The chattering classes of Lisboetas, who gathered in downtown Lisbon cafés, speculated whether membership of the European Community would come quickly enough to save the country, or whether it would have the opposite effect and destroy it. Aspiration, fear, nationalism, uncertainty were all part of the equation that centred upon questions about Portugal's past and present, and in which direction its future lay.

With the Portuguese colonies gone, and with a world increasingly linked together in multi-state political and economic blocs, it was a decision between isolation versus integration into Europe. For many Portuguese, however, it was also a case of modernity versus tradition. The fear of losing Portuguese customs, culture and tradition to the unfolding new pan-European identity was hard for many to accept, particularly the older generations.

Lots of Portuguese, however, were indifferent to the debate about membership, and this was a source of immense frustration for many foreign diplomats in Lisbon. The British summarized developments in 1983:

> For Portuguese who think about the matter, membership remains a political imperative for a country still feeling its way towards an effective form of democracy. Business opinion in the more energetic north of the country is beginning to see also an economic inevitability about membership and eventual benefit for those who can meet the competition. This is a change of climate, but is also accompanied by growing frustration over delays and a determination that the Portuguese negotiation should be finished by 1984.[1]

Those Portuguese who strongly supported membership argued that, surely, European aid would transform the country and move it forwards into the modern world. A quick tour of the city revealed to even the casual outside observer that something was amiss. The empty decaying buildings made Lisbon resemble more East Berlin than the once glorious capital it had been in past centuries. Drastic action was required to save the city, and the wider country, from becoming a living museum of past glories and modern failings. The outside world looked on in the hope that there would be a wake-up call and the political and economic elite of Portugal would start to address the ills of the country. It was to be initially disappointed.

Portugal, as a result of the political crisis caused by the resignation of the Prime Minister, wandered into 1983 with a caretaker government and a severe economic recession.[2] Neither situation was what the country needed as it moved towards membership of the European Community. On the positive side, the political shift from a centre-left to a centre-right government had at least helped solidify Portuguese democracy in terms of the orderly hand-over of power from one side to the other.

While the political leadership awaited the General Election, the economy showed signs of further deterioration at a time when European bureaucrats were calculating the potential cost of Portuguese membership to the rich club. In short, there appeared an all too real danger that the country could effectively go bankrupt before it reached the safe bosom of the European Community.

At the General Election, which was held on 25 Monday April 1983, the Socialist Party and the Social Democrats (PSD) between them gained two-thirds of the votes cast.[3] The shifts in voting patterns from the previous elections were not large enough to give the Socialists the overall majority that they had hoped to obtain.[4] The failure to secure an overall majority was hugely disappointing for the Socialists, although not a totally unexpected development.

In the end, the Socialists, led by Mário Soares, increased their share of the vote to over 36 per cent, with the PSD at just over 27 per cent. The Communists saw their share of the vote increase to 18 per cent, with the centre-right party of the CDS being perhaps the biggest loser. In terms of seats in the National Assembly, the Socialists became by some margin the largest single party, with 101 seats to the 75 seats for the PSD. Once again, the Portuguese population turned out in large numbers to cast their votes, with 79 per cent of the electorate voting.[5]

The majority support for the parties of the centre was the main message that the country sent to its political leaders. This was welcome news indeed for the Western and European powers, whose support for Portugal's ailing economy was vital if its economic ills were to be addressed. Indeed, several international bankers put off the signature of a $300 million loan to Portugal until the new government took office in June.[6] The increased scrutiny of the Portuguese economy by international bankers did not stop there. Representatives of the International Monetary Fund (IMF) were in Lisbon applying the finishing touches to a very large bailout package for the country.

The IMF bailout was much needed. By May 1983, Portugal's foreign exchange reserves were so low that they could effectively only pay for two weeks of essential imports.[7] In light of this stark reality, the government took the decision to sell off some of the gold that the state had acquired during the Second World War, in order to reduce the impact of the crisis.[8] The first $480 million of IMF stand-by credit was released to help pay for the country's imports and to meet the ever increasing repayments of the interest on foreign debt.[9]

On the political front, after much negotiation and burning of the midnight oil, a centrist coalition was cobbled together that included the Socialists and the PSD. It represented something of a government of national unity, which, while normal in some other countries facing severe economic difficulties, was a first for post-Revolution Portugal. With nearly two-thirds of the popular support, the government enjoyed the biggest majority since any of the 15 governments since 1974. Ego, internal party squabbles and, to some extent, ideological differences were to make the management of the government far from easy for Mário Soares, who was once again installed as Prime Minister.

Naturally, the major issue on the agenda for the newly sworn-in Cabinet was the economy and the need for the formation and implementation of an austerity programme. Privately, Soares informed the British that the Portuguese people would accept austerity if it were carefully explained to them.[10] It was with some relief that the British Embassy reported back to London that Soares' assessment appeared to be, at least, initially correct.

Soon after coming to power, the new Minister of Finance, Ernâni Lopes, set out the austerity programme that was to last until the autumn of 1984. As a result of the programme, the value of real wages dropped by approximately 10 per cent, and there was an increase in the number of companies going bust, a rise in unemployment and evidence in Lisbon and the rest of the country of real hardship.[11]

Austerity came as something of a shock to the Portuguese, many of whom still clung to the idea that the 25 April Revolution would lead to improvements in the economic situation of the majority of the population. Instead, it opened the economy even more to the pressures of economic cycles and to calls for greater transparency and scrutiny from foreign governments and financial institutions.

Lisbon was no longer able to hide at the western edge of Europe, now that representatives of the IMF were making regular visits to the Portuguese capital in order to receive updates on the progress of the austerity programme. As ever, Soares was good at charming and reassuring them that everything was in hand. During this period, the British were much impressed by Soares' steady hand and his attention to economic matters, as the British Ambassador, Hugh Byatt, wrote: 'He has settled in with energy and confidence showing himself ready to delegate and supported by a stronger staff [than previously].'[12]

What soon became clear, however, was that while the Portuguese were good at taking the medicine of austerity, the government appeared much less interested in implementing the programme of structural reform that came as part of the plan, nor did they have the ability to do so. Reducing red tape for employers, labour reform and cutting the size of the state sector were overlooked to a large extent. The government, in short, appeared bent on dealing with the problem on the surface, but not its root cause.

Just over the horizon from the austerity programme was Portugal's hoped-for accession to the European Community. By 1983, the political negotiations to make this happen were about two-thirds complete.[13] Agreement still needed to be reached on the key issues of agriculture, fishing and the budget. There also remained the complexities of Portugal joining at the same time as Spain, and the linkage between the two sets of negotiations in European eyes remained a source of great frustration for Lisbon.[14]

The Soares-led government had initially hoped for an entry as early as possible, even without the Spanish, but it was soon apparent that this was not going to happen. Portuguese–Spanish relations during 1983 were in a state of deep tension, largely caused by the complexities of the European negotiations and the need for both Lisbon and Madrid to establish arrangements as to their trading relationship within the European Community.[15]

In November 1983, Soares hosted an Iberian Summit in Lisbon with the Spanish Prime Minister and fellow Socialist, Felipe González. The summit made some progress, but trade and fishing issues remained largely unresolved. The difficulties of Iberian neighbourly relations were further complicated by the negotiations for entry into Europe. At times, Lisbon and Madrid were seen to be competing against one another in order to gain the best terms from the EEC. This became something of a frustrating experience for the European powers. After the Iberian Summit in Lisbon the British Ambassador noted in a dispatch back to London: 'A framework has been established and, if used, the two Iberian neighbours may be looking more towards each other as allied already in NATO and sooner or later partners in the Community.'[16]

The Portuguese–Spanish rivalry (for that was what the relationship really amounted to) was of course nothing new. The two Iberian states had both undergone difficult transitions from authoritarian rule to democracy at approximately the same time. In 1983, Socialist leaders were in power in both Lisbon and Madrid (although the Portuguese Government was a centrist coalition), but the two countries remained like distant cousins who had once been connected to each other through marriage.

To some extent, the negotiations to join the European Community that were being conducted simultaneously by both countries were seen as exercises in competition between the two states. Put simply, Portugal and Spain each hoped to secure better terms of entry than the other. This was particularly apparent in the previously mentioned negotiations about agriculture and fisheries.[17] Despite reassurances from the key European powers that the Portuguese and Spanish accessions were not related to one another, and with strong support from London for Portuguese membership in particular, there was a growing feeling in Lisbon that the negotiations were indeed inter-related.

The frustration about the slow pace of finalizing the terms for Portuguese membership of the European Community grew with both Soares and the Minister of Foreign Affairs, Jaime Gama, talking publicly of the need to find alternatives to membership if the negotiations did not move forward in the near future.[18] In reality, this was merely political theatre to try to help speed the talks along. Around 66 per cent of Portuguese exports went to countries from the European Community, and for Portugal there was no real alternative to membership of the Community.[19] In private, Gama conceded this point to the British, but the sense that the Community was dragging its feet over the enlargement negotiations did not go away.[20]

In Lisbon, as the autumn days began to grow shorter and the nights became colder, the full effects of the austerity programme started to be felt by the Portuguese. The pain of austerity was mixed with the knowledge that the country had little alternative but to take its medicine in the hope that the treatment would be over, as claimed by the government, by 1985.[21]

On a positive note, foreign banks retained confidence in Portugal, although there was a fear that the Portuguese would attempt to cherry-pick the agreed austerity plan with the IMF, and choose not to implement the most economically painful part of it.[22] Bankers expressed scepticism that the problem of restructuring the economy would ever be addressed.[23] By the end of 1983, Portugal had helped to reassure the IMF and other international financial institutions by cutting the country's current account deficit by one-third.[24]

Throughout the later part of 1983, the Prime Minister, Mário Soares largely held his nerve amid the increasing social costs of the austerity programme, and the complexities of selling the programme, as well as Portugal's membership of the European Community, to the population. Gone were the histrionics that had irritated many diplomats and European leaders during the immediate post-Revolution period. Internal divisions within the Socialist Party increased as the pressures of governing the country rose, but Soares showed at the party's congress, held in October 1983, that he remained firmly in control of the party.[25]

Maturing as a political leader, Soares in 1983 had one eye on the next Presidential Election, which he hoped to contest as the Socialist Party's candidate.[26] The British claimed that Soares, as a result, wanted to leave the Prime Minister's office by the end of 1984 to prepare for the Presidential Elections.[27] Regardless of the accuracy of this claim, it looked difficult for Soares to be elected as President after heading a government that had been forced to implement a painful and increasingly unpopular austerity programme. There also remained the thorny question for Soares as to what the incumbent, President Eanes's political intentions were, in light of the fact that he would be able to stand for an additional term himself.

Put simply, Soares remained wary of President Eanes and there had been tension when the government clashed with the President over the appointment of a new Chief of Staff.[28] Eventually, a compromise was reached, which ensured that the elected government's control was maintained. This outcome was seen as further confirmation of the principle of civilian control over the military being accepted by the President.[29] Hugh Byatt wrote on the consequences of the crisis as well as the changes to Presidential powers: 'The powers of future Presidents will be slightly reduced over military appointments, but the system remains "semi-presidential" and I doubt if it will move further towards full parliamentary control.'[30]

In 1983, modern Portuguese democracy was under a decade old. The competition for influence and power between the Presidency and the government was, by and large, a product of attempting to define the rules of the game. The fact that a resolution was found, albeit to the detriment of President Eanes, represented a positive sign for the future of democracy in Portugal.

What worried outside observers the most about Soares' intention to run for the Presidency, was that he would be tempted for his own political motivations to try to re-inflate the economy too soon.[31] With his eyes on the Presidential Election, it was widely believed that Soares would not want to court too much unpopularity by strictly adhering to the austerity programme.

Soares hoped that the worst of austerity in terms of increased unemployment and reductions in the real value of wages would be over by the time of the election.[32] The Communists, and the unions they controlled, made it clear that the focus of their campaign would be unemployment. For the most part in 1983, however, the unions had been unable to exploit the impact of the austerity programme for their own political gain: workers were simply too afraid of losing their jobs to join national protests against the cuts.[33]

Arguably 1983 had been the most difficult and testing year for Portugal since the Revolution. As the Christmas lights were turned on in downtown Lisbon to usher in the festive season, there was a hope that the worst of the austerity programme was behind the country. Sadly, this was not the case. While the IMF and the bankers were satisfied with Portugal's efforts, the full domestic impact of the austerity measures was still to be felt.[34]

What Portugal appeared to need the most at this important moment was good government and political stability. Internal feuding in both the major political parties threatened to derail this hope, and as the year ended, a number of 'marginal but emotional issues such as abortion or local government' could potentially blow the government off course.[35]

What Difference Does It Make?

On 25 April 1984, the Portuguese marked the tenth anniversary of the Revolution that had transformed Portugal from an authoritarian state to a democratic one. The Revolution had transported Portugal out of the past ages and into the modern world, but in 1984 its place in the democratic club of nations remained far from secure. It was, as a result, a time of quiet stock-taking and muted celebrations across the country.[1]

In Lisbon, the 25 April Association honoured the leaders of the Revolution in a separate celebration to the official one, which was organized by the government.[2] The impression given by the staging of dual events was of a separation, or a divorce, between the revolutionaries and the political ruling class of the country. The former group was left to indulge in its nostalgic recounting of the events of the Revolution, which was somewhat soured by the bitterness at being left marginalized in the post-Revolution national narrative. The latter group remained focused on the present-day troubles, and there were plenty of those for it to worry about.

The prediction that the worst of the social costs of the austerity programme would be felt in 1984 proved to be accurate. To make matters even more difficult for the Portuguese, there was little evidence that there were better times to come in the foreseeable future. For many Portuguese, the merits of the austerity programme remained abstract. 'What difference does it make?' was a common response to questions about potential support for

austerity. Despite the hardships caused by the austerity programme
the majority of the population remained, by and large, passive and
the trade unions were unable to foment major labour unrest.[3]

On this score, Soares' prediction from the previous year, that the
Portuguese would accept austerity, was proved correct. Educating
the population about the potential benefits of the policy, however,
remained a work in progress. Portugal continued to take its
economic medicine in the hope that this action alone would cure
its illness. Few suspected that it would, but given the IMF theory of
'no pain, no gain' there was no realistic plan B to consider.

Not for the first time, at a moment of dire national need,
Portugal's party political leaders were, at times, more interested
in wrangling with one another than addressing the needs of the
country. Having a President and Prime Minister who were both
personally and politically opposed to each other exacerbated political tensions, and threatened to overshadow important ongoing
debates on constitutional reform.[4]

The Soares and Eanes relationship was often reduced to a second-
rate *telenovela* plot. Neither man covered himself in glory, but constant
speculation about the future political intentions of Eanes continued to
impact upon daily political life. Several observers believed that Eanes
would form a new movement to try to run against the government
after he left the Presidency. As the British Embassy noted:

> The constitution prevents President Eanes from standing for
> a third consecutive term at the end of 1985, when he will
> still be under fifty. The future of this withdrawn, prudent but
> undoubtedly ambitious man has become an intriguing ques-
> tion. Some of his former supporters have launched a movement
> designed to appeal across the spectrum to a grassroots urge
> for decency and honesty . . . Eanes has been characteristically
> cautious about giving this his blessing, but has virtually said
> that he will enter active politics when his mandate ends.[5]

With a Presidential Election just over the horizon some Portuguese
politicians, however, were fast becoming austerity-weary, with

many of the sceptics coming from within the ranks of the governing parties. The political leaders of both the Socialist Party and the
Social Democrats also started to focus on the forthcoming election.

Badly needed economic reform and modernization programmes
were postponed, or shelved altogether. The minimum was done
to please the IMF and the international banks, but the tone had
changed.[6] Both the Socialist and the Social Democrat leaderships
turned on each other and the bickering in the ruling coalition
parties brought the government to a standstill by August 1984.[7]

Soares complained about the problems of working with the PSD,
who he believed were not shouldering their share of the responsibility.[8] Eventually he challenged them to take more responsibility or
to leave the coalition.[9] This led to a political crisis when it looked
as if either Soares might resign, or the PSD would leave and go
off sulking into the shadows. In the end, both parties pulled back
from the brink and continued with the ruling coalition.[10] It was,
however, a government in decline, and its ability to deal with the
ongoing financial crisis was compromised by the near-constant
distraction of both intra- and inter-party disputes.

Outsiders watched events unfold during 1984 with some trepidation. The British rather scathingly commented on the political
infighting: 'Personal feuding imposes great strains on the still imma-
ture political parties. Their management is a demanding affair for
the leaders and government business suffers accordingly.'[11]

Within the Socialist Party, Mário Soares remained very much
the number one. Despite some internal opposition to both his
style of leadership, and his seeming commitment to the austerity
programme, Soares kept a tight grip on the control of the party. The
same could not be said for the Social Democrat leader, Carlos Mota
Pinto. His leadership was questioned and, in 1984, he survived
two leadership challenges. In truth, he was little more than a transitional leader who was described in the most unflattering terms,
along with the party he led, by the British Ambassador to Lisbon:
'He is a weathercock figure swinging to what he believes to be the
prevailing wind: ineffective as Vice-Prime Minister and scarcely
functioning as Defence Minister. Management of the PSD [Social

Democrats] takes all his time, and it is no easy coach to drive. Its leadership is composed of groups of self-styled barons and its philosophy is lazy.'[12]

These were extremely strong words indeed from the diplomat, who could no longer contain his frustration at the Social Democrats and their internal disputes. In reality, change was just around the corner for the Social Democrats, in the form of Cavaco Silva, who would soon come to dominate political life in Portugal for a decade. In the meantime the Minister of Finance in 1984, Ernâni Lopes, produced a plan for economic recovery that centred upon the reform of the 'inflated, over-borrowed and largely unprofitable' public enterprises set up in the immediate aftermath of the Revolution.[13]

In addition, the plan called for a modernization of the woefully performing agricultural sector. Here one simple statistic illustrated the sad and sorry state of affairs in this key sector of the Portuguese economy. In 1984, the agricultural sector employed 26 per cent of the working population, but produced only around 4 per cent of Gross Domestic Product (GDP).[14] The plan, however, dodged the bullet of dealing with arguably the most controversial area of reform: the labour laws. In this area, there was a constant call for reform from the IMF and other international financial institutions.

In essence, by making it virtually impossible to reduce workforces that were greatly inflated by recruitment in the wake of the Revolution, the labour laws constituted a major cause of unprofitability in both the state and private sectors.[15] In reality, few of these reforms were implemented by the government, who were afraid to rock the ship prior to potential membership of the European Community, which many hoped would change the economic realities of the country with the arrival of large amounts of aid and subsidies.

In 1984, to paraphrase Sir Winston Churchill on the Second World War (again), Portugal had reached the beginning of the end of its quest for membership of the European Community. As the negotiations began to reach a conclusion, however, tensions remained high as Portuguese leaders tried to extract both the best deal possible for the country, and a better deal than their Iberian cousins. This was a very real case of high-stakes diplomacy, which was played out in smoke-filled rooms by negotiators who were acutely aware that the outcome of the talks would shape the future of the country for generations to come.

In this respect, Mário Soares began to escape from behind his desk more, under the guise of overseas visits to shore up support for Portugal's terms for entry to the European Community. Given the divisive state of internal Portuguese politics in 1984, such overseas 'charm visits' must have been a most welcome relief for the Prime Minister. It was Ernâni Lopes, however, who continued to be Portugal's 'Mr Detail', leading the small team negotiating the terms for accession.[16]

The negotiations remained a bumpy ride for the Portuguese, and suspicions of Spanish motives that had been brought up during 1983 rose to new levels during 1984. All of this had a quite dramatic and negative impact upon Portuguese–Spanish relations at this crucial juncture. The essence of the problems remained the potent mixture of impatience and frustration felt by the Portuguese negotiators over the continued slow pace of the negotiations.

The biggest source of annoyance for Lisbon remained that above all, its negotiations had to wait upon the Spanish ones with the Community.[17] Traditional Portuguese suspicions over Spanish motives started to border upon paranoia. Lisbon, for example, feared that Madrid might try to reassert historical fishing rights in Portuguese waters.

The mounting Iberian crisis of confidence between the two nations was not helped when during the course of 1984 Spain cancelled three ministerial visits to Portugal.[18] Further evidence of the deteriorating relations between Lisbon and Madrid came when an Iberian Summit between Soares and González, which was originally scheduled for November 1984, did not take place.[19] The forgotten summit meant that the negotiations between Portugal and Spain about their future relations when both joined the Community were delayed.[20]

Lisbon was more reassured by the visits of European leaders to Portugal that did take place during the course of 1984. The three heavyweight giants of European politics, Helmut Kohl, Margaret Thatcher and François Mitterrand, all visited the country. As well as providing Mário Soares, and other members of the government, with much-needed moral support for Portugal's struggles with the austerity programme, all three publicly and enthusiastically endorsed Portugal's rapid accession to the Community.

All three leaders were also competing for a bigger share in the Portuguese market. Britain had seen its share contract and was only Portugal's fourth largest supplier of goods.[21] Portuguese exports to its oldest ally were rapidly increasing, and during her stay in Lisbon, Thatcher called for greater British investment in the Portuguese economy.[22] The seriousness with which the three leaders took trade links with Lisbon was a timely reminder amid the economic chaos of austerity that Europe expected Portugal to get back on its economic feet one day soon.

Soares was also warmly welcomed in European capitals, and was a guest of Mrs Thatcher in London in November. During the course of their meeting, Thatcher reaffirmed her strong support for Portugal's rapid accession to the Community. Soares welcomed all of this – coming as it did at the same time that there was evidence that the French were cooling on the idea of rapid Portuguese accession.[23]

There was an additional reason for Thatcher's strong support for Portugal at this juncture. As Britain's war with Argentina over the Falkland Islands in 1982 had shown, London needed continued access to the defence facilities on the Azores.[24] During the course of the war, the Azores had served as an important supply point for the British task force as it sailed into the South Atlantic to confront the Argentine forces that had invaded the British-controlled Falkland Islands. Thatcher never forgot those who had helped Britain during the conflict, and those who had not.

On a strategic level, London also acknowledged the need to keep Portugal in the Western Alliance. This was still the era of the bipolar international system of the Cold War. Portugal was also useful as a partner in Southern Africa, where it retained excellent contacts.[25] The British were open about Portugal's usefulness in Africa. As the British Ambassador to Lisbon reminded the Foreign Office in London:

> Lisbon continues to be a useful listening post for lusophone [Portuguese-speaking] Africa although it is necessary to sift genuine information from rumour. During the year [1984], the Portuguese have been used by both the South Africans and the Americans in establishing contacts. Portugal's human links with their former colonies are real and it remains in our interest to encourage their maintenance.[26]

In reality, 1984 was not a vintage year for Portuguese relations with Africa. President Eduardo dos Santos of Angola snubbed Portugal by visiting Madrid and avoiding a similar trip to Lisbon.[27] It was a blow on which the Portuguese put as good a spin as possible, but it hurt Soares to see Spain succeeding in signing trade and fishing agreements with Angola.[28] The Angolans remained suspicious of Lisbon's attitude to the official Angolan government enemy, UNITA.[29] President Eanes tried his best to keep communications open with Luanda, but in 1984 there was no direct meeting between the two respective Presidents.[30]

Portuguese relations with another of its African colonies, Mozambique, were more promising. Soares undertook an official visit there in September, which was viewed as a qualified success.[31] There was a clear lack of personal chemistry between Soares and his hosts, with whom Soares had very little in common. Inter-African politics got in the way of better relations, which were overshadowed by the suspicion that came from South Africa that some powerful individual Portuguese were helping the Mozambican rebel movement in its conflict with the government.[32] To compound this there were rumours circulating in diplomatic circles back in Lisbon that two members of the Portuguese government had had telephone conversations with a member of the rebel movement.[33]

Overall, the major fear in London was that the democratic instinct in Portugal might falter in the wake of the ongoing economic crisis and this might lead to a more neutralist Portugal.[34] The British, as a result, were keen to be seen encouraging the country – which they described as 'an old friend and modern ally' – towards greater economic stability.[35]

The linkage between the economic crisis and the threat to democracy remained abundantly clear to the European powers at the time. With the Communists, and other far-left parties, consistently securing around 20 per cent of the vote in national elections, the threat of a leftward shift towards Moscow was a real and present danger. Likewise, nobody wanted to see a return to the old authoritarian ways that had dominated the modern history of the state from 1933 until the 25 April Revolution in 1974.

Away from politics and the ravages of the austerity programme, it was an unusual year for the country that was not without its moments of drama, success and near misses. During the early summer, Lisbon and the rest of the country was gripped by football fever. As the evenings grew longer and balmier in June the nation's football team was competing in the European Championship in France, and had a very real chance of winning the tournament. This represented Portugal's best hope of clinching an international tournament since its near miss in the 1966 World Cup in England. For the duration of the 1984 European Championship, Lisboetas were glued to their television screens.

The centrality of football to the Portuguese nation was always at its most visible when the national team was performing well. Esplanade cafés in downtown Lisbon placed television screens outside, and ordered in extra kegs of beer. Outside Portugal, the Portuguese national team was perceived as being full of highly skilful individual players, tinged with a streak of ill-discipline and hot Latin temper. As a team, the players often did not gel well together and under-performed.

In France, for once, the team exceeded expectations. It managed to get past the initial group stages without crashing out of the tournament and reached the semi-final of the competition. Given the large number of Portuguese emigrants working in France, the team was the best supported of the foreign outfits.

On 23 June 1984, Portugal took part in the semi-final against the hosts, France, in Marseille. The match was to become one of the most important in Portuguese football history. As UEFA described it: 'Arguably the most vivid match in the competition's history, in many ways it resembled the famous 1970 FIFA World Cup semi-final between Italy and West Germany as one team held sway for much of the match only to concede a late equaliser.'[36]

It was the Portuguese who grabbed the late equalizer, when Rui Jordão headed in his goal of the championship to temporarily silence the partisan Marseille crowd.[37] Playing in their white away kit, the Portuguese team took the lead in extra time when Jordão volleyed in from close range. At that moment, a real upset looked to be a distinct possibility, but the French equalized before Michel Platini grabbed a dramatic late winner.

The Portuguese lost but, as UEFA wrote, 'there was great honour in defeat for Portugal'.[38] The French went on to win the tournament by defeating Spain in a dour match in the final. Few, however, remember the final – rather that the Portuguese national team brought much credit to a country that was feeling the economic effects of the austerity programme. Football continued to offer a sense of escapism for the lower-income workers in the country, who were the group that was arguably suffering the most during the economic crisis.

Football was not the only sport to dominate the headlines during the long hot summer of 1984. During the summer Olympic Games in Los Angeles, the Portuguese long-distance runner, Carlos Lopes, won the marathon. His victory brought Portugal its first Olympic gold medal. Lopes won a race held in hot and humid conditions by a margin of some 200 metres in an Olympic record time of 2.09.21.[39] His victory prompted ecstatic celebrations back in Lisbon.

Upon his return, Mário Soares awarded Lopes the *Grã-Cruz da Ordem do Infante*. Lopes almost did not make it to the Olympics. Just prior to his departure for the games, Lopes suffered a fate common to many Portuguese pedestrians – he was run over by a car in Lisbon. As his official Olympic profile described the event: 'Only 15 days before the Olympic marathon, Lopes was on a training run when a car hit him. He rolled over the hood and his elbow crashed through the windshield. Fortunately, his injuries were minor.'[40]

Thankfully, Lopes was able to continue with his preparation programme for the marathon. Lopes' victory helped put Portuguese long-distance running on the map. More successes were to follow and in recent decades the country has produced a number of world-class marathon runners, both male and female.

Arguably the most curious sporting event of the year in Portugal was the return of the Formula One Grand Prix circuit to Lisbon. The race was held at the Estoril track on 21 October 1984, and represented the sixteenth and final round of the Formula One season. The arrival of the super-wealthy Formula One circus in a country still haunted by austerity made for a series of strange contrasts.

Large ocean-going yachts were moored off the coast at Cascais, and a steady stream of private jets and helicopters brought the drivers, their large entourages and the international jet set into Estoril. It was Portugal's first Grand Prix since 1960, when it had been held on the Boavista street circuit in Porto, and again the event promised drama.

The Austrian driver, Niki Lauda, needed 2nd place or better to win the Driver's Title, and gained this when British driver Nigel Mansell lost control of his car and spun off the track with 18 laps to go. Lauda, as a result, took the Driver's Title by the narrowest of margins – half a point – from his team-mate, the Frenchman, Alain Prost.

The point-scoring drivers of the Portuguese Grand Prix won a total of 13 world championships between them, and the three drivers who were on the podium that day were all (at least) triple World Champions from different eras: Niki Lauda was approaching the end of his long Formula One career, Alain Prost was at the peak of his, and the bright-eyed Brazilian, Ayrton Senna, was at the very beginning of his exciting career that was sadly to end in tragedy. Indeed, the real story of the Portuguese Grand Prix was the arrival of Senna on the podium. The young Brazilian was driving a Toleman-Hart car that was considered to be one of the slowest performing in Formula One.

The Australian journalist, diarist and author, Clive James, who attended the race for the *Observer* newspaper, described the scenes at Estoril that day:

> Before dawn last Sunday the vendors of cakes and fizzy drinks were in position beside the road leading to the circuit at Estoril. They weren't rich, and in the morning most of the people who bought what they had to sell weren't rich either. A lot of people came by car but almost as many came on foot, looking bedraggled and stepping carefully, because not all the mud had dried to dust. Slogans daubed on walls exhort the Portuguese to live always in the spirit of some day or other in April. It's a worthy sentiment, but the occasional splurge can't hurt. The international grand prix circus is the biggest splurge there is. 'Blam blam!' yelled an outlandish engine being tested in the distance. Money was being burnt. The traffic jam inched impatiently towards it. The pedestrians shuffled dust. The police were outnumbered – always a sign, in Portugal, that the crowd must be very large.[41]

The race helped put Portugal on the map of the Grand Prix, and for a generation people flooded to Estoril each year to watch the Grand Prix, as much as the rise of the driver that they most came to watch, Ayrton Senna. The following year, in 1985, Senna claimed his first Grand Prix Title by winning the Portuguese Grand Prix at Estoril, driving a distinctive black Lotus. The race took place in driving rain and the legend of Senna's driving skills in the rain was born on that April day in Estoril, which Senna reminisced later was his greatest wet-weather drive.[42]

So Portugal was back on the Grand Prix circuit, and the race helped highlight to an outside world that the country was becoming a part of Europe. Ten years on from the Revolution, the country was still waiting to see the real economic gains from democracy, but the political system remained intact and entry to the 'rich club' of the European Community was just around the corner.

The year of 1985 would be Portugal's last outside the bosom of the Community, and the political leadership needed to prepare the country for the major changes and challenges that lay ahead. This was to prove to be a tricky job for a government that remained deeply divided across party lines, and with the two main parties both experiencing mounting internal disputes as well.

12

Road to Nowhere

In many aspects of the political and economic life of the Portuguese nation, the year 1985 was one of transformation and the onset of a decade of relative political stability for the country that had not enjoyed such a luxury since the Revolution. The year also marked the end of Portugal's solo journey and the final stretch of its road to integration into the European Community with all the changes, good and bad, that would be entailed by membership.

The year also marked the start of the end of austerity with signs of improved economic indicators and hope for much-needed genuine economic reform. Most Portuguese might have missed the 'green shoots of recovery', but the IMF and the international bankers appeared happy with Portugal's efforts, and international confidence returned to the nation's economy. Not everything was transformed, and many old problems lingered unresolved and unaddressed, but the country was shifting, albeit with typical Portuguese indifference, towards the modern world.

Politically, the first part of the year was dominated by the slow collapse of the Soares-led government.[1] The eventual demise of the government was made all the more certain following the annual PSD Congress in the spring of 1985, during which Cavaco Silva was elected as leader of the party. The former Minister of Finance decided to formally withdraw the party from the coalition shortly after assuming the party's leadership.[2]

This left President Eanes with the decision between trying to put together a new government of technocrats – as he had done on two previous occasions – or leaving Mário Soares in charge of a caretaker government over the summer months.[3] After toying with the former idea, President Eanes opted for the latter one and dissolved the National Assembly on 12 July 1985, leaving Soares in office until the General Election scheduled in the autumn.

It was only after the Portuguese returned from their long August breaks at the beach that the election campaign moved 'reluctantly' into full swing.[4] August in 1985 remained very much the month of shutdown across the country, when whole cities temporarily migrated to the beach for sun, sea and fun. The political and economic life of the country (with the exception of the tourist sector of the economy) ground to a near halt. Any campaigning, such as it was, moved to the Algarve where the political elite vied for time on the television news in staged interviews, and wore open-neck shirts to local political rallies during their holidays.

The General Election was to be Portugal's final one prior to membership of the European Community, and the member states scrutinized the campaign and the results far more vigorously than in previous elections. Two issues topped the agenda: who would be most punished for the social and economic pain caused by the two years of the austerity programme, and how would the electorate react to the new PSD leader and his platform of economic liberalization and reforms. To complicate matters, the emergence of a new third-way party supported by President Eanes, entitled the Party of Democratic Renewal (PRD), ran in the election. The basic message of the PRD was that the two major parties had failed to deliver, and that the electorate was tired of the in-fighting among the existing political elite.[5]

The result of the election, which was held on 6 October, came as a surprise to many of the observers who had covered the campaign.[6] The first shock was the collapse of the Socialist vote, which was down from 37 per cent to just 21 per cent. The second largely unforeseen result was the performance of the PRD, which captured 18 per cent of the vote and became the third largest party.[7]

Here a large part of the electorate embraced the populist appeal of a party that promised a new beginning in Portuguese politics. The biggest winner of the election, though, was Cavaco Silva, whose PSD party saw its share of the vote rise to 29.9 per cent to become the single biggest party in the National Assembly.[8]

The result represented a personal triumph for Cavaco Silva, with the party having campaigned largely on his personality. The PSD fell short of an overall majority and were reliant upon support from other smaller parties. This made life difficult, but not impossible, for the government with the PRD often abstaining on key votes and offering tacit support to the government. Hermínio Martinho, the 39-year-old farmer who led the Democratic Renewal Party, stated that his party would give Cavaco Silva enough support in Parliament to form a government, but it would not be willing to formally join a coalition.[9]

'We're going into the opposition to transform Portuguese politics,' Martinho informed the media on the morning after the election. As the *New York Times* put it: 'his party is a populist group with leftist leanings but no well-defined ideology. Although it is closely associated with President Eanes, the President is barred from campaigning while in office.'[10] Prior to the election Cavaco Silva had made it clear that he would not enter into any new coalition with the Socialist Party.[11] Eventually, Cavaco Silva could rely upon the support of the Christian Democrats, who won 10 per cent of the vote, but he was still left short of an overall majority.

The election represented a major setback for the Socialist Party, and its candidate for Prime Minister, António Almeida Santos, as well as casting fresh doubts on Mário Soares' efforts to secure the Presidency.[12] Soares did not lead the Socialist Party in the election as he prepared to seek the Presidency in the elections in 1986. In retrospect, given the struggles that Portugal experienced during the tenure of the Soares-led government, it made it difficult for the party not to be punished by the electorate. It was widely believed that the apportioning of blame by the electorate for the severe economic crisis that the country had faced over the previous two years was central not only to the General Election, but also to the next Presidential Election.

Cavaco Silva, in withdrawing the PSD from the governing coalition so quickly after assuming the leadership of the party, was able, in the eyes of the electorate, to distance himself and the party from the previous two years' difficulties. As the *New York Times* coverage of the election summarized, 'the Socialists were apparently hurt at the polls by their economic policies, which resolved a foreign-debt crisis but brought on a recession. The unemployment rate exceeds 10 per cent, and inflation has eased only to about 17 per cent.'[13]

The timing of the rise of Cavaco Silva could not have been better from his perspective, with the financial aid from the European Community set to start flowing into Portugal soon after he assumed office. The one concern that the generally supportive British had about a Cavaco Silva-led government was that it would try to inflate the economy too soon for electoral reasons, just as they felt Cavaco Silva had done when he was Minister of Finance in 1980.[14]

Earlier in the year, and after many false dawns, the final agreement for Portuguese accession to the European Community was reached on 29 March 1985.[15] The agreement coincided with the agreement for Spanish accession to the Community. Even as his government was crumbling, Mário Soares, who had staked his political career on membership, was able to hail the agreement.[16] In a radio interview he said, 'within five years, Portugal will be a completely different country – and certainly a much better one for all Portuguese'.[17]

Despite the reassurance from Soares, many Portuguese remained uneasy about membership. While many industrialists and farmers supported the agreement, others expressed concern that the transition might damage Europe's poorest country.[18] As the British Ambassador wrote: 'There was pleasure that Portugal was at last accepted as an integral part of Europe tinged with concern as people began to grapple seriously with the economic impact of impending membership.'[19]

The real impact on Portugal of membership remained unclear. The European Community made it clear that its forthcoming poorest member (Portugal's GDP per capita was only 24 per cent of the EC average) would not become a net contributor.[20] The British worried that the internal political uncertainties during 1985 meant that Portugal's first year in the European Community would be 'close run' as it delayed the preparation of potential projects that would attract European funding from the outset.[21]

The agreement for Portugal's entry was met with widespread relief by the European powers, mainly on the grounds of the resolution of the more complex issues regarding the related question of Spanish membership.[22] The agreement itself was formally signed on 12 June 1985 in a ceremony in the Renaissance cloisters of Jerónimos Monastery in Belém. Soares hailed the signing of the treaty as being 'one of the most significant events of contemporary Portuguese history. We shall symbolically make a new departure with Portugal returning to the European fold and playing its rightful part in its dynamism and progress.'[23]

Soares' triumph, however, was short-lived.[24] The PSD, soon after the ceremony finished, formally left the coalition government – as they had stated they would do – and the country moved swiftly onwards, towards the General Election that would see the Socialist Party lose power for a decade.

Portugal's importance to the European Community and to NATO was highlighted in 1985 by the steady stream of international dignitaries who visited Lisbon during the course of the year. On 28 January, Tancredo Neves, the President-elect of Brazil, paid an official visit to Portugal. Neves, however, was to fall gravely ill before his inauguration and died soon after. In March, as the winter chill departed Lisbon, Queen Elizabeth II of the United Kingdom made an official visit to Portugal.

The subtext to her visit was the continued British efforts to outdo the French to become Portugal's third largest supplier after the United States and West Germany.[25] The Queen was always good for a trade boost, and her visit helped Britain achieve its goal of overtaking the French. The visit also helped to remind the Portuguese that Britain remained its oldest ally. The British Ambassador, Hugh Byatt, wrote lyrically on the visit:

> The State Visit by Her Majesty the Queen and His Royal
> Highness the Duke of Edinburgh provided a splendid climax to
> a very active period in our bilateral relations with Portugal. The
> occasion will endure in the minds of a new generation here.
> It was doubly welcome to the government and people coming
> as it did after a long winter of frustration over economic
> austerity and delays in the negotiations with the European
> Community.[26]

By happy coincidence, the last day of the visit coincided with the news that the Portuguese negotiations for membership of the European Community had been concluded.[27] In another sign of the good health of Anglo-Portuguese relations, nearly one million British tourists visited Portugal during 1985.[28] This figure helped push the Portuguese tourist sector forward after a couple of difficult years caused by the international economic recession.

Britain was not alone in looking towards the Portuguese market. The United States was keen to develop its trade position with Lisbon as well as to help retain Portugal's commitment to NATO. On 9 May 1985, President Ronald Reagan visited Lisbon. During the course of the day, President Reagan gave a typically fiery speech to the National Assembly: patriotic, rousing and fatherly. Parts of the speech succinctly summed up Portugal's role in the modern world and the problems and challenges that the democratic nation still faced:

> We must do more than today celebrate the daring and renown
> of the Portuguese past. For the events of the last decade suggest
> that you're once again embarked on an adventure, a great
> adventure that all the world is watching closely. Once again
> you're charting a new course, not just for Portugal but for all
> others, especially those peoples of the Third World with whom

your long-established ties permit you to speak with a special
trust, wisdom, and candor.

President Reagan continued:

> In little more than a decade, your nation has moved rapidly
> through stages of development that illustrate the history of this
> century – from far-flung Empire and dictatorship to a confron-
> tation with totalitarian ideology to a decisive turn to democratic
> self-rule. While it's always hard to distinguish between the
> ripples of daily events and the great tides of history, I will still
> venture a prediction. Future historians will recognize Portugal's
> journey as the journey of our time, the journey of our century.
> For you, the people of Portugal, have chosen freedom. You have
> elected to embark on a great adventure in democracy.[29]

On the question of Portugal's contribution to the Western Alliance
President Reagan went on to say:

> Today Portugal's contribution to the Western Alliance remains
> of critical importance. Your geographic location is strategically
> vital, your armed forces are modernizing to expand their role in
> NATO – all of this is further testimony that martial skill and
> a love of national independence are more than just parts of the
> Portuguese past.
>   Yet even your contributions to the alliance are superseded by
> the example of what you're doing now. Yes, democratic Portugal
> has faced political problems and social problems and economic
> problems, and, no, democracy, particularly in its earlier years,
> does not always go smoothly. But this is true of any nation and
> especially any democracy. In my country, we've learned over
> and over again that democracy can only work when it is judged
> not in the short run but over the long term, when we keep in
> mind the principles upon which it is based and remember how
> right Winston Churchill was to remind us that democracy truly
> is the worst form of government, except for all the others.[30]

President Reagan made similar comments during his lunch with
Mário Soares at Sintra Palace, and at the state dinner with President
Eanes at the Ajuda Palace.[31] Portugal's commitment to NATO, to
which President Reagan had referred in his speech, was highlighted
when the NATO Ministerial Summit was held in Estoril from 6 to
7 June 1985.

The summit was a chance for the Portuguese government both
to show off the country's skills at hosting such summits, with all the
security and organizational skills required for such international
events, and to underscore Lisbon's continued commitment to its
membership of NATO. The honorary President of NATO and
West German Minister of Foreign Affairs, Hans-Dietrich Genscher,
was keen to thank the Portuguese:

> We have to thank Portugal for the generous and proverbial
> hospitality, which is being accorded to us during our visit.
> The Portuguese Government impressively demonstrated its
> commitment to the Alliance, which is based on the long
> Atlantic tradition of the country. On 1st January 1986 we shall
> also be able to welcome Portugal in the European Community
> as a new member who can give us so much from its history,
> its culture, its international standing and the strength of its
> democracy.[32]

The summit represented another opportunity for Soares to shine on
the international stage, at a time when internally his government
was starting to collapse.[33] Over the years several Portuguese Prime
Ministers have used the trick of deflecting attention away from
imminent domestic difficulties by hosting international summits,
arguably most spectacularly José Sócrates.

As the mild autumn days grew shorter and attention turned
towards the election campaign, Portugal, and the watching outside
world, was provided with a tragic reminder of the desperate need
to modernize key parts of the country's ageing infrastructure. On
11 September there was a major rail crash in Mangualde near
the Moimenta-Alcafache station, involving the international

high-speed train between Porto and Paris, and a local train going to Coimbra. The two trains collided and the crash resulted in a heavy loss of life.

Train crashes can happen anywhere in the world. And unfortunately they do. What made the Portuguese accident all the more shocking was the lack of communication technology for the drivers, stationmasters and the control centre in Coimbra. All appeared unable to talk with each other. Communication was only possible by way of landline telephones and signalling systems, and these were also inadequate. Had better systems been in the place on the trains, at the stations and from the control centre, the accident could have been prevented.

Moreover, anybody who travelled on Portugal's increasingly fast rail lines during the mid-1980s couldn't fail to notice the lack of automatic level crossings – the crossings were mainly manned only by old ladies waving red flags. Membership to the European Community would help transform Portugal's rail and road systems, but it took time and in 1985 the country remained a long way behind the rest of Europe in this area.

New railway lines, roads linking the interior to the coast, and the coast to Spain – and from there the rest of Europe – were an urgent priority, as Portugal prepared to enter the European Community on 1 January 1986, following eight years of detailed and difficult negotiations.

The Portuguese, and fellow newcomers Spain, along with the rest of Europe, held their breath to see exactly what the impact of Europe's poor joining the club of the rich would be for all concerned. Would membership prove to be the road to nowhere for Portugal, or would it be the salvation of the nation as Mário Soares hoped? Whatever the outcome, a new chapter in Portuguese history was about to begin.

PART FOUR

Absolute Beginners

13

Holding Back the Years

On a cold, damp and foggy New Year's Day in 1986 the border signs came down along the Portuguese–Spanish border crossings, and were replaced by the now familiar road signs of blue background and yellow stars, organized in a circular form. Each new EC sign was carefully unveiled as if the New World had been discovered.

Members of the local border communities waved mini EC flags with as much enthusiasm as they could muster. Yellow and blue balloons were released into the wintry, grey sky and floated away in the chilly wind before popping and falling to the ground.[1] Among Portuguese officials at the border crossings, there was a sense of pride that Portugal had done it, coupled with a fear that the Spanish would flood the Portuguese market with agricultural produce from Galicia, Andalusia and Catalonia.

Welcome to the brave new competitive world of the European Community. In Spain, membership of the European Community was greeted with typical enthusiasm.[2] 'This New Year is a special one for us Spaniards. Today we begin to share a common destiny with the rest of Europe,' Prime Minister Felipe González said in a televised statement.[3] Around 14,000 candidates applied for nearly 200 European Community jobs given to Spain. Spaniards flocked to language schools to learn new languages, and newspapers ran daily special features on each of the member states of the Community.[4]

In Madrid, there was a quiet consensus that Spain had secured a good deal in the negotiations for accession to the Community.[5] This was certainly the case in the agricultural and fisheries sectors, where it had fared much better than the Portuguese.

In Lisbon, as orange-and-cream-coloured buses sped from junction to junction trying to make as many traffic lights as possible, there was a sense of normality on this historic day. It was a public holiday and many Lisboetas remained rather tender from the previous night's revelries. A jump into the unknown: the single biggest development since the Revolution. Yet there appeared to be apathy among the population. No fireworks, no marching bands, few speeches, and no real sense of national achievement.

On television, political leaders smiled with their mouths and talked of the importance of the date, the challenges ahead and the pitfalls that the country needed to avoid. In truth, the smiles on the faces of the politicians signified more a sense of relief than of pure joy. The country was in Europe after eight long years of arduous, complex and often frustrating negotiations, which produced a treaty so detailed that it would require a forklift truck to move a hardcopy of it.[6]

Despite some belated efforts from the government, and the media, to educate the Portuguese about what lay ahead, most people remained blissfully ignorant of the potential changes, positive and negative, to their everyday lives, that membership would eventually bring. To the man in the street, on the farms and in fishing boats, there remained a degree of scepticism and fear of the unknown.[7] Portugal in truth was not a nation of revolutionaries; rather, a country whose people were generally content with the status quo of daily life and routine.

Change was only embraced slowly, and for those who grew up in the era of the Estado Novo there remained an isolationist streak in their mind-set. Many Portuguese appeared intent on trying to hold back the years and to remain in a time capsule that was characterized by conservative tradition.

Across Europe, political leaders hailed the accession of Portugal and Spain into the Community for different reasons. For Margaret

Thatcher, the larger the Community, the more difficult it would be for it to move towards a federal European state, to which she was fervently opposed. The French and the Germans also welcomed the Iberian bloc, although there was some concern about the impact of letting in an additional two poor countries (Greece had already joined), and how much Portuguese membership would cost the Community financially.

This was still the era of the Cold War, and it would be folly to divorce the entry of the Iberian nations into the European Community from the conflict with the Soviet Union. President Reagan regarded the entry of Portugal and Spain into the Community as confirmation of their entrenchment into the democratic Western European bloc in its fight with the Eastern bloc.[8]

The Cold War mentality did not stop there. The immersion of Portugal into the European Community was viewed as the best means of protecting Portuguese democracy. In the era of the Cold War, the relative strength of the Communist Party in Portugal – despite incurring losses in the General Election in October 1985 – remained a troublesome worry for the leaders of the Western world. Few European leaders took Portuguese democracy for granted.

The core aim of membership of the European Community for the Portuguese government was to change one brutal fact: that in 1986, Portugal was still by some way the poorest country in Western Europe.[9] This despite some important improvements in economic indicators: a healthy current account surplus, a fall in inflation (but at 12 per cent it was still the highest in the EC), and unemployment steadying at around 10 per cent. The debt burden, however, remained huge and the economy was still the weakest in Western Europe.[10]

Economic data is open to interpretation and political spin, but when taken together the overall picture was of an economy that had survived austerity and was on a road to recovery. However, the improvements would not end Portugal's role as the poor man of Europe. Put simply, Portugal looked to the EC to help strengthen and modernize/reform its economy.[11]

One of the major initial goals of the Cavaco-led government was – according to the British – to show the Portuguese that membership had brought 'immediate financial benefits to Portugal'.[12] To a large extent, this was none too difficult to achieve. Portuguese membership had been set so that the country would be a net beneficiary from Europe rather than a contributor. By the end of 1986, it was predicted that the balance of transfers would register £150 million or more in Portugal's favour with that figure doubling in the following year.[13]

The majority of the initial funds that came from the EC were regional and social funds. Agriculture was not so well catered for, and this was a source of complaint. The Portuguese delegation in Brussels did the best it could to maximize the returns for the country, but it was not easy. One EC Commissioner rather cruelly described the delegation as 'a sardine among sharks'.[14]

According to British sources, the delegation 'gave a good account of itself'.[15] But its attempts to secure more funds for Portuguese industry did not really get off the ground. It was a steep learning curve for the Portuguese, and the delegation had to learn the rules of the game and build alliances within the Community.

Spain remained Portugal's chief concern within the Community.[16] There were few signs of an improvement in political relations between the two Iberian neighbours, but the two Prime Ministers did at least manage to meet in October 1985. Entry into Europe brought a high level of competition from Spain, and a greater Spanish penetration of the Portuguese market.[17] Good news for Madrid – not such good news for Lisbon. The Spanish problem aside, Portugal's initial year in the EC was of a positive nature.

The year 1986 also marked an important anniversary in Anglo-Portuguese relations: the 600th anniversary of the signing of the Treaty of Windsor on 9 May 1386. The Treaty of Windsor (not to be confused with the Anglo-Portuguese Treaty of 1373) is the diplomatic alliance signed between Portugal and England, which established a pact of mutual support between the two countries.[18].

To mark its anniversary Queen Elizabeth II hosted the Portuguese President and Prime Minister at Windsor Castle for a luncheon ceremony.[19] Margaret Thatcher also attended the lunch, as did other key members of the British government.[20] It was a timely reminder as to how seriously the British still took their ancient treaties with the Portuguese.[21] It also provided Margaret Thatcher with the opportunity to quiz the Portuguese leaders on their impressions of the first months of Portuguese membership of the Community.[22]

The two Portuguese leaders that attended the formal luncheon with the Queen were the right eye of Portugal, Prime Minister Cavaco Silva, and the left eye of the country, President Mário Soares. The latter had been elected as Portugal's first post-Revolution civilian President on 16 February 1986, having defeated Diogo Freitas do Amaral in one of Portugal's closest elections. Soares' victory was a triumph for both the man and the Socialist Party, which had been so soundly beaten in the General Election in the previous October.

At the start of the Presidential Election campaign, Soares trailed badly in the polls and his primary aim was to make it to the second round. His victory set up a Portuguese version of cohabitation, where the Prime Minister and the President came from different political parties.[23] Initially, there were fears that the 'bad blood' that had previously existed between Cavaco Silva and Soares would make the cohabitation arrangement unworkable. In reality, the relationship worked much better than expected.[24]

To a large extent, this was down to the fact that Soares did not meddle in politics as much as his predecessor, President Eanes, had done.[25] Instead, Soares put his energies into developing the ceremonial role of the Presidency – taking a six-day voyage on a training sailboat, and holding court in Guimarães, a historic city in northern Portugal, for ten days.[26] At the time, such gestures were widely applauded by the Portuguese public, who were more used to an austere and distant Presidency of military figures, such as President Eanes.

The Cavaco-led government survived its first year in office, but found it difficult to get the major parts of its legislative programme through the National Assembly.[27] From time to time this led to the Prime Minister's frustrations getting the better of him in making rather 'high-handed declarations on the respective roles of the

[National] Assembly and the government'.[28] The government won a vote of confidence in the National Assembly in June, but still found it difficult to get its medium-term economic plan passed in November.

A number of factors kept Cavaco Silva in power, centring upon the lack of an appetite for new elections from the opposition parties – with the exception of the Communists.[29] At the time, opinion polls indicated that if new elections were called the PSD would win a handsome victory, but again would fall short of obtaining the overall majority they needed to push their legislative programme through the National Assembly. The biggest potential losers in a second poll would have been the PRD, who would have lost most of their seats in the National Assembly.

So the year of transition in Portugal was dominated internally by an effective stalemate in national politics, as the mainstream political parties tried to avoid new elections. As a result, tough decisions on the economy and the reform of the state sector were postponed during 1986 as the initial economic boost from membership of the European Community, and a more favourable international economic outlook, helped Portugal plod along.[30] The Prime Minister confided to the British Ambassador in Lisbon that he saw little hope of being able to implement any more radical policies aside from achieving an agreement to end the entrenchment of the public sector.[31]

As Cavaco Silva strolled around the garden of the Prime Minister's Office and his official residence (a small building behind the National Assembly at São Bento), his thoughts were most probably dominated by two key political words: timing and trigger. The former referred to the most opportune time for the government to call new elections, and the latter to the issue or event that would act as the trigger for sending Portugal to the polls.

In politics, the trick with the selection of the trigger has always been to choose an issue that can be readily understood by public opinion.[32] In 1986, the Prime Minister felt that there was no such issue. Moreover, the time was not yet ripe to achieve the goal of obtaining an overall majority in the National Assembly. Instead,

Prime Minister Cavaco Silva waited and waited, and busied himself with lots of foreign trips and hosting European and international leaders in Lisbon: a by-product of Portugal's new status as a member of the European Community.

In foreign affairs there was much for the government to consider and decide upon. As the British admitted: 'On Africa, five of whose countries are former Portuguese colonies, Portuguese views are usually worth listening to: within the [European] Community, their ideas are very close to ours on what policies should, and should not, be applied to Southern Africa.'[33]

Portugal continued with efforts to try to develop ties with Angola and to strike a deal with the Chinese over the future of Macau.[34] On East Timor, Lisbon adopted a harder line, which, according to the British, achieved little except some irritation at EC/ASEAN (Association of Southeast Asian Nations) meetings.[35] At the United Nations, the Portuguese voted with the major European powers on the Middle East, and continued to abstain on votes relating to the Falklands Islands.[36] In truth, much of Portugal's foreign policy continued to be guided by its membership of NATO and by its status as an Atlantic power.

Indeed, the Portuguese were keen to remind all that while they might be one of the two new boys in the European Community, the country was one of the founder members of NATO.[37] Naturally, the air base on the Azores were still important for the Western powers, who continued to use the facilities as a staging point for the United States' large military presence in Western Europe. With the Cold War still very much active, there was also the potential for another outbreak of hostilities in the Middle East that would require US military supplies or intervention that would have come through the base on the Azores.

The Portuguese continued to take their NATO role very seriously and in this respect the country had moved on from the period of the immediate aftermath of the 25 April 1974 Revolution, when it looked as if its membership of NATO was in peril. Despite the fact that Portugal was strongly pro-NATO, its relations with the United States remained somewhat cool.[38]

The Portuguese were disappointed in what they saw as a lack of commitment from Washington.[39] Supporting evidence put forward by the government in Lisbon included the slowness in appointing a new US Ambassador to Lisbon, and financial cuts imposed by the US Senate over how much the Americans paid for the use of the air base in the Azores.[40] It would take a visit to Lisbon by the US Secretary of Defence, the old US Ambassador to Portugal, Frank Carlucci, in February 1988 to help get relations back on track for a time.[41]

Portugal's first year as a member of the European Community passed without as much drama and upheaval as many had predicted. Change did come to the country, but it was mixed with a fair degree of continuity as well. However, the political stalemate between the government and the National Assembly brought uncertainty to the country at a time when strong leadership was required.

Towards the end of the year Cavaco Silva started to mature as a Prime Minister, no doubt buoyed by his good performances on the international stage. He started to resemble the strong leader that many felt the country needed to help navigate it through the difficult and vital decisions it would have to take in the years that followed. The newly crowned President Soares had also considerably matured politically, and his reinvention of the role of President – towards a more ceremonial model – brought stability to the hitherto thorny and grey area of Presidential–Governmental relations.

To some extent, the shock of joining the European Community – and for many Portuguese this is exactly the emotion that it created – meant that there was a need for some short-term postponement of painful decision-making and economic reforms. The transitional period was set to last until the next election, after which tougher decisions would have to be taken.[42] This aside, many countries were complimentary about Portugal's first year in the Community. The British wrote: 'The UK firmly supported Portuguese membership of the EC, and this first year's experience has helped confirm the rightness of our direction. Portugal should remain a stable, unassuming and democratic partner in both the

Community and NATO, offering us an accessible market and useful military facilities.'[43]

At the end of 1986, Lisbon remained very much a Portuguese city and the transformation into the European city it resembles today (along with Porto) was still some way off. Entry into the European Community, however, had started a process of change that would eventually transform the country in both predicted and unpredicted ways. The direction and speed of this change would largely be decided by the outcome of the subsequent General Election.

In the meantime, as Portugal celebrated its first Christmas as a member of the European Community, there was a quiet sense of pride in Lisbon that at last it had been able to join the EC and that all appeared to have gone relatively well. In the subsequent years, Portugal would elect and send representatives to the European Parliament and play a much more active role within the institutions of the Community.[44]

14

With or Without You

As the cold, stormy winter winds from the Atlantic died down, and the first warm sun of 1987 burnt away the morning mist over the city of Lisbon, the long-expected political crisis broke out in Portugal. Springtime in Lisbon brought to a dramatic end the political impasse that was characterized by the inability of the minority government to pass its legislative programme, and the reluctance of the parties to push for fresh elections.

While the political crisis was all too predictable, its causes and consequences were not so clearly envisaged by Portuguese or foreign commentators. The crisis started in March 1987 when ex-President Eanes (who now headed the PRD) put down a censure measure on the PSD-led minority government. The British felt Eanes's action to be highly questionable. As the Ambassador pointed out:

> We had not reckoned on the political naivety of Eanes . . . He put down a motion of censure on Cavaco's PSD minority government in March, without attempting to concert tactics with the other opposition parties. This both wrecked any prospect of a coalition with the Socialist Party, and presented Cavaco with the opportunity to appeal for a decisive vote of confidence in his premiership.[1]

In short: game, set and match to Cavaco Silva and the PSD. The resulting General Election served as a decisive moment for the

Prime Minister in establishing his authority, and for several of
the leaders of opposition parties who would eventually depart the
political scene.

On 19 July 1987 Cavaco Silva and the Social Democratic
Party (PSD) won the first single party overall majority since the
25 April Revolution. It was a stunning victory that ushered in a
period of political stability not seen since the Revolution. When
all the votes had been counted, the PSD had gained just over
50 per cent of the votes and 148 of the 250 seats in the National
Assembly.[2]

Cavaco Silva returned to office safe in the knowledge that he
would be likely to remain for the full four-year term. This stability was widely welcomed internationally, where it was viewed as a
necessary ingredient to complement an improving economy and
to manage the challenges that lay ahead with membership of the
European Community.[3]

Writing the day after the election, the *New York Times* summarized the appeal of Cavaco Silva during the campaign as being seen
as a strong leader. As the newspaper put it:

> He was a tough-talking father figure who lectured voters that
> the nation faced grave problems if the Social Democrats did
> not receive a majority. The tactic worked. But it was that
> kind of authority that earned him a reputation, as one writer
> described it, of being 'so prone to self-congratulation that his
> detractors often call him and his government arrogant'.[4]

The use of the phrases 'father figure' and 'authority' by the newspaper was interesting and represented a throwback to the authoritarian
era of Salazar. That didn't mean that the Portuguese were turning
their backs on democracy, but there appeared a longing for strong
and decisive leadership, which Cavaco Silva had promised during
the campaign.

Support for Cavaco Silva, and the PSD, was largely drawn from
the middle class, young professionals and the elderly.[5] To these
groups Cavaco Silva and the PSD represented a new start and a

repositioning of the country away from the political, social and economic baggage of the Revolution.

The buzzwords of the Social Democrats in 1987 were 'reform' and 'change'. A third word could be added to this list, 'modernization'. In 1987, there was a clear majority support for all three, and the PSD promised during the campaign to deliver on all of them. It called for reform of education and labour laws, the restructuring of agriculture and the tax system, as well as the privatization of several state enterprises – especially those that were nationalized in the immediate aftermath of the Revolution.[6] In short, a repositioning of the country away from the Socialist-style economy of the post-Revolution era and a turn towards the development of a new liberalized one, in tune with the economic reforms taking place in Britain and the United States.

While the programme was clear, its implementation faced difficulties. Under the terms of the Constitution, which was drafted in 1976, a two-thirds majority in the National Assembly was required to make some of the changes that the new PSD government was proposing. So on top of social and economic reform, the government sought to attempt to modify the Constitution as well.

Reform and change would not prove easy, and internationally there was concern that the government would find it harder than expected to implement its radical programme – even though it enjoyed a clear overall majority in the National Assembly.[7] Change is never easy, and in Portugal, the major obstacles had been deliberately put in place after the Revolution to protect the left-wing nature of the democratic state.

The dominance of the PSD was further confirmed in the election for the European Parliament, which was held on the same day as the General Election. The PSD emerged as the single biggest party and won 37.45 per cent of the vote, a percentage that brought the party ten out of the total twenty-four seats. Pedro Santana Lopes, a future Prime Minister of Portugal and leader of the PSD party, headed the PSD European list. Taken together, the two elections indicated a shift in Portuguese public opinion towards the centre-right.

After the new PSD government took office following its success in the General Election, there was some initial disappointment among diplomats based in Lisbon over the apparent lack of activity as Ministers prepared to start implementing their respective programmes.[8] This fallow period was partly caused by the summer shutdown in Portugal that followed on the heels of the intensive early summer period of election campaigning.

To some extent, President Soares helped fill the vacuum. Always a great traveller, he managed to fit in state visits to the Soviet Union and Spain, and spent two weeks touring the Alentejo in the south of Portugal. All of this generated positive headlines in Lisbon and by the end of the year the President's popularity was even higher than that of the Prime Minister. In continuing to develop the ceremonial side of the Presidency, Soares was able to maintain the positive start to cohabitation with Cavaco Silva, as the latter focused his attentions on the economy.[9]

On this score, the economic news for Portugal was much improved. While the country remained the poorest in Western Europe, the Prime Minister was at least able to report to the Portuguese that they were living in one of its fastest growing economies.[10] Indeed, there were indications of a slight overheating of the economy and the government took action to try to correct this danger.

Improvements in most key economic indicators illustrated that the health of the economy was improving, albeit from a very low starting point. Inflation fell, but still remained well above the European Community average, and unemployment fell to 8.5 per cent, the single biggest fall within the EC.

Crucially, Portugal looked good to foreign investors.[11] As the British noted, 'inflows of foreign capital contributed to the astronomical, and unhealthy, rise in shares quoted on the Lisbon Stock Exchange'.[12] The balance of trade deficit, however, widened. Portugal managed to export more in 1987, but this increase was outpaced by rises in imports.[13]

All in all, it was a much better time for the economy than the country had endured in previous years. Much of the economic improvement reflected the impact of the austerity programmes, a better international economic climate and, in part, Portugal's entry into the European Community.

Portugal's second year in the European Community delivered far more tangible results than its first year. On the ground there was greater evidence in terms of developments in infrastructure, all of which were financed by structural funds and loans from the Community. All of this financing fell far below the amounts of Community funding going for similar projects to Greece and Ireland. As one diplomat wrote in praise of Lisbon, 'refreshingly, it is not the Portuguese style to rattle the begging bowl too loudly'.[14] The Prime Minister adopted a low-key approach to European Community meetings compared to the leaders of the other new boys in the club.

Two problems, one internal and the other external, remained largely unresolved, which continued to worry the government. The internal problem concerned the impact of Portuguese membership of the EC on its agricultural sector, and externally there were heightened fears over the Spanish penetration into the Portuguese market. Cavaco Silva was at least able to negotiate for EC compensation to help offset the effects of the Common Agricultural Policy (CAP) on Portugal.

Iberian neighbourly relations, however, remained frosty, despite the successful state visit of President Soares to Spain. In contrast, the visit of Prime Minister Cavaco Silva to Spain was only saved from possible postponement by a last-minute Spanish decision to cancel a proposed nuclear laboratory (it was described as a 'dump' by Lisbon) to be located near the Portuguese border.[15] Continued suspicion in Lisbon of the Spanish flooding the local market with goods did not recede during the course of the year.

Privately, many European diplomats called for King Juan Carlos of Spain to play a more active role in encouraging détente between Lisbon and Madrid.[16] The King had been educated in Estoril, and still undertook frequent private visits to the Lisbon coast. A full state visit, it was hoped, would do much to improve relations and remove (mainly) Portuguese fears and anxieties about their Iberian neighbours.

During the course of 1987 Portugal was also treated to the visit of the most talked-about Royal couple of the era, the Prince and Princess of Wales. Naturally, it was Diana Princess of Wales who attracted most of the attention of the cameras. The Royal couple arrived in Portugal on 11 February 1987 for a four-day state visit. The weather in Lisbon was not welcoming for the Royals, with an Atlantic storm battering the city with high winds and torrential rain.[17] Trees on the roadside were uprooted and blocked the motorcade carrying the Royal couple to their first official welcoming ceremony outside the Presidential Palace in Belém.[18] Arriving only ten minutes late, they fared better than President Soares, whose (British-made) Presidential Range Rover broke down in Belém and had to be unceremoniously pushed off the road.[19]

The Presidential guard of honour, which was soaked to its skin, tried its best to go through its welcome routine, but the rain had got inside the band's brass instruments. Brave attempts at the national anthems were soon aborted: the band and guards were stood down and marched away to dry off back in the warmth of their nearby barracks.[20]

Sadly for the Royal couple, the inclement weather followed them for nearly the entire four-day tour, preventing them from going on any of their famous walkabouts, until the party reached Porto on the last day of the tour. It was only possible then because the Prince and Princess broke with the official programme and went on an impromptu walkabout in the hope of meeting part of the large crowd that had gathered to get a glimpse of them.[21]

Bad luck dogged the Royal tour during their trip to Sintra near Lisbon. Low-lying cloud, wind and rain coming off the Sintra Mountains greeted the party as they arrived at the National Palace.[22] British television reported the supposed spectacular views that nobody could see. An unveiling at the Palace by Prince Charles did not go to plan when the cloth refused to budge.[23]

The Royal tour of Portugal included a formal theatre trip, hosted by President Soares. Princess Diana caused a sensation among invited guests, as well as among fashion followers, by wearing a bowtie around her bare neck. President Soares arrived with his clip-on bowtie not properly done up and hanging down off his collar.[24] Recovering from his initial dress faux pas, President Soares proceeded to charm Princess Diana.

The rest of the visit comprised the usual mix of sightseeing and visits to good causes, as well as a trip to the British Council in Porto.[25] Though the Royal couple were in Portugal for ceremonial duties, the main purpose of their visit was to foster Anglo-Portuguese trade links.[26]

At the height of her fame, Princess Diana was perhaps the most iconic woman of the era and the press paid as much attention to her wardrobe as to the trip itself. It was during this trip to Portugal that rumours of marital difficulties between the couple started to become more public, after local hotel staff revealed that they slept in separate bedrooms during their stay in Lisbon.[27] Four days in a wet and windy Portugal in February, in all likelihood, did little to help their crumbling marriage.

Such was the media attention devoted to Princess Diana that for a few days in mid-February, photographs and television footage of her, containing the backdrops of Lisbon and Porto, dominated the international news. All of this proved very useful in promoting tourism to Portugal. British business was also given a boost by the trip.

During his visit to Portugal, Prince Charles opened the British Industrial Exhibition, which was claimed to be the largest all-British trade exhibition held in Western Europe since the Second World War.[28] In a sign of the growing importance of the Portuguese market, Britain was not alone in making concerted efforts to sell its products to Portugal. Indeed, Britain, despite its huge trade fair, had seen only a slight increase in its sales to Portugal, and had dipped one place in the league table of exporters to Portugal: behind West Germany, Spain, France and Italy.[29]

For the Portuguese, political and trade relations with ex-colonies remained paramount. With the exception of East Timor, where events took a turn for the worse, there were signs of improvements.[30] A meeting between the Portuguese and the Foreign Ministers of its former African colonies led to improved relations, as did the long overdue visit of the Angolan leader to Lisbon.[31]

During the course of the year Portugal and China ratified their agreement on Macau (based largely on the British agreement with China over Hong Kong).[32] The hope in Lisbon was that this would lead to warmer relations with the Chinese, and the development of further trade ties.

Ever keen to get his passport stamped, President Soares visited Brazil in the hope of boosting trading links with the economic powerhouse of South America.[33] All in all, Portugal was making strides in developing trade ties with the outside world. The left-wing dominated post-Revolution era was rapidly fading into history.

To some extent, this sense was increased when one of the major symbols of the Revolution died in the early part of 1987. The musician José (Zeca) Afonso passed away on 23 February 1987. The broadcast of his song 'Grândola, Vila Morena' on the radio had signalled the start of the 25 April Revolution. It was a beautiful song that highlighted both his role as a folk singer and as a political activist. The pure tone of his voice, and the simple arrangement of the piece, made it one of the most haunting songs composed and performed by a Portuguese musician. Zeca's music lived on after his death; his popularity continued in Portugal, and grew in other countries.

In 1987, the Portuguese group Madredeus made their first album, 'Os dias da Madredeus'. The record was an eclectic mix of traditional Portuguese music and modern folk music. At the centre of the group was the vocalist Teresa Salgueiro whose rich and enchanting vocals cast a spell over both listeners to the record and audiences at live concerts. At first, the band – many of whom had played in more mainstream Portuguese pop/rock bands – started playing in small theatres and concert halls across Portugal. Their appeal quickly spread overseas, particularly after they made a film, *The Lisbon Story*, with the German filmmaker, Wim Wenders in 1994. The success of the film, for which the band provided the soundtrack and in which they also acted, put their music in front of new audiences.

For much of the 1990s Madredeus became one of the most internationally recognized symbols of Portuguese culture. Touring extensively across North America, in Europe, Asia and in some of Portugal's former colonies, the group went from strength to strength before Teresa Salgueiro left the group in 2007 to pursue a solo career. The band had experienced personnel changes prior to Salgueiro's departure, but, in truth, it failed to recover from the loss of its prime asset.

The band's back catalogue of songs remains a soundtrack to the era that saw the isolation of Portuguese culture end, and the start of its exposure to European and international audiences and critics. In subsequent years, more Portuguese musicians, artists and writers would follow this path to international recognition. To a large extent, membership of the European Community, while potentially threatening the uniqueness of Portuguese culture, did at least offer access to new audiences that had not been exposed to Portuguese culture before.

All in all, a sense of positive and creative energy in political and economic life, as well as in the arts, characterized Portugal's second year as a member of the European Community. Reporting to the Foreign Office in London, the British Ambassador quoted an interesting finding in a British newspaper poll:

> Incredible as it might seem to anyone who has sat through a single evening of fado, the Portuguese emerged from a recent poll in the *Daily Telegraph* as the most optimistic people in Europe. More than half of them expect that 1988 will be a better year than its predecessor. I hope they are right, but the outcome is not solely in their hands.[34]

In truth, the Portuguese economy remained vulnerable on two fronts: any deterioration in the international economic climate, and too much attention from its European Community partners.[35] In other words, there were fears from both sides of the economic problematic scales of a new recession created by international factors or overheating. Cavaco Silva, as a result, would need to use all of his economic skills to keep the economy on its track of 'measured development'.[36]

The fear was that he might be tempted to, as the British put it, 'rush at the fences too quickly'. In reality Cavaco Silva, with his strong majority in the National Assembly, was busy planning to space out his reform plans over the full four years of his government. No other post-Revolution Prime Minister had yet enjoyed such a luxury.

15

All Around the World

As the country moved towards the end of the final years of the 1980s, one of the most traumatic events for Lisbon, and the rest of the country, came from an unexpected source. On 25 August 1988, a fire destroyed much of Chiado, the historic shopping district of the city. The flames from the intense fire could be seen across the city, as much of central Lisbon came to a standstill.

The wooden structures of several of the buildings, and a lack of fire sprinkler systems in the shops affected, meant that the fire spread quickly. The narrowness of the streets also increased the speed with which the fire engulfed Chiado. At one point, the whole area appeared threatened. Lisbon-based international news agencies praised the bravery of the firemen who fought the blaze, but were strongly critical of the fire trucks and equipment, most of which were over 30 years old.[1]

The *New York Times* reported the fire as the biggest disaster to hit the city since the earthquake of 1755.[2] While the comparison with the earthquake was a little overstated, the fire caused extensive damage to a large area, but the loss of life was limited. It was, however, the city's worst single fire incident for centuries in terms of damage caused to buildings.[3] The City Council summarized the damage inflicted by the fire:

The fire caused the destruction of 18 buildings, some of which were quite emblematic of the commercial activity of the city:

the Chiado Stores, the Eduardo Martins Store, the Ferrari
Pastry Shop, the Batalha Shop, and other shops dedicated
to traditional commerce. Many offices and houses were also
destroyed. It is estimated that about 2,000 people lost their
jobs. There were about 1,150 men and 275 vehicles fighting the
fire. There were two casualties and 73 injured, most of whom
were fire-fighters.[4]

An ashen President Soares visited the site of the fire some hours
after it had been put out and announced that the area would be
rebuilt. The world-renowned Porto-based architect, Álvaro Siza
Vieira, was chosen to lead the reconstruction project, with a focus
on exterior continuity – to return the area to its former glory, mixed
with interior modernity. This mixture of tradition and modernity
meant that, today, the now nearly fully restored buildings mirror
their historic predecessors, but inside contain many of the modern
interior fittings of twenty-first-century businesses, homes and
shopping malls.

The reconstruction project has been widely applauded and the
area is once again one of Lisbon's main attractions for tourists and
local shoppers alike. Back in 1988, the lessons of the fire, as well as
those from the Moimenta-Alcafache train crash in 1985, were that
while Portugal was modernizing at a rapid rate and integrating into
Europe, much of its infrastructure remained in desperate need of
updating.

In political terms, the years of 1988 and 1989 were in-between
years during which money flowed into Portugal from European
Community funds.[5] Much of the promise of the government to
reform the economy was partially met with some 14 structural
reforms on the statute book in 1988 alone.[6]

Despite increasing internal problems and a number of distracting alleged seedy sexual, political and financial scandals, the
government remained secure and set on a course to serve out its
full four-year term. The increase in the number of scandals in the
government coincided with the launch of a new weekly newspaper
in Portugal, *O Independente*.

The paper, with its links to the right in Portugal, ran headlines in almost every edition accusing a member of the government and other politicians of corruption or the misuse of public funds. Some politicians were found to be guilty of the charges that resulted from the allegations, but others were acquitted and sued the newspaper for libel.

The era of the tabloid political scandal had reached Portugal. To complicate matters, one of the young journalists, and the newspaper's second editor, was Paulo Portas, who went on to lead the CDS (Centre Democrats) political party. Relations between Portas and several leading PSD politicians, including Cavaco Silva, have remained extremely problematic ever since.

Back in 1988–9, the government did not have it entirely its own way politically. There was widespread labour unrest in response to its economic reform policies, which culminated in a closely observed General Strike in March 1988.[7] The reform of the tax system, which was central to the government's programme, proved to be the singular most unpopular policy, particularly with Portugal's middle class. The development of the middle class, particularly in urban areas, had been one of the leading challenges of Portuguese democracy. Many felt that the government's tax reforms would leave them the worst off of all the socio-economic groups in the country.[8]

The opposition parties, while making something of a recovery, still looked in various degrees of disarray, with strong internal squabbles and leadership battles distracting them from potentially denting the absolute majority of the PSD in the subsequent election scheduled for late 1991.[9] Despite the unpopularity of key parts of the government's economic programme and the rise in scandals, which were heavily covered by a new generation of investigative reporters and newspapers, there appeared little prospect of an immediate large-scale political realignment.

Arguably the most important change made among the opposition parties was the resignation of the leader of the Socialist Party, Vítor Constâncio, on 22 October 1988 and his replacement on 15 January 1989 by Jorge Sampaio, a politician of Sephardic Jewish origin.[10] Sampaio was viewed as a stronger potential alternative

Prime Minister to Cavaco Silva than Constâncio, who was seen as a rather dour technocrat.

Writing in 1989, the British viewed Sampaio as 'intellectually well qualified to take on the Prime Minister and a good public speaker'.[11] The key to the future political fortunes of the Socialist Party lay in reconnection with the middle-ground electorate, and the election of the highly articulate Sampaio represented a good start for the party in trying to achieve this aim.

The catalyst for Portugal's economic development was its membership of the European Community.[12] For Lisbon, this was the transitional golden age of membership when funds flowed into the country, and before the bills from Brussels started to come in.[13] By 1988, the funds received from the European Community represented more than 1 per cent of total GNP.

Economic indicators provided mixed news regarding the health of the economy. Inflation reached nearly 10 per cent and was the highest within the Community.[14] The current account was in the positive, but only kept out of the red by the large amount of receipts from Portuguese emigrants and by spending from tourists. Agriculture was the worst-hit sector, with the country suffering an unusually rain-soaked summer.[15]

Continued concerns in Lisbon about relations with Madrid and potential Spanish penetration into the Portuguese market continued. During the course of 1988, the Portuguese were miffed by the decision of the European Community President Jacques Delors to appoint a Spanish (and not Portuguese, as the Portuguese media had hoped) Commissioner.[16] The British noted that following Delors' decision: 'The air was thick with references to Aljubarrota, the battle where, with English help, the Portuguese routed the Spanish invaders in 1385.'[17]

There were some signs of a kind of political rapprochement between Spain and Portugal at this time. An Iberian Summit held in November 1988 was moderately successful in appeasing Portuguese fears and anger.[18] In 1989, King Juan Carlos made the highly anticipated state visit to Portugal, during which enthusiastic local crowds greeted him.

In defence matters, Portugal was less than happy with draft guidelines regulating Spain's role within NATO, and there were other niggles between the two Iberian neighbours with the institutions of the Community. In reality, however, Spain was Portugal's biggest trading partner, and after Britain, the second largest foreign investor in the country.[19]

Any visitor to the two Iberian capital cities at the end of the 1980s could not fail to notice the different pace of modernization and renewal in each city. Madrid looked to be five years ahead of Portugal, with major Community-funded public works programmes either finished or well under way. Lisbon retained its old-world charm, but the city was becoming something of an ageing faded beauty in desperate need of repair. Buildings in central Lisbon continued to suffer from the effects of pollution and decades of neglect.

There were suspicions in Lisbon that the faster pace of change in Spain, since the Iberian nations had joined the Community, was a result of the better deal for accession that the Spanish had managed to negotiate with the Community. In reality, the rate of modernization and renewal in Lisbon was slowed by incredible amounts of red tape, in particular the slow pace in the granting of planning permission and continued disputes over the ownership of derelict buildings. Inter-family disputes and complications of disputed ownership resulting from the 25 April Revolution were among the most common excuses.

For his part, Cavaco Silva remained suitably reluctant to shake the begging bowl in the Community, and kept a low profile at Community summits. He did undertake special pleading for the Portuguese textiles sector at the European Council in March 1988, where he requested special consideration be made for 'ultra peripheral' European Community nations.[20]

It simply wasn't the Prime Minister's style to plead national poverty – the Spanish leadership had fewer qualms about adopting this tactic. Cavaco Silva viewed membership of the European Community as not so much a gravy train for the country, rather a means to drag Portugal into the modern world through his programme of economic liberalization and social and welfare reforms.

At the start of 1989, Portugal was at the midway point between joining the European Community and the end of the transitional period for most parts of its membership which was due to finish on 1 January 1992. On this same day, Portugal was to start its Presidency of the Community – and the introduction of the European single market was also on its way.[21] These were crucial times for Portugal, as the British Ambassador reminded the Foreign Office: 'The Prime Minister has bleakly summarized the difficulties to be overcome as: Portuguese firms' lack of international experience, the excessive influence of the state, uncertainty over agrarian reform, inadequate labour legislation, insufficient professional training and a not very efficient financial market.'[22]

To the average man in the street in Portugal, the period was characterized as being free of political and economic crisis. Despite a violent confrontation in Lisbon between one police force division and another, whose members were protesting for the right to form a trade union, all remained quiet on the western edge of Europe. The resulting inter-police violence – policemen attacking other policemen – made headlines around the world, but was not representative of the state of the country.

The most serious danger the average Portuguese faced, according to the British, was to die in a traffic accident.[23] In 1989, Portugal was the country with the highest death rate on the roads in the European Community, as well as having the highest rate of pedestrian deaths.[24] To make matters worse, many Portuguese drivers were taking advantage of the improved access to credit to buy top-of-the-range hatchbacks that were simply too fast and too badly driven for Portugal's ageing roads.

In overseas policy, Lisbon continued to follow the European line.[25] It welcomed the dramatic developments in Eastern Europe, but warned about the potential impact on competition that Portugal would face as a result of the political changes in the region. In Africa, Portugal continued to be a useful source of information for the West, especially on developments in Angola.

President Soares briefed the new US President, George H. W. Bush, at the US Ambassador's residence in Tokyo, Japan, on 23

February 1989.[26] Specifically, President Bush pressed his Portuguese counterpart for information on the effects of the potential withdrawal of Cuban forces and civilians from Angola. Soares updated the Americans on the likelihood of a Cuban withdrawal, its effects on Angola and the peace process in the country.[27]

Soares' meeting with Bush was part of a Portuguese effort to play a more active role in Africa.[28] As ever, the Americans were grateful for Portuguese information on the country, though President Bush did not share with the Portuguese the US intelligence assessments of the developments in Angola.[29]

Portugal attempted to improve relations with all its ex-colonies in Africa, with regular visits by Ministers to the continent. In Angola, during the course of 1988, a mini-Marshall Plan was proposed by the Portuguese Ministry of Foreign Affairs to help try to support Angola's economic recovery. Some foreign observers, however, unkindly described the plan as a scheme for spending other people's money.[30]

Relations with other ex-colonies continued to be uneven. In East Timor, the pressure grew on the Portuguese government to try to do more as a result of the Pope's visit there, and discussion continued with the Chinese over Macau.[31] The Chinese were said to be very grateful to the Portuguese 'conciliatory attitude' towards the massacre at Tiananmen Square, which took place on 4 June 1989.[32] Much of the rest of the world chose to shun the Chinese for some time after the massacre.

As the decade of the eighties drew to a close there were still a great many problems to address, especially in one key area. The British summarized these: 'Work on the country's infrastructure, financed to a large degree by European Community funds, continued, but the country still suffered from overcrowded and badly surfaced roads, bad public transport and bad telecommunications.'[33]

Unusually heavy rains during November and December of 1989 across much of Portugal led to a further worsening in the condition of the roads.[34] There was a promise of much still to come from the European Community, with ambitious plans for new motorways to better link the country from north to south and from east to

west. Work also started in widening key national road routes, and
the construction of new bypass roads to divert traffic around rural
towns and villages. Portugal was on the move with the promise of
greater things to come.

Politically at the very end of the decade there were signs that the
government was suffering from mid-term blues. Added to this was
the heightened public perception of the Prime Minister as 'distant
and disdainful'.[35] As a result of both factors, there was a steady
decline in support for the government. This coincided with an
improvement in the fortunes of the Socialists.

The Socialist Party made gains in the European Elections in
June 1989 and was the clear winner in the local elections held in
December of the same year.[36] The British foresaw that, with the
increase in the possibility of a Socialist-led government emerging at
the next General Election in 1991, Cavaco Silva might be tempted
to 'conduct a rather less vigorous economic policy'. In other words,
he might postpone some key reforms until after the election.[37]

Lisboetas started to talk in the future tense. How long would
Cavaco remain as Prime Minister, and how would the city be
further transformed by funds from the Community? Moreover,
would the two-line metro system that served parts of the city ever
be expanded? Details of planned future infrastructure projects
(both real and not so real) were published in the newspapers, as
well as allegations of corruption involving the misappropriation of
Community funds. Corruption, at all levels of society, remained,
and blighted the development of the city and wider country.

Portugal was slowly becoming more outward looking and hoping
to show its new-found international credentials by hosting major
events: international summits, sporting and cultural. Almost overnight the world was interested in all things Portuguese, and there
were examples of success stories in many of these fields.

At the 1988 Olympics, the Portuguese runner Rosa Mota won
the gold medal in the marathon. Small, stocky and looking as if
she could run for ever, Motta's victory was a source of great pride
to the Portuguese – their long-distance running pedigree was of
the highest order. Another world-famous Portuguese woman, the

artist Paula Rego, had an exhibition of her works hosted by the Gulbenkian Foundation in Lisbon. Rego's paintings, with their strong feminist undertones, were controversial back in the 1980s. Today, they fetch some of the highest sums of money paid at auction for a living artist.

By the end of the decade, Portugal appeared good at producing individuals who were able to excel at world-class levels in sports and the arts. The trick for the government, and for the population, lay in transforming Portugal into a world-class country before the end of the century. Collectively there remained much work to be done if this was to be achieved.

At the end of the 1980s Portugal was moving forward. The problem remained, however, that much of the rest of Europe was moving forward at a greater pace than Portugal. If the country was not careful, it would risk getting left behind altogether. Catching up with Europe became the challenge for the subsequent decade as the Community moved towards both expansion and deeper financial and political integration.

PART FIVE

Fields of Gold

16

Wicked Game

In 1990, William Jefferson Clinton set out with gusto on the campaign trail for the Presidency of the United States. His campaign would almost implode before it got off the ground, and he ran after that point as the 'Comeback Kid' – going on to win the Presidency two years later.

Portugal had its own 'comeback kid', Cavaco Silva, who engineered a recovery of his own and the government's fortunes, that led him to a third consecutive election victory in the General Election of 1991. Equally importantly, the government won an absolute majority.[1]

Prior to the General Election, which was held on 6 October 1991, President Mário Soares 'romped home' with a landslide in the Presidential Election held on 13 January 1991.[2] The re-election of the so-called 'left eye and right eye' of Portuguese post-Revolution politics helped provide a degree of stability for an electorate who endorsed cohabitation – Portuguese-style.

In reality, there was never any real doubt that Soares would win a second term, and Portugal's European partners welcomed his re-election.[3] The PSD decided not to put up a candidate against Soares, and this decision effectively guaranteed him the Presidency for a further five years. 'He was and remains immensely popular, a man of the people, with an easy and straightforward manner,' according to the British; and he wanted to transmit his personal popularity to boost the Socialist Party.[4]

No matter how hard he tried, Soares failed to achieve this aim, which he believed would strengthen his own political position. Despite this, he remained one of the most influential post-Revolution political figures in Portugal.

The other part of the cohabitation 'dream team', Cavaco Silva, started his comeback during the course of the previous year. At the start of 1990, the Prime Minister and the PSD struggled to gain traction, with opinion polls indicating that the government had lost considerable ground.[5] There was much debate as to the main reasons for this decline, all of which centred upon the image problems of Cavaco Silva.[6] The Prime Minister suffered from a poor and somewhat detached public image that made him appear aloof and disinterested in the struggles of the everyday man on the street.[7]

By the end of the year, however, the government had clawed back much of the ground it had lost, and was running neck and neck with the Socialist Party, with the Prime Minister enjoying a higher poll rating than the leader of the Socialists, Jorge Sampaio.[8] The fact that Sampaio had won the race for Lisbon Mayor appeared something of a double-edged sword. It looked, in short, as if Sampaio should not have taken on being both the Leader of the Socialist Party and the Mayor of the capital city at the same time.[9] The British pointed out the obvious: 'It is too much work for one man and since Lisbon's problems appear insoluble, its Mayor only earned brickbats. And Lisbon is in a bad way, with holes in the streets, the pavements collapsing, water mains bursting and buildings falling down, not to mention the hideous traffic jams.'[10]

Sampaio's difficulties aside, and despite the opinion poll increases in support for both the Prime Minister and the PSD, the government's report card for 1990 was not entirely positive. Scandals continued to linger, especially over the alleged misuse of funds in the Ministry of Health. In carefully apportioning blame at the time, the British Ambassador wrote in a dispatch to the Foreign Office: 'The scandal over the misuse of funds in the Ministry of Health rumbled on, touching in particular . . . the former Minister of Health (herself under some suspicion) and the present Minister of Finance (who is not).'[11]

The government, however, was still riding the lucky wave of ongoing growth in the economy, based on the continued increase in the influx of funds from the European Community.[12] Economic indicators generally made for good reading with near full employment, an absence of any serious labour disputes (except on the trains and by air traffic controllers), but inflation continued to be a major worry, running at over 14 per cent.[13]

Sadly, the economic indicators did not translate into an improvement in the living standards of the vast majority of the Portuguese people.[14] To make matters worse, Portugal was still waiting to see major improvements as a result of EU funding in infrastructure – particularly in roads and telephones.

Anybody who tried to buy a phone and get a line connected in 1990 could recount the continued problems in the telecommunications sector in Portugal. Waiting lists to get connected of around six months, and then a choice between a black or a green handset, appeared to belong to the 1970s.

While much of the rest of Europe marched towards new and deregulated telecommunications markets, Portugal looked as if it might, once again, be left behind in the reform of a crucial sector of the economy. There was also a setback for the government in another important area: alcohol. During the course of 1990 the sale of Centralcer, the producers of Sagres beer, was not a total success.

The first major phase of the process of European Monetary Union (EMU) was introduced on 1 July 1990, when exchange controls were abolished and capital movements within the European Community liberalized. The government, as a result, introduced measures to help Portugal deal with the EMU, which aimed to bring inflation down and to reduce the public sector deficit.[15] In addition, the Bank of Portugal was given a large degree of independence from the government.[16]

There were some concerns in the government over the pace of reform and the shift towards a political union of the Community. Portugal, however, kept most of these thoughts to itself – despite lobbying from London to join its more sceptical approach to the EMU and Community political union.[17] In reality, the Portuguese government was afraid of getting left behind in Europe, and also fearful that such a stance could prejudice the flow of Community funds to Lisbon.[18]

Much of the media coverage for the start of the EMU was soon overtaken by the events of 2 August 1990. Far away from Portugal, Saddam Hussein's Iraqi armed forces invaded Kuwait and set in motion a series of diplomatic and military events that became the first major war of the post-Cold War 'New World Order'. The build up to the Persian Gulf War of 1991 might have seemed very remote to the Portuguese watching events unfold on CNN and RTP.

The Portuguese Government was quick to show solidarity with the Western powers over Iraq. Cavaco Silva granted the Americans unrestricted use of the air base in the Azores, which the Americans used as a staging point for the build-up of military equipment and personnel in the Middle East.[19] From the outset of the crisis, Cavaco Silva was keen to support the Americans, but was uneasy about becoming directly involved in the Gulf.

Two key factors dictated this position: fear over the inadequacies of the Portuguese armed services, and potential domestic criticism over fighting another overseas war.[20] Portugal's colonial wars, conducted during the era of the Estado Novo, were still fresh in the minds of many of the older generation.[21] On top of this, Portugal remained totally dependent on imported oil. Following the Yom Kippur Arab-Israeli War of October 1973, Portugal had paid dearly for allowing the Americans to use the Azores as a staging point for its massive airlift of arms to Israel during the course of the year.[22]

The events of the Persian Gulf War dominated the first part of 1991. Portugal managed to achieve its aim of keeping its head down, while providing useful assistance to the US-led Allied Coalition.[23] The Portuguese claimed that its cautious approach to the conflict would help its Presidency of the Community in its dealings with the Arab world.[24] In reality, Cavaco Silva navigated Portugal astutely during the course of the war.

Without having committed anything more than the Azores base to the Coalition, he had gained the appreciative thanks of the US administration led by President George H. W. Bush. With the United

States emerging as the sole superpower at the end of the Cold War this was an important achievement. In the past, US–Portuguese relations had been characterized by a lack of empathy on both sides that dated back to the era of Salazar and his dislike of all things American.

As Portugal settled back to domestic issues during the spring and summer of 1991, it was clear that the government had started to prepare for a General Election campaign that would lead to its third straight victory. At the centre of the government's political message was the promise of more stability.[25] The linkage between political stability and economic prosperity was constantly highlighted, and to some extent, this message was an accurate reflection of the state of the country in 1991.

Economic growth rates were slightly down from previous years, but importantly, they were still above the average growth rate in the Community.[26] As in the previous year, there was no major labour unrest and the tripartite-agreement reached between the government, employers and the unions remained relatively intact. Salary increases remained ahead of inflation, but not by much, and by the end of the year there were signs that the increases were slowing down. As ever, the budget deficit remained too high for Portugal's own good, as was the balance of payments deficit. Both negative economic indicators appeared to have little political impact on the government.

Better news for the government was that unemployment continued to fall and was at about 4.2 per cent, which all in all was equal to virtually full employment.[27] Equally importantly, foreign investment in the country remained strong. This investment was drawn partly from funds from the European Community and also from increases in investment from the private sector.[28] The results of these investments were starting to be felt across the country.

Crucially, the new Lisbon to Porto motorway was completed just prior to the election. This important step linked Portugal's two major cities together for the first time. The old *Route National* (N1) road, for so long crammed with slow-moving lorries spewing out black smoke and crawling along its single-lane winding route, had been a death trap for motorists.

Many Portuguese, however, complained about the price of the tolls between Lisbon and Porto (taking the train remained a cheaper option) and simply refused to use the new motorway. Sadly, to avoid the tolls, many motorists and the old rickety lorries simply continued to use the old N1 road, so little really changed. Still, the new motorway was good for the fleets of fast Mercedes cars that raced from one city to the other at speeds approaching 200kph (120mph).

All the other new motorways that have been built in the country have consistently matched the pattern set by this first new completed motorway in Portugal. Over the subsequent years hugely ambitious motorway projects were launched – linking Lisbon to the Algarve, Lisbon to Spain, the centre of the country (Leira, Coimbra, Viseu, Aviero) to Spain.

More recent projects have included linking Porto to Spain (both northwards and eastwards), as well as linking other northern cities such as Braga to Porto and onwards to the rest of the country. These projects have included the construction of hundreds of tunnels and viaducts that often wind their way through the mountain regions of the country.

Foreigners arriving in Portugal by car noted the quality of the motorways (in stark contrast to those of Spain), admired the long viaducts, painted in bright colours, and wondered why they pretty much had the motorway all to themselves. In short, the development of the extensive motorway system has made it easier and quicker for lorries bringing foreign goods to get into and across Portugal, but has still had little other impact. The *Route National* roads, which are free to use, remain overcrowded, poorly maintained and dangerous for both drivers and pedestrians. Portuguese motorways have some of the highest motorway toll charges in Europe, and until that changes, they will remain largely empty of local traffic.

At the start of the 1990s the vision was to create a European Community-funded motorway system and that these new super-highways would link the different parts of the country together. The first part of the vision was realized, but not the second. Most Portuguese simply cannot afford, or are not willing, to pay to use the motorways.

Foreigners wonder why there is a need for tolls at all, as the European Community (the European taxpayers) paid for the construction of the roads in the first place. Anyhow, the creation of the new motorways at the start of the 1990s gave both President Soares and Prime Minister Cavaco Silva the opportunity to be seen cutting ribbons and officially opening new stretches of road.

By the time autumn arrived in Lisbon, and the colourful new election posters went up around the country, it was clear that the recovery in the fortunes of the Prime Minister and the government was near complete. The big question during the campaign, as a result, was whether the government would be returned to power with another absolute majority in the National Assembly.

The Prime Minister regarded the obtaining of an absolute majority as vitally important to maintaining political stability ahead of taking on the Portuguese Presidency of the European Community in 1992.[29] During the campaign, Cavaco Silva led from the front, heavily defending his government's economic record, but at the same time reminding the electorate that his programme of economic liberalization and social reforms was not complete.[30] It represented a classic case of a government appealing for a further term to finish implementing its programme from the previous election.

In the international arena the government enjoyed strong support. In London, there was a sense that Cavaco Silva was introducing the necessary structural reforms to the Portuguese economy.[31] There was also a feeling that Sampaio, and some of his Socialist colleagues, sat too close to the Communists in Portugal.

Continuity and stability were the order of the day, although there was some disappointment over Portugal's failure to align itself with London over the issue of monetary union in the Community.[32] Other European leaders were generally supportive of the government for similar reasons. Nobody wanted a change in power in Lisbon so close to the first Portuguese Presidency of the Community.

President Bush personally telephoned Cavaco Silva on 11 October 1991 to congratulate him on the PSD victory in the General Election, which had taken place on 6 October. The transcript of the conversation reveals both the strong support of President Bush for Cavaco Silva, and the importance the Prime Minister attached to winning an absolute majority at the election:

> PRESIDENT BUSH: Hello. How are you, my friend?
>
> PRIME MINISTER CAVACO SILVA: Fine, thank you, and you?
>
> PRESIDENT BUSH: Well, I feel like I'm not a very good friend because I should have called sooner to congratulate you on your stunning victory.
>
> PRIME MINISTER CAVACO SILVA: Thank you very much. That is very kind. I knew that you were following the situation in Portugal.
>
> PRESIDENT BUSH: Yes, I was for two reasons. First, I was anxious to see how it would go on the issues, and second, on a personal basis because you are a friend. I was glad to see you prevailed and that you have this clear vote of confidence just before Portugal takes on the Presidency of the EC. I just wanted to call up and wish you well and say well done.
>
> PRIME MINISTER CAVACO SILVA: It was a good victory. I think it is for the best for Portugal now, as we need political stability. Since we are now going to have the Presidency of the Community, it was very, very important to have a majority. You understand I am very pleased. To get a majority is difficult.
>
> PRESIDENT BUSH: I think it was wonderful.[33]

President Bush wasn't the only American who followed Portugal closely. For some years American musicians, especially in the field of jazz, had been visiting Lisbon on a regular basis.

By 1991, Lisbon, along with Porto, had become very much part of the international tour circuit for major groups. In February 1991, Miles Davis, the legendary jazz trumpeter, visited Lisbon to

Lisboetas pour on to the streets of the capital to support the 25 April 1974 Revolution.

Crowds gather in Lisbon's main square as news of the Revolution spreads through the city.

Refugees returning to Portugal arrive at Lisbon airport in 1975.

Henry Kissinger leaves Lisbon following his private trip to the city in 1980.

Pope John Paul II about to start his visit to Portugal in 1982.

Portuguese Prime Minister Mário Soares at the signing of the accession of Portugal to the EEC on 12 June 1985, at the Jerónimos Monastery in Belém, Lisbon.

Queen Elizabeth II on the steps of the Portuguese National Assembly at the start of her state visit to Portugal in 1985.

US President George H. W. Bush arriving at the Portuguese National Assembly in 1986 with Prime Minister Cavaco Silva.

In 1987, students at the University of Porto provide a traditional welcome to the Prince and Princess of Wales by laying their cloaks on the ground for the royal couple to walk over.

King Juan Carlos I of Spain during his state visit to Portugal in 1989 at the National Assembly in Lisbon.

US President Bill Clinton stands with President Jorge Sampaio at the Torre de Belém in Lisbon on 30 May 2000.

British Prime Minister Tony Blair arriving for the Azores Summit in 2003 is met by his Portuguese host José Barroso.

At the Summit Meeting of NATO Heads of State hosted by Portugal in 2010, US Secretary of State Hillary Clinton, President Barack Obama and the President of the European Commission José Barroso.

Cristiano Ronaldo takes a selfie with the Portuguese football squad and President Cavaco Silva ahead of their departure for the 2014 World Cup.

Present-day Portugal is
an attractive mixture of
the old and the new.

The Portuguese
flag flying over the
National Assembly
building in 2015.

play a concert at the Coliseum, the city's leading venue for concerts at the time. It was to be one of Davis' last concerts; he died later in the same year at the age of 65. Following the concert, Davis' band jammed at another of the city's most famous venues, The Hot Club, which attracted both local and international jazz acts.

Politically and culturally, Portugal readied itself to take the Presidency of the European Community. Lisbon was about to become centre stage for the six-month duration of the Presidency, with the city hosting meetings and summits. Naturally, all of this provided the opportunity to construct a new arena in which to host such prestigious events.

In Lisbon, there was a quiet sense of pride that, after decades of being totally, or partially, removed from the European continent, it was set to become the centre of attention of its European neighbours. In a sign of the importance of the Presidency, Cavaco Silva chose to keep his Cabinet largely intact following his election victory. Any potential major reshuffle in the government was postponed until after the Presidency.[34]

17

Under the Bridge

When it comes to hosting international events, the Portuguese do not do anything by halves. So in January 1988, the government took the decision to build the Cultural Centre of Belém to act as the host venue for the Portuguese Presidency of the European Community, which started on 1 January 1992. The building faced the River Tagus and looked towards the venue that had formerly been the flagship of highlighting the achievements of Salazar and the Estado Novo – the Portuguese and the World Exhibition of 1940.

Standing out in the gardens at the front of the somewhat austere façade of the Cultural Centre building, it is possible to see examples of Portugal's historical achievements: the monument to the discoverers, a reminder of the Golden Age of Portuguese history, and the 25 April Bridge (formerly the Salazar Bridge). The bridge is a modern wonder in all its red metallic glory, spanning the river and linking the old world to the new, marking the western edge of mainland Europe. A more evocative location could not have been chosen by the planners, who wanted to reshape Belém's image as a leftover decaying relic from the 1940 exhibition, which was fast fading into nostalgic irrelevance.

Following the Presidency, one of the buildings was designated to become the nation's leading venue for world-class modern art, putting the city of Lisbon well and truly on the international art circuit. Other Iberian cities remained far ahead of Lisbon in this respect. Madrid, Barcelona, and later Bilbao with its Frank Gehry-designed Guggenheim Museum, all hosted and housed important international collections that helped attract tourists from all around the world.

The ambitious aims in Lisbon were to try to match these cities with the creation of a state-of-the-art building that would be able to house both a permanent collection and temporary exhibitions. It all appeared to bode well for those who had a vision of the potential for the Iberian city of light to become an important centre for international art. Before all of this could be developed (or not), Portugal had to get through its Presidency of the European Community and show the potential of the city, and the country, to a slightly sceptical outside world.

Naturally, the Portuguese Presidency of the Community dominated everything in the government's agenda from January to June 1992. Both the government and the other member states of the Community approached the Portuguese Presidency, as the British said: 'with great trepidation and, in private, many had misgivings about their [Portugal's] ability to cope'.[1] The British went on to pay tribute to Portugal's efforts:

> But they did cope, and well. Some of their success may have
> been due to the advice and training given to key officials by
> their partners including ourselves. Some was due to the support
> of the Council Secretariat and the Commission. But much
> was also due to the hard work and dedication of officials and
> Ministers together with a willingness to spend the money first
> and find out where it would come from afterwards.[2]

On this note, the plans to convert the buildings into an art gallery and wider cultural centre at the end of the Presidency lay temporarily in tatters: a victim of the 'spend first and raise the money afterwards' financial planning culture in Lisbon. At the end of the Presidency, the buildings to host the new Cultural Centre of Belém lay empty with no money left to convert them to their intended purpose.[3] That said, they had proved a spectacular success for hosting the key meetings of the Portuguese Presidency. In some respects, the Portuguese were blessed with well-deserved good fortune during the six-month period of the Presidency.

International events generally worked in Portugal's favour by not producing an inordinate number of crises for the Community to wrestle with and resolve. Many feared at the start of 1992 that there would be a major crisis in the Soviet Union, which would have drawn in the Community. This did not materialize.[4] Events in Yugoslavia started to dominate the headlines – as they did for many years after. There were several instances of internal political upheaval in member states that produced unexpected difficulties for the management of the Community by the Portuguese.

By and large, however, these internal difficulties were not as bad as those faced by the British, who succeeded Portugal in the Presidency in July 1992.[5] Overall, the Portuguese Government managed to 'keep the train on the rails' and achieved an acceptable outcome at the European Council held in Lisbon.[6] At the end of it all, there was a palpable sense of relief in Lisbon and a feeling of pride that, at least, the country was better known again in the world.[7]

In identifying the Portuguese heroes of the Presidency, Cavaco Silva took many of the plaudits for his unfazed, unruffled, states-man-like approach – even when things (as often happens in Portugal) did not go exactly as planned. The main hero, however, was the Minister of Foreign Affairs, João de Deus Pinheiro.

The British, in particular, had been highly critical of Pinheiro's conduct as Minister of Foreign Affairs citing, among other examples of questionable judgement, his decision to stay on the beach when Iraq invaded Kuwait.[8] The Minister got his reward for his strong performance during the Presidency, when Cavaco Silva was able to name him as Portugal's nomination for European Community Commissioner in the second part of 1992.

This promotion worked well for the Prime Minister, who was able to appoint his political protégé, José Manuel Durão Barroso, to take over from Pinheiro as Minister of Foreign Affairs. Although Cavaco Silva didn't know it at the time, his appointment would launch the international career of arguably the most important Portuguese bureaucrat of the modern era.

One of the superior skillsets of Durão Barroso was his linguistic ability, which made him able to converse with the leaders of Europe in their native language. Personable, keen to ingratiate himself with foreigners, highly ambitious and a modernizer – Durão Barroso would emerge as a potential likely successor to the Prime Minister, and a man whose list of contacts would carry him all the way to the top in Brussels.

The other new boy on the block was António Guterres, whose domestic and international career coincided with that of Durão Barroso. In 1992, Guterres succeeded the increasingly hapless Jorge Sampaio as Secretary-General of the Socialist Party. Sampaio was rather unceremoniously dumped by the party in favour of Guterres, as the former simply could not deal with the cut and thrust of daily political life and could not break the stranglehold that Cavaco Silva and the PSD held over the electorate.

His successor, Guterres, also struggled to make an impact during the first months in charge of the Socialists.[9] In reality, it was initially a very difficult time to be leader of the opposition in Portugal. Europe, and much of the rest of the world, was watching the Portuguese Government perform its tasks on the international stage with great aplomb.

Cavaco Silva, who, prior to the Portuguese EC Presidency, was virtually unknown outside the country, became an internationally recognized leader, and a regular on the television news throughout Europe. In Portugal, there was a widely accepted centre-ground consensus to support the government during the six months of the Presidency.[10]

Although, in time, Guterres' cautious and consensual style of leadership and policy-making would come to be vindicated, it was a difficult introduction at the very moment that Cavaco Silva was at the peak of his power and popularity. Portuguese society had changed as well, since the last Socialist Government. It might not have been much wealthier, but it was more aspirational, with a growing professional middle class that regarded itself as the new powerhouse of the nation. New top-of-the-range cars, new roads, meals out in restaurants and trips around the shopping malls brought the new international brands to the country.

These changes were not unique to Portugal, but for the Socialist Party there was a need to modernize the party and present a new vision that looked towards the twenty-first century, and not backwards over its shoulder at the 25 April Revolution. This was the task which Guterres faced, and which Sampaio had failed to fully comprehend.

Guterres' efforts at modernizing the party would eventually have an impact not only upon the Socialist Party in Portugal, but also in Britain – when a few years later, a young Tony Blair would introduce similar changes into the British Labour Party. In the meantime, Guterres provided an early indication of his own personal international ambitions by getting himself nominated as the Vice-President of the Socialist International in September 1992.

The government was acutely aware that its strength during 1992 presented it with an opportunity and moved to introduce some key reforms to the economy and the state. The reforms included proposals for the reduction in the size of the bloated civil service, as well as cuts to the armed forces. Even though the government moved with great caution, both proposals ran into considerable opposition. The military reforms led to the resignation and early retirement of several senior key officers. The result, however, fell well short of achieving the government's objective of creating a professional armed service in Portugal.[11]

The government tried to introduce, with mixed success, key reforms in other public sectors. In higher education, and following much noisy student protest and strikes, it introduced limited fees for places at universities, which were means-tested on parents' ability to pay.[12] In healthcare, it was clear that hospitals were wholly inadequate to deal with the demands made on them by the public.[13] The government here made little dramatic progress, and the state-run hospital buildings continued to deteriorate: leaking roofs, unrepaired cracked windows. Doctors made their money in the private sector, and many only worked the minimum hours required in the public sector. Healthcare in Portugal, in short, remained very much based on the patients' ability to pay for their treatment.

Despite the only partial success of the government's reform plans, it could at least point to the relatively healthy state of the Portuguese economy at the time. An international economic recession bit into Portugal's main export markets, which impacted on the economic data for the country. The growth rate fell to 2 per cent, a figure that was not at all bad, given the difficulties being experienced in many other parts of Europe.[14] Unemployment remained low, and interest rates were down to 16–17 per cent. While this was still high, the fall was at least giving some breathing space for business without helping to fuel higher rates of inflation.[15]

The key to Portugal's relatively healthy years in terms of the economy lay in it largely avoiding the chaos surrounding the introduction of the European Exchange Rate Mechanism (ERM), which was introduced in the spring of 1992. At the time, the escudo entered the ERM at a rate lower than the Portuguese had wanted (and indeed blamed the British for this development), but it withstood the market turmoil that became known as 'Black Wednesday', which led to the British exit from the ERM on 16 September.

Later the escudo, along with the Spanish peseta, was devalued, but it largely maintained its value against other currencies in the ERM with the help of the Bank of Portugal's reserves. In a precursor to the Portuguese rationale in joining the euro single currency years later, the government justified its policy towards EMU (European Monetary Union); as the British said, 'The government remained determined that Portugal should be ready for the final stages of EMU and avoid relegation to a second tier of the European Community.'[16]

Away from the bright lights of the political and diplomatic arenas, Portugal had to face up to another transport accident that resulted in a tragic loss of life. On 21 December 1992, when attempting to land at Faro Airport in poor weather conditions, Martinair Flight 495 crashed and the fuselage broke into three pieces. As a result of the crash, 56 people were killed and some 106 seriously injured.

There was controversy over the main cause of the crash. High winds, thunderstorms and a flooded runway were initially blamed, but later pilot error became a potential cause of the fatal crash.[17] In reality, while the weather conditions were considered to be freakish, anybody who has landed at Faro Airport, with its close proximity to the sea, understands just how windy it can get on landing at this exposed site.

The accident was a sad ending for a year that had put Portugal on the front pages of the international media for the right reasons. As well as European Heads of State visiting Lisbon, several other VIPs paid a visit to the city. Guns 'N' Roses played a concert to an ecstatic crowd of fans at the Sporting Lisbon football stadium (Estádio José Alvalade) in the city. By the early to mid-1990s, Lisbon was very much part of the stadium rock circuit, with concerts being held at the city's major football stadiums. Faith No More also played, as did the 'King of Pop', Michael Jackson, in September 1992.

All of this meant that Lisbon, once a backwater, became very much part of the international pop scene. The only downside was the high price of the tickets, especially for Michael Jackson's 'Dangerous' tour, which put them out of reach of the pockets of many Portuguese. A new generation of Portuguese youth were growing up very much linked to Europe and North America musically.

The onset of the digital age and the CD was at hand, and those old locally produced cassette recordings were increasingly confined to the dustbin. It was largely a one-way street as, with the notable exception of Madredeus, Portuguese singers and bands found it difficult to break into overseas markets. Even fado music was in the doldrums, and it would be a decade, or more, before a new generation of singers would come through to help internationalize the genre and seduce audiences all over the world.

The year of 1992 represented the year when Lisbon and Portugal appeared to be more closely connected with Europe. The Presidency of the EC and the EMU illustrated that Portugal was determined to remain at the centre of Europe. There was good news from the

Community for Portugal, when agreement was reached to continue to supply the country with Community funding until the end of the century.

The government, as a result, was able to take planning decisions based on financial realities. What followed in 1993 was more complicated, with the full effects of the European economic downturn reaching Portugal. With its closer economic connections with the Community, it could be said that when Europe caught a financial cold, Portugal got the flu.

The period of the cohabitation was coming to an end and the outside world wondered how long Cavaco Silva would remain in power before handing over the reins to his successor.[18] It was widely presumed that he would do this in good time for the next General Election, to give his successor an opportunity to get his feet under the desk.[19]

The timing of the Prime Minister's resignation had to be carefully managed, as during 1993, the poll advantage over the Socialists started to narrow and eventually disappeared.[20] There were a number of reasons for this including the 'Cavaco fatigue factor', the decline in the economy, normal mid-term blues, sleaze and the increasing effectiveness of António Guterres in presenting alternative policies to those of the PSD.[21]

Constitutionally, President Soares was not able to seek a third term, and so speculation also started about the likely successor as President. Personal relations between the Prime Minister and the President deteriorated over the course of 1993, and by the start of 1994, as the British Ambassador wrote to the Foreign Office in London, 'Whenever the government has been wounded, President Soares has rushed to the scene with his salt jar.'[22]

The marriage of convenience that had been the backbone of a decade of political stability and economic advancement was ending in a bitter divorce, the after-effects of which would continue for years. Both men were busy securing their respective legacies in the post-Revolution narrative of the state.

Their swords would cross again, but for President Soares the twilight years were fast approaching, and power was rapidly slipping away from him and towards the leader of the Socialist Party, António Guterres. Like many political leaders, however, Soares did not comprehend the generational changes that were taking place and, as a result, did not exit the stage with noble grace.

In retrospect, 1992 and 1993 were the years of transition when Portugal fully committed itself to Europe and the path that was laid out towards monetary union. This path was not without dangers for a small nation and weak economy, like Portugal, and the British for one were disappointed that Portugal did not join the Eurosceptic camp. Instead, Cavaco set the country on course to remain inside the ERM and to potentially join a single currency when the time came to introduce it.

The driving force in decision-making concerning the newly branded European Union for Cavaco Silva was his concern about Portugal being relegated to the European Union's second division.[23] With the state of the Portuguese, and European economies, worsening throughout 1993, remaining within the European Union's first division came to be no easy task for Portugal.

The stakes were getting higher, as the country's left eye and right eye prepared to depart – or be dragged – from the political stage. The batten would be handed on to the next generation, for whom the 25 April Revolution was little more than a distant memory.

18

Fake Plastic Trees

Walking around the centre of Lisbon during the long hot summer of 1994, it was impossible not to be impressed at the cultural energy and buzz that emanated from the city. Tourists sitting at esplanade cafés along the city's main thoroughfare, Avenida da Liberdade, could not fail to notice that on their red chairs emblazoned with the beer logo of 'Sagres' or 'Superbock' were the words, 'Lisbon 1994: European City of Culture'.

Public spaces in the city had undergone something of a make-over prior to the start of the year, with the grey drabness of the urban landscape having been replaced by colourful hoardings and decorations. Grafitti was cleaned up wherever possible, and key buildings in the city given a new lick of paint. Attempts were made to cover some of the derelict buildings with large canvases that hid the unsightly face of urban decay, but in real terms did little to resolve the underlying problems of the poor condition of many of the buildings in the city centre. While the focus of attention was on the city of Lisbon, the celebration of the cultural capital of Europe was treated as an event of great national importance.

President Mário Soares viewed the one-year celebration as an opportunity to reorientate Portugal's national identity away from the periphery and towards the centre of Europe.[1] In short, democratic Portugal wanted to show Europe there was a new Portuguese national identity that, while respecting elements of the country's historical past, was forward looking, dynamic and prepared for the road towards closer European integration.

It was as if Lisboaetas were saying that they were cool with the past (both good and bad times), relaxed about the present, and looking forward and prepared for the changes that the future would bring. The shift away from a more outdated version of Portuguese identity was not sparked by Lisbon's year as Europe's cultural capital; rather the year represented the first screening, or premiere, for an international audience and the move towards a new, more Eurocentric Portuguese identity.

Two years earlier, Lisbon had won the right to host an even bigger international celebration – Expo 1998. This event was to become the most important international fair that the city would host since 1940. It would also lead to a much-needed modernization of the transport infrastructure in Lisbon, and the urban regeneration of a hitherto under-used part of the city along the bank of the River Tagus. Much of the middle part of the decade of the 1990s, as a result, was spent in preparing the city for the events that were expected to bring millions of visitors to the city. In other words, parts of Lisbon resembled a building site for much of this time.

At the centre of the hugely ambitious Expo project was the construction of a new bridge across the River Tagus, the Vasco da Gama Bridge, which was to be the longest bridge in Europe. There was also to be a new underground line built for the Lisbon metro, including some seven stations that linked with the city's trains and buses, and a new train station and terminal at the Expo site, Gare do Oriente, designed by the Spanish architect, Santiago Calatrava. With the benefit of hindsight, the plans appear to be a trifle over-ambitious for a country that, despite all the funds from the European Union, still remained one of the poorest nations in Europe.

The physical and financial imprint that all of this would leave on the city and the country was significant, but the Portuguese appeared hell-bent on maxing out on the projects for international events. It was as if the transformation of the city would take place under the guise of a large party to show off the country's wares to foreigners. Naturally, there was strong competition to win the contracts to create this piece of new Lisbon.

The British were feeling especially pleased with themselves for winning arguably the biggest tender of them all: the contract to build the Vasco da Gama Bridge.[2] Portugal's other European partners were keen to get in on the work, with foreign companies viewing the Expo project as a golden opportunity to establish a foothold in the Portuguese market. The whole project, the sum of the parts, was meant to create a new micro-city that would serve as a route map for the transformation of the rest of the country.

The year 1994, as well as being the year in which Lisbon tried to connect itself culturally with the rest of Europe, was also the 20th anniversary of the 25 April Revolution. A time for quiet reflection and a stock-take on the pluses and minuses of the democratic era? Not quite. The Portuguese were reminded of the dramatic day in grainy black-and-white television documentaries shown on the news, which were run on the new SIC and TVI channels, and in extensive coverage of the anniversary in the local and national press (but not in the international press).

For most Portuguese discussing politics, while drinking their after-dinner *bicas* in the new yuppie restaurants that had sprung up in downtown Lisbon, the only topic of interest was, when would Cavaco Silva throw in the towel and stand down as Prime Minister. There was an increasingly deep-rooted belief that he harboured ambitions to run for President, and would resign as Prime Minister in good time to prepare for the next Presidential Election, which was scheduled for 14 January 1996.

There were two related obstacles to Cavaco Silva's prospects of winning the Presidency: the increasing unpopularity of the government from early 1994 onwards, and the poor health of the Portuguese economy. After a tough year in 1993, the economy made something of a recovery during 1994 with exports up and the construction sector improving. Other positive signs included a falling rate of inflation at around 5.2 per cent for the year, and a reduction in the deficit to 6.8 per cent (still too high to meet the terms for convergence set out in the Maastricht Treaty).

Included in the bad news column was falling investment, a decrease in the real value of salaries, and consumption that was sluggish – with car and retail sales falling.[3] The biggest hope for the government was that the injection, in 1994, of £8 million of EU Structural Fund money per day would help boost growth. In electoral terms, the government was counting on this money to help kick start the sluggish economy.[4]

As Portugal's economic and political links with Europe deepened, it was also clear that it was reluctant to abandon its ties with Africa. 'Portugal's head is in Europe, but its heart is in Africa,' wrote the British Ambassador.[5] His assessment of Portugal's foreign policy was spot on. As he went on to argue: 'There has been quite a lot of soul searching about whether Portugal simply abandoned Angola and Mozambique carelessly to Communism. The truth is they did, but the political climate at the time explains it, even if it does not justify it. Personal ties often remain strong. There is an even stronger commercial interest (particularly in Angola).'[6]

In 1994, the Portuguese remained somewhat sceptical over the question of the implementation of the Angolan Peace Agreement. President Soares continued to criticize the Angolan Government, and was seen by Angolan President dos Santos as being too close to the leader of UNITA, Jonas Savimbi.[7]

East Timor continued to make headlines in Portugal, as the Portuguese Government attempted to implement confidence-building measures and organize a dialogue between the parties concerned.[8] So while Portugal was becoming more immersed in Europe, and for that matter in NATO as well, it still dealt with its ex-colonies in Africa and beyond. Bringing peace to these lands and developing lucrative markets for the Portuguese to exploit continued to be the dominant thrust of Portugal's policy aims in these areas.

In January 1995, Prime Minister Cavaco Silva announced his decision to stand down as leader of the Social Democrats. Although the decision had been widely trailed it still sent shockwaves through the political establishment in Lisbon. Outsiders voiced concerns that, after ten years in power during which the country had enjoyed unprecedented political stability, it might return to the black old days of rapid turnover of minority governments.[9] In reality, these fears were not realized.

Instead, following the General Election, which was held on 1 October 1995, there was an orderly transition of power from the Social Democrats to the Socialist Party. Even though the Socialists fell four seats shy of winning an overall majority, it was nonetheless a spectacular victory that would extend, and not end, the period of political stability in Portugal. All of this was illustrated by the calm reaction of the Portuguese Stock Exchange to the result, and the stability of the escudo in the days following the election result.[10]

The election represented a personal triumph for the leader of the Socialist Party, António Guterres, and the scale of the victory allowed the new Prime Minister to largely achieve his ambition of putting together a government of centrists, rather than Socialist Party 'stalwarts'.[11]

The British were impressed by both the new Prime Minister, and what it saw as a maturing in Portuguese democracy, which the result of the election appeared to confirm. In a dispatch to the Foreign Office, the newly arrived British Ambassador to Portugal, Roger Westbrook, wrote comparing the situation in 1995 to that of 15 years previously when he had served in the Embassy in Lapa:

> António Guterres has, so far, proved to be a better performer and power-broker than anyone expected. And there is some evidence that, once people saw which way the tide was flowing, they decided that the best electoral outcome would be a strong Socialist Government rather than a weak one. Many Social Democrat (PSD) supporters thought that and switched horses. This suggests that Portugal and the Portuguese have matured politically since the chaotic 70s and 80s that I knew so well. Desperate to protect the gains achieved since accession to the Community, a good many voted strategically.[12]

During the election campaign, despite the attempts of both main parties to highlight the differences between them it was really a Coke versus Pepsi branding style election, with a consensus between the parties that Portugal must make the first wave of European Monetary Union (EMU).[13] In this respect, by the end of 1995, the Portuguese economy was making steady, but unspectacular, progress towards meeting the strict criteria for EMU.

The economy was becoming more solid following a difficult few years. Inflation was running at below 4 per cent and Portugal's GDP per capita was 65 per cent of that of Britain, up from only 25 per cent in 1980.[14] The biggest problem, however, remained the deficit and the European Union predicted in 1995 that the Portuguese economy would not be ready in time for economic convergence.[15]

In order to achieve this the government had to cut the deficit, which was running at 5.6 per cent of GDP in 1995, to 4.3 per cent in 1996, and to 3 per cent in 1997. It was a tall order for any government. Local commentators suggested that in order to achieve this it would require a cut of 20 per cent in public spending in 1996 alone, as the government had ruled out raising additional revenues through a hike in taxes.[16]

The road towards EMU was to prove a rocky one for Portugal, with the key criteria being the self-imposed need to meet its 3 per cent target, for fear that if it did not make it to EMU, Portugal would not remain in Europe's first division. In retrospect, it is important to understand that Portugal's goals were motivated by a nationalistic pride in making EMU rather than by economic aims.[17] To some extent, this became an important feature to understand once the single currency started to unravel following the major recession at the end of the first decade of the twenty-first century.

As for the architect of Portugal's economic strategy, the ex-Prime Minister, Cavaco Silva, the shift from the Prime Minister's office towards the Presidency did not go as smoothly as he had hoped when he announced his decision to stand down as Prime Minister. After ten years in office there was a strong anti-Cavaco sentiment among many Portuguese. This voter fatigue was compounded by the economic difficulties that the country had faced during the final years of his decade in power.

To make matters worse for his prospects, there was a feeling among some Social Democrats that he had not given his whole-hearted support to his successor as leader of the party, Fernando Nogueira, and that had helped the Socialists win the General Election in October 1995.[18] At the end of 1995, the British predicted (as well as most opinion polls) that Cavaco Silva would lose the Presidential race to the Socialist candidate, Jorge Sampaio, who for the previous six years had served as the Mayor of Lisbon.[19]

The Presidential Election took place on 14 January 1996, with the only two candidates being Cavaco Silva and Jorge Sampaio. The latter secured a famous victory over his old political foe, winning by a handsome margin of 53.9 per cent to 46.1 per cent. The result could hardly be described as being based on generational politics: both candidates were born in the same year – 1939.

As one of the many consequences of the result, it sent Cavaco Silva into political exile, and it would be a further ten years before he finally secured the Presidency in 2006. It also brought to an end the era of Portuguese cohabitation, now that both the President and Prime Minister hailed from the same political party.

It was also the first time in living memory that either Portugal's left eye, Mário Soares, or its right eye, Cavaco Silva, did not occupy at least one of the major offices in the land. To some, this presented another sign of the maturing of Portuguese democratic politics.

There were two additional positive signs for Portuguese democracy that took place during the course of 1995. The first was the decision of the Guterres-led government to send 900 soldiers to Bosnia. 'They [the Portuguese] could hardly afford to do so, but equally could not afford not to be there,' argued Roger Westbrook, who viewed the decision, which was one of the new government's first, as being brave.[20]

It was, as the Ambassador reminded London, 'Portugal's first essay into European military affairs since it had sent its ill-fated divisions into the trenches of the 1914–18 War'.[21] It was also Portugal's first overseas force since the dark days of its colonial wars in Africa.

The decision to send the force to Bosnia, as a result, was not taken lightly, but for Portugal's European partners, still struggling to deal with the fallout from the collapse of the former Yugoslavia, it was the correct decision.[22]

The second sign was the opening of the Salazar Archive at Torre do Tombo (the Portuguese National Archives) on 25 July 1995. The archive contained all the diplomatic documents, correspondence and personal papers of the former leader of Portugal. During much of the 1980s, there was an uncomfortable silence regarding all things related to the Estado Novo and to Salazar. The opening-up of the archive led to more serious scholarly work on the period of Portugal's history from 1933 to 1968, and to the publication of new and important works that increased the debate and understanding about Salazar and the Estado Novo.

Dealing with the past is a vital component for nations struggling with present-day realities and looking forward to the future. Merely sweeping the good, the bad and the ugly from the era of Salazar under the carpet was not good for the health of Portuguese democracy. From 1995 onwards, however, new generations of Portuguese scholars have shown considerable interest in developing a better understanding of this important period in Portuguese history. There remain bitter and deep divisions, however, in the academic and political world over the merits, or otherwise, of Salazar and his contribution to Portugal.

In some respects in 1995, the country was too wrapped up in the present tense and worried about the future to pay much attention to the past. The present and future challenges that the nation faced related to the budgetary implications of meeting the convergence criteria, which dominated the daily agenda of the new government.

Partly as a result of these challenges, and the resulting economic pain, the British noted that during the course of 1995 a degree of Euro-scepticism emerged in Portugal.[23] There was very real fear as to where the European leaders were driving the union and a sense that the small nations, such as Portugal, might get lost on the way to a stronger European super-state. Ironically, decades earlier,

Salazar had expressed the very same fears in the post-Second World War order, when he had tried to keep Portugal isolated from the rest of Europe.

The challenges that Portugal's democratic leaders faced at the end of the century centred upon how best to continue to make Portugal relevant in a fast-changing Europe, where rich and poor nations had to converge to share a single common currency. It would not prove easy for the Portuguese government to succeed in this challenge. The stakes were getting ever higher for the small nation at the western edge of Europe to remain at the centre of European development.

19

Don't Look Back In Anger

Throughout 1996 and 1997 Lisbon prepared for the party of the century in 1998, its big moment on the international stage when the city would, for all of four and a half months, become the talk of Europe and the wider world. Thousands of new red chairs were readied for the city's cafés, this time emblazoned with the words 'Expo 98' on the backs.

Evidence of the works programme was everywhere and, being Portugal, the big question on the lips of many Portuguese and foreigners was, would it all be finished on time? The general sentiment in Lisbon was along the lines that it would be all right on the night.

There were, however, political problems attached to the immense project, and even more so with the change of government from Social Democratic to Socialist. And then there was the question of who was going to foot the final bill for the grand project? The planning authorities were determined to avoid the difficulties that had characterized the previous Expo, held in Seville in 1992, especially with the transformation of the site in the post-exhibition era to create permanent buildings and infrastructure.

As Lisbon prepared, the Portuguese Government could point to some relatively good economic news, as it continued its quest to meet the criteria for entry into the EMU in the first wave. The annual inflation rate of 3.1 per cent was well within the target range and growth was at around 2.5 per cent. Crucially, the deficit

reduction was on course as well with a prediction of the deficit at
2.9 per cent for 1997, and debt at 68 per cent.[1]

All of this made good reading for the Guterres-led Government
which, for much of 1996, continued to enjoy a political honeymoon,
caused by the improvement in the economy and the continued
disarray within the ranks of the Social Democrats following their
electoral defeat.[2] Both factors, however, were seen for Guterres as at
best soft factors, which allowed the government to find its feet and
prepare the ground for the harder times to come.

Guterres' consensual style continued to prove successful. The
Prime Minister's authority was not challenged in the National
Assembly during the course of 1996, and his popularity with the
voters appeared to have been consolidated.[3] His major headache
remained with the Council of Ministers. Guterres had appointed a
good number of non-party technocrats as well as representatives of
the old-style (left-wing) Socialist Party.

The mutual distrust and personality clashes that characterized
relations between these two ruling groups of Ministers provided
constant gossip for the chattering classes in Lisbon, as well as the
media. 'Guterres' imperative to find solutions which upset as few
people as possible provides fertile ground for such comment,'
Roger Westbrook argued in his summary of the year dispatch back
to London.[4]

In foreign affairs, the government enjoyed some good luck
and made a solid start. The Community of Portuguese Speaking
Countries was formed but, as the British argued, 'In the first six
months of its existence achieved precisely nothing'.[5] In Bosnia,
Portuguese forces served honourably, and the attempts of
Portugal to retain a NATO Command in the country looked to
be successful.

In other areas, the European Union managed, at last, to adopt a
common position on East Timor. The icing on the cake, however,
was the election of Portugal as a non-permanent member of the
United Nations Security Council. All in all it was a pretty successful year, with Lisbon being increasingly seen as a serious player in
Africa and in Latin America.[6]

One unexpected problematic area was in Anglo-Portuguese relations. The Portuguese took offence at Britain's apparent lack of support for Portugal's entry to the Security Council. Some Portuguese reports claimed that Britain had actively opposed Portugal's election. [7]

There were additional complications, caused by differences between the British government of John Major in London and the Portuguese Government, over the pace and scope of European integration.[8] As most diplomats and commentators suspected, these little local difficulties between the 'oldest allies' turned out to be short-term and good relations were soon restored, notably after the election of Tony Blair in Britain in May 1997.

While Guterres seemed to sail through effortlessly, and rode his luck on domestic, economic and foreign affairs, on the other side the Social Democrats could not seem to do anything without shooting themselves in the foot.[9] Their political leadership squabbled incessantly with one another and/or with other parties of the right. In this respect, Paulo Portas from the CDS was a catalyst for trouble, as he and some of the Social Democrats appeared hell-bent on score-settling from the era of Cavaco Silva.

The leader of the Social Democrats in 1996 was the highly articulate Marcelo Rebelo de Sousa, who was elected on 31 March 1996. A man of great energy, drive and ability, Rebelo de Sousa set to work to try to rebuild the party, which was still recovering from having lost both the General and the Presidential Elections.

Against the wishes of many in his own party, he attempted to solidify the centre-right and far-right under his leadership with a coalition with the CDS. It represented a brave attempt to build a potential winning coalition for the next election and was known as the Democratic Alliance, which had originally been formed in 1979 by Rebelo de Sousa's political patron, Francisco Sá Carneiro.

It proved 'a bridge too far', with the animosity between the Social Democrats and Portas proving too strong, and the Alliance broke up amid much rancour. Rebelo de Sousa remained head of the Social Democrats until José Manuel Barroso replaced him in 1999. Despite all the squabbling, the Social Democrats' consistent demand for a national referendum on the introduction of the single currency in Portugal remained the only real hope for a meaningful debate over Portugal's future participation in Europe.[10]

At the end of 1996, the British colourfully summarized the prospects for Portugal in 1997, as they put it:

> Prime Minister Guterres also faces challenges ahead. His honeymoon has been almost indecently protracted. But 1997 will be the year in which he and the Portuguese people have to learn to live together in their comparatively modest house within a comparatively modest income and both go out to work each day to bring home the *bacalhau*.
>
> We must see how they get on together. I suspect that there will be a number of rows, not least over domestic expenditure. And Mother-in-Law, in the shape of the traditional Socialist Party membership, will not hesitate to put her sharp-tongued pennyworth into the argument.[11]

The British then went on to offer Guterres some political advice.

> But argument can clear the air and be constructive. It is only from experience of the rough and tumble of leading his party, steering the parliament and guiding the nation that Guterres will finally learn that he cannot be all things to all men all the time. Once he has learnt to be tougher in his leadership, he should emerge at the end of the year successful in the local government elections and all the more secure in his position as Prime Minister.[12]

Discipline was the key word for 1997, with both main political parties wanting Portugal to be in a position for European Monetary Union on 1 January 1999. During the course of the year, Portugal's modest economic improvements continued, with GDP growth higher than the rate of inflation – about 3.5 per cent versus 2.2 per cent. Other good news came in the form of a rise in

Portugal's per capita income during 1996–7, from 53 per cent of the EU average to 70 per cent.[13]

Moreover, the structural and cohesion funds from the EU had played a vital role in this improvement by contributing 3 per cent to Portugal's GDP.[14] With Portugal still pushing for entry in the first wave of the EMU, both the Socialists and Social Democrats were in a state of unofficial truce, which robbed Portugal's political life of much of its colour and competitive nature.

The subjects that were the most contentious, constitutional reform, regionalization and abortion, cut across party lines causing internal divisions inside the two main political parties.[15] While there was a scandal involving the Deputy Prime Minister, António Vitorino, which received a great deal of press coverage and provided gossip for the chattering classes, it appeared to have little impact upon the voting public. It did lead to Guterres having to reshuffle his Ministers, leading to slight changes in the balance between the technocrats and the old school of Socialist Party.[16] In the end, Vitorino was acquitted of the charges of tax evasion, and went on to become the European Commissioner for Justice and Home Affairs.

The political truce was briefly interrupted by the campaign for the local elections held in December 1997. Both of the main party leaders appeared satisfied with the outcome of the elections, with Guterres able to claim a mid-term lead, and Rebelo de Sousa able to demonstrate enough improvement in the performance of the Social Democrats for him to keep his job as leader of the party.

These were the good times for the Socialists with, for the first time since the 25 April Revolution, a single party controlling the National Assembly, the Presidency and the majority of local municipalities. Guterres grew more assertive in his leadership style (as the British hoped he would) and continued with Cavaco Silva's programme of liberalization and privatization. In a sign of Portugal's growing confidence, Guterres adopted a more activist foreign policy, and not only in terms of sending Portuguese forces to Bosnia.

Membership of the UN Security Council was used for maximum benefit and Portugal also hosted an important NATO Foreign

Ministers Summit. Within the EU, Portugal's interventions grew
in confidence and they started to put forward proposals and not
merely respond to those from other member states.[17] Guterres
also moved to deepen relations with the United States at the same
moment that the country was moving towards closer economic and
political ties with Europe.

More confident, forward-looking and no longer a prisoner
of its history, Portugal in 1997 looked, on the surface, to be the
very personification of a modern democratic state. In reality there
remained two very different Portugals. As the British Embassy in
Lisbon noted:

> Short stay visitors to Lisbon see a thriving city of new river-
> side developments, streets clogged by thousands of new cars,
> a rapidly expanding metro system and new hi-tech buildings.
> Tourists find a growing and ever more varied range of leisure
> options. It is an image of a country which fits well into Portugal
> of 1997, a country of low unemployment, low inflation and
> healthy GDP growth.[18]

The report then went on to describe the other Portugal in the eyes
of the British:

> But a look beneath the surface reveals a very different Portugal.
> The education system, one of the weakest in Europe, turns out a
> poorly prepared workforce. Old-fashioned management practices
> persist, leaving a large group of middle managers temperamen-
> tally unable to take the most straightforward decisions.
>   Outside the major cities, the rural poor make even their
> low-income urban brothers look distinctly comfortable.
> Depopulation of the more remote areas has left some coun-
> try areas with an ageing, poorly educated sub-class eking out
> a subsistence existence. Our EXPO visitors next year [1998]
> should not be too blinded by all the glitz.
>   Much remains to be done to update work practices and to
> dispel the ingrained belief that taxes are to be avoided and the

state/employer is there to be milked at every turn. Failure to change attitudes will cost Portugal dear following the tougher competition that will surely come post-EMU and post-enlargement. The Socialist government has made a start but Portugal remains, for the time being, a country of Two Nations.[19]

To some extent, the notion of 'two nations' could be applied to several European countries, but the extent of the divide between the two in Portugal was huge. By 1997, it was clear that the input of European funds into the economy was benefiting urban Portugal far more than rural Portugal. Socio-economic divides in the country were increasing as Lisbon, and Porto, modernized and moved towards the twenty-first century, while the rural Portugal, characterized by the donkey pulling the plough, remained lost somewhere in the nineteenth century.

The danger in all of this was that a large part of the country was once again getting left behind, with little prospect of any better quality of life in democratic Portugal than in the era of the Estado Novo. New motorways made it easier for British, French and German lorries to reach Portugal with their consumer goods for the urbanites, but most of those living in the rural areas couldn't afford the tolls to carry themselves beyond their homesteads.

The challenge of doing something for the underbelly of the country was as important for the country as making Expo '98 a memorable and exciting experience for all those who passed through its gates. It was a challenge that, while not forgotten, was often pushed into a distant second place by both the main political parties in Portugal.

One area that provided hope was the Portuguese wine sector. Largely disorganized and not producing wine in sufficient quantities for export, there were examples of small vineyard companies developing ties with large overseas supermarket chains. The quality of the wine was varied, and the preference of the supermarkets was for Portuguese table wine, which could be sold at prices that undercut the more traditional French table wines that were available in a similar price bracket.

In Britain, however, Portuguese wine became trendy, with all the leading supermarkets buying up large amounts of low-priced Portuguese red wines, and selling them under the labels of the supermarket's own brand. The demand for higher quality wine came later and, here again, the Portuguese suffered from the reality that their wines were not produced in large enough volume to be able to satisfy the export market. Increased competition from New World wine, especially in the mid-price range, meant that market opportunities became more limited at the start of the twenty-first century.

In 1997, European countries were much more interested in selling their wares to Portugal and winning major contracts that were out for tender as part of the modernization of Portugal, than in buying Portuguese goods. In this respect, the British were proud to declare in 1997 that Portugal with its population of only ten million was a more substantial trading partner for Britain than China, Indonesia or Brazil.[20] Partner, however, was not an accurate description, as much of the trade was a one-way street. In 1997 alone, Britain chalked up notable success: contracts related to the construction of the Porto metro, British Telecom becoming the strategic partner of Portugal Telecom, water treatment contracts and the introduction of around 75 small to medium-sized British companies into the Portuguese markets.[21]

In return, the only notable Portuguese successes were the acquisition, in 1996, of the sporting goods retailer Lillywhites by Jerónimo Martins. After Lillywhites got into financial difficulty they subsequently sold the company in 2002. The British case was not unique; Portugal's European partners, including the Spanish, all hoped to exploit new opportunities in the Portuguese market.

Arguably Portugal's most notable export at the time was the footballer Luís Figo, who was starring in the successful Barcelona team that dominated Spanish football from 1997 until the end of the decade. In 2000, Figo made a hugely controversial move to Barcelona's arch-rival, Real Madrid, where he continued to win trophies and in the same year won the Ballon d'Or. Figo was the leader of Portugal's 'Golden Generation' that won the FIFA World Youth Championship in 1991.

In the era before the rise of José Mourinho and Cristiano Ronaldo, Figo was probably the most famous Portuguese man in the world. In Portugal, his name could be heard in discussions about football that continued to dominate the conversations of Lisboetas above the impending arrival of the euro currency.

Many of the other members of the 'Golden Generation' of Portuguese football stars became household names across the globe. Comparisons were often made between these Portuguese stars and the free-flowing Dutch sides of the 1970s: both were said to contain great individual players, but to lack team spirit and discipline. Since retiring from football Figo has retained a high international profile, often commenting upon changes in international football and the need to introduce reforms to the game.

Like many Portuguese footballers, and unlike most British players, Figo is articulate in several languages and can deal with multi-lingual press conferences. At the end of the 1990s, as Portugal was fast becoming a much better known country, his football abilities, especially in Spain, helped raise the profile of Portugal even higher on the international stage.

Portugal's global profile was about to rise even further, with the opening of Expo '98 in Lisbon. Despite continued concerns over footing the bill, the city, and the country, got most things ready on time. While it was an international festival, it was clear that it would provide a golden opportunity to highlight Portuguese talent to the outside world. The event represented the culmination of nearly a decade of work to bid, win and develop the project, but also illustrated the changes that were taking place in parts of the country. The British rather sourly warned: 'The summer [1998] will be dominated by the shenanigans of Expo, but come October, the realisation will dawn that the General Election is but twelve months away.'[22]

In other words, the political truce that had characterized the years of 1996 and 1997 was set to end as the main parties started, once again, to jostle for position to compete to lead Portugal into the twenty-first century.

PART SIX

No Surprises

Overload

Lisbon enjoyed its moment in the sun. Expo '98 was the spectacular success that its planners, and the government, had dreamed about since its conception. The weather was excellent, and tourists were greeted with deep blue cloudless skies for most of the summer. The city's hotels overflowed with guests, and room rates reflected the new reality: Lisbon was the hippest city to visit during the summer of 1998.

The statistics were quite staggering, with 141 countries represented in the individual pavilions linked by Expo's theme, 'The Oceans: A Heritage for the Future'. There were five themed pavilions, which attracted huge crowds, with the Oceania Virtual Reality Pavilion proving to be the most popular throughout the Expo. Álvaro Siza Vieira, the architect tasked with saving Chiado following the fire that destroyed much of it, worked on the Pavilion of Portugal.

By the time Expo closed on 30 September 1998, the total number of visitors had passed the 10 million mark. At the conclusion of the event, the mood in the city was upbeat, with many Lisboetas believing that Expo had placed the city firmly on the international cultural map. What next? A world-class art venue, and an attempt to steal the thunder from the city's two Iberian big brothers, Madrid and Barcelona?

As the gates closed on the exhibition and the diggers and cranes reappeared to transform the site into offices, housing, and the mandatory shopping centre, the city waited to see if the transformation would prove successful. The trouble was that the world moved on very quickly. Many of the visitors to Expo turned out to be one-timers who ticked Portugal off in the 'have visited' column of their colourful notebook, never to return to the city or the country.

In reality, there appeared little strategic planning to motivate and inspire return visits. As the tourists left the city there was a quiet sense of Expo having proved to be an expensive missed opportunity for placing Lisbon firmly and permanently at the centre of the international scene of arts and culture.

What followed was a deep sense of anti-climax, or party hangover, that was to last for a number of years, before the city started to prepare for its next international adventure: the hosting of the Euro 2004 football competition. In reality, there was a sense of overload and a need to return to the basics of repositioning Portugal in the modern financial and political world.

The award of the Nobel Prize for Literature in 1998 to the Portuguese writer, José Saramago, was lauded in the Portuguese press, and welcomed by some of the Portuguese elite who got somewhat over-excited by the international endorsement of an important area of Portuguese culture. The award of the prize to Saramago highlighted the continued deep divisions within the country among the left and the right.[1] Saramago, a member of the Communist Party, lived in 1998 on the Spanish island of Lanzarote, following an earlier spat with the Portuguese Conservative establishment and the Catholic Church over the publication of *The Gospel According to Jesus Christ*.[2] Nonetheless, the Portuguese took the prize with great pride, even if most of the population had not read any of his books. The award of the Nobel Prize for Literature to one of its own, however, did little to alter the anti-climactic feeling that characterized Portugal during the autumn of 1998.

The prospect of making the criteria to join the euro, in the first phase, appeared to shake Lisbon out of its hangover. The introduction of the euro on 1 January 1999 as the new currency – with Portugal locked into the single European monetary policy – represented a very real, but risky, achievement for the nation (Greece was not able to join until two years later). The introduction date marked the start of a three-year transition period prior to the full introduction of euro notes and coins – but legally the escudo had already ceased to exist.

This represented a giant step into the unknown for the member states of the EMU, but for Portugal, it was particularly risky given the difficulty it had experienced, and the sacrifices it had made, to enter in the first wave. Economically speaking, Portugal became in 1999 very much a part of the centre of Europe, and the all-new powerful European Central Bank would, in part, dictate its future financial dealings.

The Guterres-led Government suffered a seemingly similar hang-over from the heady days of Expo, but revived its fortunes in time to win the General Election, which was held on 10 October 1999. The Socialists were tantalizingly close to winning a historic absolute majority in the National Assembly, falling short by only one seat.

The election represented as much a continued vote of no confidence in the Social Democrats as an endorsement of the government. José Manuel Durão Barroso had succeeded Marcelo Rebelo de Sousa as leader of the Social Democrats on 27 May 1999, but in the short time prior to the General Election, he was unable to rally the party and its supporters.

The most notable statistic of the election was the record low turnout, with only 61 per cent of voters bothering to cast their votes. The apparent apathy of the Portuguese voter in 1999 was a worrying development in the democratic period, and a reflection of the lack of clear blue water in ideology and policy terms between the two main parties of the country.

During the first six months of 2000, Portugal held the Presidency of the European Union. Amid all the international events in Lisbon related to the Presidency, arguably the most high profile was the EU–US summit, which brought US President Bill Clinton to Portugal. President Clinton was in the twilight of his second, and final, term in office, but came to Lisbon for the summit to meet with the Israeli Prime Minister, Ehud Barak, who was also in the city.

Obsessively, the President was doing the groundwork for his summit at Camp David between the Israelis and the Palestinians later in the summer. Upon his arrival at Lisbon Airport on 30 May 2000, the President paid tribute to his Portuguese hosts: 'And at the dawn of a new century, Portugal again is leading the way, strengthening the European Union while preserving our transatlantic partnership, building peace in the Balkans, supporting democracy in Russia. Portugal has been a strong voice for peace and stability throughout the world.'[3]

The rest of Clinton's visit was taken up with a state dinner hosted by President Sampaio and by the summit. Prior to his departure, the President held a press conference during which he again paid tribute to his Portuguese hosts and their organization of the EU Presidency. The majority of the questions from the press, however, concerned the Middle East.[4]

As the biggest star of politics departed Lisbon, and the Portuguese Presidency ended, there was once again a sense of anti-climax as the realities of everyday politics returned to the country, and the end of 2000 was characterized by a feeling of political apathy among the Portuguese.

This apathy continued through to the 2001 Presidential Election in which, as expected, the Socialist Party's candidate, President Jorge Sampaio, was re-elected to a second term in office. Sampaio's triumph in the first round of voting, held on 14 January 2001, was marred by low voter turnout for the election, with only 49.71 per cent of voters casting their ballots.

To some extent, the predictability of the outcome of the election put off some voters from driving to the polling stations, but there was a sense of a deeper malaise in Portuguese democracy that needed to be addressed by its political leaders. In reality, things got worse, particularly over the course of 2001, before there were signs of recovery. Indeed as the British summarized in dramatic terms: 'Portugal ends 2001 becalmed, without political leadership and with major question marks about her future economic identity and performance in the looming Iberian space.'[5]

The report went on to address the question of Portuguese versus Iberian identity: 'The cartoonist who sliced the Portuguese flag into two equal halves with the banner of the Spanish department store "El Court Ingles", which has just opened in Lisbon, struck a nerve because of its self-evident truth that Spanish investment is huge and Portuguese worry about becoming an economic region of Spain.'[6]

The total sum of both statements was that Portugal was in deep trouble, with a political leadership that was failing to offer meaningful leadership, and an economy that was rapidly falling behind that of its Iberian big brother and was vulnerable to a de facto Spanish takeover. The heady days of the summer of 1998, when Portugal was the centre of attention, with the promise of Expo being a launch pad for the economy, appeared a long way back in the past.

As the year 2001 ended, the Prime Minister, António Guterres, departed the political stage following the Socialist Party's mediocre showing in the local elections held in the middle of December. For many observers, Guterres had failed to deliver on his early promise as Prime Minister.[7] By the end of 2001, the Portuguese made it clear that they had grown tired of his consensual kind of leadership and wanted a stronger leadership style.

It was a sad exit for a personality who had been seen as a great modernizer of the Socialist Party, in the same mould as Tony Blair in Britain, but who, like Blair, never really commanded total support or admiration from within the Socialist Party he led. In the end, Guterres would settle for a career in the equally choppy waters of United Nations diplomacy and administration, where he has served as the UN High Commissioner for Refugees. Prior to that, he served as the President of the Socialist International. His leadership style and bureaucratic organizational abilities were better suited to both these jobs than to the cut-and-thrust of party politics, and he achieved a great deal of success in both posts.

The tragic catalyst for the decline in the fortunes of the Socialists had come earlier in the year, on the night of 4 March 2001, when the Hintze Ribeiro Bridge collapsed in Entre-os-Rios, Castelo de Paiva, killing 59 people.[8] The cause of the collapse was said to be decades of illegal sand extraction that had weakened the bridge's supporting pillars. Much of the blame was cast on the government, who were in charge of the maintenance of the bridge.[9] Guterres was given a hostile reception when he visited the location, as the *Guardian* newspaper wrote:

Dozens of local people screamed expletives at the Prime
Minister, blaming the government for the deaths. Guterres
rejected the accusation and said he has ordered an official
inquiry. 'No one of good faith would think there was any type
of personal blame,' Guterres said. But local residents of the
rural town in northern Portugal, about 180 miles north of the
capital Lisbon, say the bridge was unsafe.[10]

According to British sources, the collapse of the bridge resulted
in six Ministerial resignations and became a symbol of the
declining fortunes of the Socialist Party.[11] Whatever the political
fallout, it served as a sad reminder of the other Portugal away
from the glitz of Lisbon. The fact that there had been repeated
warnings about the safety of the bridge made the events all the
more unacceptable.

The impression given was of a rural Portugal in which much of
the infrastructure was dangerously out-of-date, poorly maintained,
and where building regulations were often overlooked by officials
willing to turn a blind eye in exchange for a thick brown enve-
lope stuffed with cash. The transformation of Portugal from the
Estado Novo to a democratic country had done little to end the
brown-envelope culture.

The appalling events in the United States on 9/11, to which
the Portuguese government responded stoutly, led to a short-term
revival of the party, but this did not impact upon the longer-term
decline in its fortunes.[12] In 2001, there was strong support for a
European army, with some 80 per cent of Portuguese polled indicating their support for the establishment of such a force to meet
the new threats of the present day and the future. In other words,
the Portuguese remained good European citizens who travelled
with the integrationist flow and rarely raised their voice in the EU.[13]

Portugal continued to be dogged by economic structural problems. They were characterized by the British in the following
manner: 'All experts agree that the tax take is too low and the public
sector too large, but there is little sign of real reform. The shakeout
in traditional industries continues as Portugal's labour costs look

increasingly high and her labour laws unduly restrictive by comparison with Eastern Europe.'[14]

The rate of unemployment ran at around 4 per cent, and the seasonal job market had to be reinforced in the Algarve and in the Douro vineyards with a steady flow of Eastern European labour. The longer-term part of the plans for European Monetary Union continued to cause Portugal problems, with the country's chances of achieving a balanced budget by 2004 seen as low.

The key statistic was that the deficit in 2001 was over 2 per cent, against a target of only 1.1 per cent. In 2001, it was widely presumed in the banking world, however, that with the Portuguese love of using their credit cards, the country would have problems when the euro notes and coins were introduced into circulation on 1 January 2002 in place of the escudo.[15]

As Portugal entered a General Election campaign following the resignation of Guterres, the Socialists could at least use some of the previously mentioned data to make a case that while the economy was not growing as fast as hoped, there were some positive signs during this difficult transition period.

A harsher assessment of the economy was that, despite promises by Guterres of systematic reforms to the economy, little had changed during his period in office. Portugal needed a strong reformer and instead got a consensus management of the economic status quo from their leader. The era was a touch mockingly referred to as 'the Guterres years of easy charm and easy credit'.[16]

The result of the General Election, which was held on 17 March 2002, produced a close finish between the two main political parties, with the Social Democrats winning 40.2 per cent of the vote, to the Socialists' 37.8 per cent. The Social Democrats were able to form a coalition with the CDS (Centre Democrats), which allowed José Manuel Durão Barroso to form a workable coalition government under his leadership. The turnover of power from one main party to the other was now a feature of Portuguese democracy.

In 2002, the implications of the turnover lay in the campaign promises made by the incoming Prime Minister Barroso, in his determination, as the British saw it, 'to carry through real transformation of the economy and the grossly inefficient and complacent public sector'.[17] There was some scepticism as to whether the new Prime Minister would make good on his election promises. The question on the lips of many observers during the spring of 2002 was, would Barroso turn out to be a Cavaco II or a Guterres II?

By 2002, it was apparent that the new Prime Minister intended to become the former. 'Barroso sowing seeds of economic transformation and not for turning', said the British Ambassador.[18] The 'not for turning' phrase was lifted from the queen of economic reformers, Margaret Thatcher. Barroso's most important European relationship during his time in office was with another reformer and modernizer, Tony Blair. Later on Blair was to become the 'Sugar Daddy' to Barroso, helping secure the Portuguese Prime Minister's appointment as President of the European Union in 2004.

In 2002, many people saw Barroso as a caretaker Prime Minister, but he acted swiftly, and with initial determination, to push through a real economic transformation of the economy, and especially of the public sector. In the process the Prime Minister became a 'resolute and respected leader'.[19] Of course, such lofty ambitions and kind words of encouragement had been uttered at the start of term for several previous governments in Portugal, but in this instance, Barroso appeared as if he might just deliver on his electoral promises.

In reality, Barroso inherited a difficult economic hand and was forced to deal with the consequences of the uncontrolled spending spree that had characterized the Guterres era.[20] Belatedly, it became clear that the deficit for 2001 was worse than initially thought, coming in at 4.1 per cent. The new government, as a result, was forced to abandon a proposed major tax cut. Moreover, it announced a rise in the top level of VAT (IVA) to 19 per cent, and set out to try to reduce the deficit to 3 per cent by the end of the year.

There was further bad news with a general economic slowdown in the country that led to minimal growth (0.5 per cent) and a near collapse in government revenues. Ministers, as a result, had to

swiftly rethink priorities and agree to painful cuts to ensure that the
deficit target was met at all costs.[21]

Despite these unforeseen economic difficulties, the government
made enormous efforts to reform Portugal's labour laws. Given
the entrenched nature of the opposition to these reforms from the
labour unions this proved to be no easy task, but Barroso appeared
determined to rid the country of the old social structures implemented on the back of the 25 April Revolution.[22]

As the economic development slowed to a snail's pace, and the
deficit widened, Portugal was hit by a crisis of confidence. Expo
'98 had put the country at the centre of Europe for a few heady
summer months four years previously. In 2002, Europe and the
world looked very different and Portugal felt in real danger of
becoming ever more irrelevant in a world of innovation and rapid
change. The British summed up this feeling at the end of 2002:

> Enlargement of NATO and the EU have left the Portuguese
> with a bad bout of peripheral small countryitis as Europe's
> centre of gravity has shifted so firmly eastward. The Bush
> administration court them because of the importance of the
> Lajes base in the Azores to the build-up in Afghanistan and
> the Middle East, and both the Prime Minister and Defence
> Minister are strong Atlanticists. This has helped the Portuguese
> case in the battle over NATO command restructuring. But
> in the EU, the Portuguese have felt bullied by the French,
> swamped by the Spanish and unloved by the British, except
> when we want something.[23]

The British Ambassador pleaded with the Foreign Office not to
forget Portugal, and said: 'Given Durão Barroso's courageous and
principled stand successively on Afghanistan, Iraq and Turkey accession, the occasional phone call from Number 10 [the British Prime
Minister] would hearten a potentially good friend and ally on the
key issues of the 2003 agenda from Iraq to the Middle East.'[24]

Tony Blair got the message, and with the development of the
Iraq crisis into full-scale preparations for a war against Saddam

Hussein and his alleged weapons of mass destruction, Barroso, the Azores and Portugal were set to become of great importance to the Americans and the British. It was, however, a little bit as the Ambassador had written; Britain only loved Portugal when it wanted something from Lisbon.

In the meantime, the Portuguese Government was busy trying to put its own house in order. Barroso wanted to create new agencies to help with high-tech start-ups in Portugal, and to hire diplomats from the private sector who would be able to promote and help sell Portuguese goods in overseas markets.[25] At the heart of his policy was the need for Portugal to modernize and to become relevant to the twenty-first century. Forward momentum and the changes to the health sector, prison reform and a long overdue overhaul of the armed forces were all near the top of the political agenda.

Barroso had the air of a man in a hurry, huffing and puffing, moving rapidly from one location to another. It was as if he was trying to give the country one great push to get it moving, only to discover that he would have to push it up a steep hill. By the end of 2002, the Prime Minister had at the very least outlined a leadership – though it was not to everybody's liking, especially the trade unions, who saw him as arrogant and something of a bullyboy.

He couldn't have cared less what the unions thought of him, as long as they didn't obstruct his programmes of reform, which is exactly what they did do. Although he could not have known it at the time, Barroso was about to cross the threshold from national to international leader. His name would become the answer to a Trivial Pursuit question: name the four leaders whose meeting in the Azores resulted in the decision to go to war against Iraq. The most common response was Bush, Blair, [José María] Aznar and what's his name?

Aside from the Iraq War, Portugal would have its own fires to fight in 2003, when Europe experienced one of its hottest ever summers. Sadly, in Portugal the heatwave led to powerful and widespread forest fires across the country, which caused terrible destruction in many rural areas.

Hurt

For Lisboetas who were not able to join the mass annual exodus from the city on 1 August 2003, the night was hard to endure, with the temperature not dipping under a sweaty 30 degrees. All over the city, the sounds of overworked, and poorly maintained, air-conditioning units could be heard humming alongside the music of bars and discotheques where tourists and unfortunate locals drank ice-cold beer and prayed for rain. At dawn, across the south of the country a tremendous freak storm unleashed a hot, strong sirocco wind, the Mediterranean wind that originates from the Sahara and that reaches hurricane speeds across North Africa and Southern Europe.

Across Europe, the heatwave of 2003 produced the hottest summer since records began. In Portugal, the temperature reached a staggering 47.3 degrees in Amareleja, and the high temperatures across the country, mixed with the sirocco wind, led to some of the worst forest fires in the history of the country. By the time they had been extinguished, the fires had destroyed around 5 per cent of the countryside and 10 per cent of the forests in Portugal. The BBC weather centre summarized the damage: 'In Portugal 215,000 hectares area of forest was destroyed. This is an area the same size as Luxembourg. It is estimated millions of tonnes of topsoil were eroded in the year after the fires and the protection of the forest cover was removed. This made river water quality poor when the ash and soil washed into rivers.'[1]

Human costs were also high: 2,100 died as the result of the heat-wave in 2003.[2] Experts argued that the devastation that occurred during the summer was made all the worse by the following six structural causes:

- The chaotic structure of small private property that encourages abandonment of many of these smallholdings
- The absence of a sustainable long-term national forest policy
- The lack of a strategy for the rural economy comprising the forestry sector
- The deterioration of the Forest Services
- Poor organisation of the fire-fighting structure and lack of specific training of fire-fighting corps
- Poor education and poor public awareness campaigns on the increased risks of forest fires[3]

The fires were a deadly blow to Portugal's rural areas, which were still struggling with the effects of land reforms dating back to the 25 April Revolution. It was clear that in 'two nations' Portugal, as the British had characterized it, the development of the country was very much still relevant. Rural Portugal struggled to come to terms with the twenty-first century, and the heatwave exposed the shortcomings of local arrangements to protect the countryside and to fight the inevitable fires that broke out during times of prolonged hot weather. The sinister undertones in all of this remained the widely held belief that many of the fires were started deliberately for planning permission purposes.

Despite the summer setbacks in rural Portugal, the Prime Minister, José Manuel Durão Barroso, continued to try to push a country that was still suspicious of change into the twenty-first century.[4] Moreover, he stood by the Allies and, according to the British, by his principles on Iraq, even at high domestic cost to his government's popularity. Barroso's support for the US-British fighting against the alleged WMDs (weapons of mass destruction) in Iraq was shown by his hosting of the Azores Summit on Iraq between President Bush and Prime Ministers Aznar and Blair, and by his decision in May 2003 to commit Portugal to sending a force to Iraq.[5]

Both decisions, to host the summit and to send a Portuguese force to Iraq, represented major political gambles by the Portuguese Prime Minister, which were taken as part of his strategy to show Portugal as punching above its weight in international affairs.

It was completely apparent what Barroso and the country gained from such a high-risk strategy during the Iraq crisis, the subsequent war and the problematic post-war era. Barroso was given the red-carpet treatment by President Bush, which was reserved for favoured VIP visitors to the White House. The Prime Minister was treated to a lunch, which was attended by all the leading members of the Bush administration: Dick Cheney, Donald Rumsfeld, Colin Powell and Condoleezza Rice.[6] More specifically, the United States continued to support the maintenance of the NATO base in Lisbon, despite the arguments against it from some European NATO members.[7]

In another sign of the fruits of Portugal's support for the Americans, Barroso's phone call to President Bush in the small hours of a Sunday morning was put straight through, even though it was within half an hour of the rumoured capture of Saddam Hussein being confirmed to the media.[8]

The capture of Saddam relieved some of the mounting domestic pressure on Barroso over his Iraq policy. The deployment of the Portuguese National Guard (GNR) to Iraq in November 2003 was a highly risky affair, from both military and political perspectives. The deployment took place following an attack on Italian forces tasked with a similar mission to that of the GNR. There were widespread public and media doubts about the wisdom of sending the force to Iraq, but the Prime Minister insisted that he would keep his promise to send a Portuguese force to the troubled country.

Militarily, it was a risky mission for the small contingent of Portuguese forces, who were both high profile and unsupported nationally, and dependent upon Italian and British forces if anything went wrong.[9] Any casualties would have caused a serious public reaction among the majority of the population who were unimpressed by the case for their deployment in the first place, and by the government's Iraq policy in general.[10]

While Barroso, and the government, tried to wave a big stick on Iraq, on European Union affairs it largely tried to keep its head down, fearing action over its failure to meet EU conditions in the Stability and Growth Pact (SGP). In 2002, punitive proceedings had been started against Portugal for allegedly failing to meet its terms within the SGP, but fines were never imposed.

By 2003, Portugal was technically in recession, with the country having some of the lowest international growth (actually minus 1.1 per cent). However, by making considerable cutbacks and imposing severe restrictions on public spending, the country was set to just about crawl under the SGP wire for 2003. All of this came with considerable social costs, but the Prime Minister appeared to have little choice but to try to meet the criteria set out by the European Union, or risk facing fines and a loss of international financial confidence.

Barroso, the man and the leader, continued to try to ingratiate himself with the European leaders, especially Tony Blair, who was at the height of his influence. Here, Barroso tried to convince other leaders that he was the man who would complete the job and, whenever he met foreign diplomats, he underscored his reforming credentials.[11] The British certainly fell under Barroso's spell, writing in glowing terms about him:

2003 has been dominated by Prime Minister Durão Barroso pursuing the Sisyphean task of rolling Portugal forward into the 21st Century. He knows that Portugal risks being left behind economically and becoming politically peripheral unless there is wholesale transformation. He has staked his political future on delivering change.

Competitiveness, innovation, labour law and public administration reform have been initiatives promoted by the Prime Minister to make a reality of Lisbon process commitments. 'Portugal 2010' seeks to bring together the various facets as part of a strategic approach to modernising Portugal. It is a brave effort. But it will stand or fall by the government's success in changing culture in the ossified and legalistic 700,000 strong public administration.[12]

In truth, as Foreign Office officials back in London noted, much of this promise had been heard before, particularly during the Guterres era, but, as one official said, 'it was startling to see how little lay behind the arras of promises'.[13]

Anglo-Portuguese relations experienced a difficult year, with the exception of Iraq. In Lisbon there was a sense among the British diplomats stationed in the city and the Portuguese government that London was ignoring its oldest ally. All of this was to change in 2004 with the Euro football championship, when the Ambassador warned the Portuguese about the arrival of English football hooligans: '. . . few are ready for the arrival of the tsunami of red and white flags, shaved heads, chants, beer and bellies that will wash over the principal squares when England plays France in the first round.'[14]

It was important to remember that Portugal was a medium-sized EU and NATO country with a population of 10 million. For the British, however, Portugal always had a higher profile with the average punter than with the British Government. As the Ambassador reminded London in the hope of persuading more Ministers to visit Portugal: 'Two million British tourists visit Portugal every year. 40–50,000 or more live here part-time or permanently. We all know someone who has been to the Algarve on holiday. Today the pleasures of the Algarve (and the 900 bars in Albufeira alone) have greater recognition than the enduring bilateral Anglo-Portuguese alliance of 1386.'[15]

The Ambassador's comments are important in that they reveal the profile of Portugal to be particularly high in Britain, especially among the population who enjoy package holidays to the sun. Portugal was always a favoured location owing to the high level of English spoken, the quality of service and hotels, the high standard of beaches and, yes, because the local beer was cheap and strong. So both the Portuguese authorities and the British government awaited the arrival of the additional hordes of football fans (and hooligans) in Portugal for Euro 2004 with some trepidation.[16]

On the surface, Euro 2004 turned out to be another international success story, despite the hurt felt by the local population at the competition's outcome, when Greece narrowly defeated the host nation to lift the cup for the first time. Portugal prepared for the tournament by building seven new stadiums and renovating a further three. The costs involved were immense, and the new stadium buildings were met with mixed receptions. Arguably, the most impressive for foreign football fans was the Estádio Municipal de Braga, with its unusual open end.

The stadium was designed by the brilliantly talented Porto-based architect Eduardo Souto de Moura. It is also known as A Pedreira (The Quarry), as it is carved into the face of the ancient Monte Castro quarry. Souto de Moura's later work would include the building in Cascais to house the works of artist Dame Paula Rego.[17] In addition to the stadiums, new five-star hotels were built in Lisbon, Porto and in other host cities. The project was as ambitious, if not more so, as that planned for Expo '98. With the Euro 2004 project, however, there appeared much less planning for the day after.

The tournament itself was a huge success in footballing terms. The sun shone, the famous deep blue summer skies were visible for most of the tournament. Fans came from all over Europe, and with a few minor exceptions there was very little trouble. Even the notoriously badly behaved travelling English fans were on their best behaviour and were closely shepherded by a well-prepared Portuguese police.

The tournament anthem, sung by Nelly Furtado and entitled 'Força', was an unusually good tune for a football song. Throughout the summer of 2004, there was a definite feel-good factor in the country as the Portuguese proudly opened their doors to the colourful array of football fans. Television coverage in Europe and around the world put the country very much in the international spotlight, with most feedback being very positive.

In this football-loving nation, many Portuguese took great pride in being seen as having organized an efficient, well-policed football experience, which highlighted the modern aspects of Portugal to the outside world. Even if their team did not emerge as victorious in the end, the Portuguese at least took consolation in beating their Iberian rivals, Spain, 1–0 in the group stages.[18]

For those people that arrived in Portugal during the second half of 2004, most expected to find a country buoyed up by the success of Euro 2004, proud of its recent achievement in staging a world-class tournament and confident about the future of the country.[19] Instead, there was widespread dissatisfaction and widespread anxiety, together with a sense of the tournament being a wasted opportunity for the country.[20]

In short, there was a hangover similar to the period that followed Expo '98. It was a good time to stock-take Portugal's progress, and also to assess where it continued to fall short in a rapidly changing continent.

In 2004, as a result of the EU structural funds, Portugal had the newest and arguably the best motorways in Europe (but also some of the most expensive). Better living standards in urban areas such as Lisbon meant that its roads were crammed full of new cars. The site of Expo '98 had been successfully transformed (though at great cost) into a new and highly fashionable suburb of Lisbon that resembled the Docklands in London.

The Lisbon metro system continued to expand, with the promise that one day the underground signs marked Santa Apolónia railway station would lead to the opening of the station there. In Porto, the new metro system was under construction. And a country in which a generation hid their savings under the bed (or for the wealthy in overseas accounts) had in 2004 a retail banking system that was as sophisticated as any in Europe.[21]

On the surface everything looked to be heading in the right direction. But dig a little deeper and the evidence for the sense of malaise that characterized the feeling in the country following Euro 2004 was not difficult to uncover. The economy was faltering – again – and the centre of European gravity was rapidly shifting eastwards.[22] The Portuguese understood that they needed to implement important reforms, but the political will to undertake this was declining – again.

Any economic growth to speak of had largely been driven by consumer debt and, in 2004, ran at an average of 118 per cent of family income.[23] The development had been uneven: the notion of the 'two nations' still existed, with rural areas dropping further behind the cities. The British noted more specific issues in 2004:

> The centrally-directed state education system is chaotic – epitomised this year [2004] by the failure to place the new teacher intake before the beginning of the academic year. Only a minority of the adult population has completed high school. The rate of functional illiteracy remains the highest in the post-enlargement EU. Social mobility is very restricted, and real wealth still controlled by the few.[24]

The final point here was important, because it essentially argued that if the 25 April Revolution, and the introduction of a democratic state, had been intended to end control of the wealth of the country by the few over the masses, then it had clearly failed to achieve its aim. The British continued with the analysis:

> The European comparisons get worse. A decade or more ago, Portugal's per capita GDP was 64 per cent of the EU average. It rose to 70 per cent in the 1990's, but after the recession of 2002–3 fell back to 67 per cent, the lowest in the old 15-member EU. The latest statistics suggest that growth was again negative in the third quarter of 2004. Productivity is only 60 per cent of the old 15-member EU average.
>
> Three of the new members – Slovenia, Cyprus and Malta – are already richer than Portugal. The Czech Republic and Hungary may soon join them. The new Baltic and East European members have a cheaper and better-educated labour force, and are strong competitors for direct foreign

investment. Meanwhile, the Portuguese see their Spanish
neighbours leaping ahead.[25]

It was a damning analysis of the state of Portugal in 2004, in which
the country was running the very real risk of being left behind
if it didn't get its act together, and quickly. To further complicate matters, Portugal lost its Prime Minister, as in 2004, José
Manuel Durão Barroso became the 11th President of the European
Commission.

On a superficial level, the elevation of Barroso to the top job in
Europe represented a great honour and recognition – not only for
the man, but also for Portugal. It was becoming usual for the big
three in Europe (Britain, France and Germany) to seek nominees
from one of the smaller countries for key EU jobs, and Barroso
was seemingly well qualified: he had served as Prime Minister and
crucially spoke good English, French and German. His character
appeared well suited to Europe's leading bureaucratic job and his
personal ambitions made it virtually impossible for him to turn
down the job when offered the position.

In Portugal, the elevation of Barroso led to Pedro Santana Lopes
taking over as head of the Social Democrats and becoming Prime
Minister on 17 July 2004. There were a number of issues related
to Santana Lopes that centred first upon the fact that he had not
been elected directly by the population, and secondly on issues
surrounding his management of the government.

To compound the difficulties, Santana Lopes was left, in effect,
holding the baby of the Portuguese economy, which as previously
mentioned was in a state of crisis.[26] After the country returned
from its traditional August holiday shut-down, what followed
throughout the autumn of 2004 was a series of political crises
before President Sampaio stepped in and essentially sacked the
government on 30 November.

President Sampaio announced that he was calling an early election for the National Assembly set for 20 February 2005. On 11
December 2004, Santana Lopes stated that the government would
resign, but would continue to serve in a caretaker capacity until

the new elections. The British noted that despite his failure to run a successful government, Santana Lopes remained 'a formidable campaigner who cannot be written off'.

There was much to play for at the start of 2005, with the Socialists ahead in the polls, making the most of internal difficulties in the government. President Sampaio's two key decisions: to hand the mandate to Santana Lopes, and then some months later to dissolve the government, remained extremely controversial. The parties of the left protested against the first decision, and the parties of the right protested against the second decision – in what was otherwise a Presidency characterized by moderation and consensus-style leadership.

Portuguese democracy in 2004 proved strong enough to be able to withstand the fallout from the political crisis, but it sharpened the divisions in the country between the centre-left and centre-right.

22

Fix You

The General Election in 2005 was never going to be easy for Santana Lopes and the government, having effectively being fired from office by a President who believed that the country needed a government with a new mandate. Santana Lopes gave it his best shot, but his rival, the new leader of the Socialists, José Sócrates Carvalho Pinto de Sousa, was also a formidable campaigner and extremely telegenic.

The election was held on 20 February 2005, and the result was not unexpected, with the Socialists winning an overall majority with 45 per cent of the vote, against the Social Democrats who dropped by 11.4 per cent to take only 28.8 per cent of the vote. The result was a triumph for José Sócrates, who ran on a platform of modernizing Portugal, in the mould of the changes that Tony Blair was introducing in Britain.

As well as traditional points of debate, such as the weak state of the Portuguese economy and unemployment, the divisive issue of abortion also became a campaign issue. The BBC summarized the debate:

> Portugal currently has one of the most restrictive abortion laws in the European Union. Only Ireland, Malta and Poland have such similarly strict legislation. The mainly Catholic country currently allows abortions up to the 12th week to save a woman's life or to preserve her mental or physical health. In

cases of rape, abortions are allowed within 16 weeks. The limit is 24 weeks if there is a risk that the child will be born with an incurable disease or deformity.

As a result many Portuguese women go to Spain for terminations or resort to illegal abortions. In a referendum held in 1998, voters upheld the existing abortion law by 51% to 49%, but the result was declared void as nearly seven out of 10 voters stayed away. The Socialists made holding another referendum part of their election platform in 2005.[1]

Abortion laws in Portugal were eventually liberalized on 10 April 2007, allowing the procedure to be done on demand if a woman's pregnancy had not exceeded its tenth week. The President signed the changes into law, following a referendum that was held on 11 February 2007, in which the majority approved the liberalization of the Abortion Law.

The debate over the abortion laws once again exposed the divisions within the country, between those who favoured a strict observance of Catholicism and others who favoured bringing Portuguese laws more into line with those of mainstream Europe. It was also a debate that was closely watched by the outside world and the international media.

'The people spoke with a clear voice,' Sócrates said in televised remarks after the polls closed. He went on to say: 'The law now will be discussed and approved in Parliament. Our interest is to fight clandestine abortion and we have to produce a law that respects the result of the referendum.'[2] The final count was 59.25 per cent in favour and 40.75 per cent against, with a turnout of just under 44 per cent of the 8.8 million eligible voters.

The split between the two Portugals was evident in the result – in many urban centres, the margin in favour of changing the law was far higher than at the national level. In Lisbon, 71.5 per cent voted in favour. There was, however, a very low turnout, which was largely attributed to the seasonal rainy weather and voter indifference.[3]

But as Sócrates took office in 2005, it was the economy that once again took priority over everything else, and it proved to be another difficult year. The fundamental problem was that there had hardly been any real growth over the previous three years. Of equal concern, when the new government took office it discovered that the budget deficit was running at over 6 per cent, a figure far worse than the previous government had let on.[4]

The country fared no better with unemployment, which was running at nearly 8 per cent, regarded as a historically high level.[5] Figures released at the start of 2005 also indicated that foreign confidence in Portugal was declining, with foreign investment in 2004 being just one-seventh of what it had been in 2000. When taken together, these statistics indicated a downward trend in Portugal's performance, which was in direct contrast, at the time, to countries such as Spain and Ireland.[6] In short, Portugal was falling further behind in Europe, and risked being shunted into the sidings of the periphery's railyard.

Youthful, eager, ambitious and articulate, Portugal's new Prime Minister aimed to reverse this decline through a curious mixture of punching above Portugal's weight on international affairs (especially European issues) and spending the country out of trouble. The British were initially impressed and called him 'a crisp, forward-thinking moderniser'.[7] Moreover, Sócrates enjoyed an overall majority in the National Assembly and he was determined to use it to maximum effect in pushing through his legislative agenda.

The major fear was that the government's attempts to tackle Portugal's structural problems would not go far or fast enough to bring about real change.[8] In truth, Sócrates did see himself as something of a Blair figure: great at giving soundbites to the media, and head and shoulders above everyone else in his own party in popularity with both the centre-left and centre-right voters. He appeared to have much fewer problems with the old guard of the Socialist Party than the previous Socialist Prime Minister António Guterres had endured.

The first years of the Sócrates-led Government were characterized by popular frustration and the realization that Portugal's structural changes were extremely entrenched after decades of failure to comprehensively address them.[9] Productivity in Portugal was around 60 per cent of the EU average and traditional Portuguese industries such as textiles, clothing and leather goods (shoes and handbags) were hit hard by the influx of cheap Chinese and Asian imports.[10]

The public administration sector continued to absorb 50 per cent of GDP, and this limited the government's room for manoeuvre in trying to modernize the economy. Employment red tape in 2005–6, left over from the era of the 25 April Revolution, inhibited growth, with the World Bank ranking Portugal 145th out of 155 countries in terms of labour market flexibility.[11]

In attempting to deal with Portugal's economic problems, the government hoped that a hike in VAT (IVA), along with a concerted attempt to address the deep-rooted issue of tax evasion, would help reduce the budget deficit to an acceptable level for the EU's Stability and Growth Pact by 2008.

In dealing with the crisis in education, the government increased compulsory schooling from 9 to 12 years and asked teachers to do more to help (never an easy point to raise with this often militant group). It also made a sizeable new commitment to the teaching of English in schools, largely in recognition of the use of English as the international language of business.[12]

The Portuguese levels of English were already high due to the early introduction of the language in schools. The fact that Portuguese televisions and cinemas subtitled English programmes and films, rather than dubbing them, as was the case in Spain, also stimulated improved levels of English. Since the late 1980s, English had replaced French as the second language of Portugal, and the levels of spoken English (and sometimes written English as well) were among the highest of the non-native English speakers in Europe.

In addressing the overstaffing of the state sector, the government introduced a scheme that had mixed results – taking only one new recruit for every two retirees in the civil service. In addition, the government raised the public sector retirement age. It also announced plans to raise Portugal's low level of professional qualifications by way of a five-year plan to effectively re-skill and re-train one-fifth of the workforce (around one million workers).

In pensions, the government promised to address what appeared to be a black hole in the pensions provision, and also to look at the sustainability of social security provision in 2005.[13] All of this sounded like good news to Portugal's European partners, but the key questions remained over just how committed was the government to reforms that could decrease its popularity, and how much opposition there would be to the reforms from Portugal's militant labour unions.

It was clear by the drubbing the Socialist Party received in the Local Elections – held just six months after its spectacular success in the General Election – that its popularity had been hit by the unpopular policy proposals. This Local Election result led, in part, to a feeling of internal disarray in the Party, which was shown by the selection of a candidate for the Presidential Elections, due to be held in 2006.

The Socialist Party risked putting forward two candidates and thus splitting the centre-left vote – handing the centre-right candidate, the ex-Prime Minister, the right eye of Portugal, Cavaco Silva, an easy victory. Indeed, the British suggested that Sócrates had more in common politically with Cavaco Silva, a liberal Social Democrat, than he did with the official Socialist candidate, the left eye of Portugal, Mário Soares (in 2006, able to run for an unprecedented third term).[14]

Partly in the hope of winning back popular support, the government announced plans for two new major infrastructure projects, both of which raised eyebrows in Brussels. The decision to build new high-speed rail links between Lisbon and both Porto and Madrid was, potentially, an extremely ambitious project, which aimed to be a game changer in connecting Portugal with the newly expanding high-speed rail network of Europe. The second proposed project was even more ambitious: the creation of a new major international airport for Lisbon, which was to be based outside the city.

Lisbon's existing airport is located in the city and it was claimed that there was little room to expand this airport with a new runway or any additional terminal buildings. Naturally, both projects required an enormous amount of investment and the government looked towards the EU to help pick up the bill. As the British noted:

> Many of these initiatives will be dependent on European funding. So the deal struck in Brussels this weekend [in December 2005 for extra funding for Portugal] will have given the government, and Portugal, more generally a seasonal fillip. But the more perceptive commentators know that Portugal's generous treatment is also a symptom of the country's relatively poor performance. Others worry about the creation of a dependency culture.[15]

The importance of this assessment lies with its last two words, 'dependency culture'. There was a growing feeling that Portugal was becoming over-reliant on European funds to sustain an economy which, without financial intervention from the EU, would be unsustainable. In this instance, the case for the high-speed rail link and the new airport fell short of being convincing for an outside world that was increasingly looking towards the East as requiring more EU structural funds than Lisbon.[16]

The process of choosing a site for the new airport was steeped in allegations of impropriety against some of the bids. The key questions remained however: did Lisbon really need a second international airport, and what would such an airport bring the city and the country? The answers were not convincing, and the project soon started to look like something of an unnecessary luxury for a city in which the existing airport was not working at full capacity.

By the middle of the first decade of the twenty-first century, both Lisbon and Porto were firmly established as favoured destinations for the 'weekenders', visitors who enjoyed a relatively new form of short-visit city tourism, fuelled by the advent and expansion of low-cost airlines. The general pattern was for tourists to fly into the city on Thursday evening or Friday morning and stay until Monday. The three-day-visit culture led to changes in existing models of tourism.

Lisbon was a natural location for city tourism, given the high quality, low price and plentiful availability of its hotels, many of which were built for Euro 2004. The city also lent itself to be seen in three days: compact, with the various tourist sites easily accessible and with the possibility of a one-day excursion to Cascais and Sintra. The high level of English, French and Spanish spoken by most waiters, shop assistants and guides added to the ease of the visit for tourists. Mass tourism from Spain was also a significant source of income for Lisbon, and with better road links in place in the north of the country, also for Porto.

Some problems remained that restricted the influx of tourists to Portugal, most notably the high taxes imposed on flight operators by Portuguese airports – among the highest in Europe. For a long time, this prevented low-cost airlines such as Ryanair establishing routes to Lisbon.

In 2005 and 2006, the Portuguese Government came under strong pressure from Spain and Britain to up its levels of security cooperation with both countries. The terrorist attack at Atocha train station in Madrid on 11 March 2004 resulted in the loss of 191 lives, and the suicide attacks in London on 7 July 2005 led to the death of 52 people (plus the four bombers). There was a great deal of frustration in Madrid and London at the levels of cooperation offered by Lisbon on the most important issue of the era, counter-terrorism.[17] As the British outlined:

> The Portuguese approach to counter-terrorism is coloured by their relatively recent experience of dictatorship. Intelligence-led interception remains controversial, and outlawed by the Constitution. But the Portuguese are making efforts to do more within existing constraints; are likely to implement EU measures on data retention . . . An exchange of visits by British and Portuguese security coordinators gave an important impetus to Portuguese movement and cooperation in this area.[18]

Phrases bandied around by security chiefs centred upon the need for Portugal to make a choice as to whether it wanted to be part of the war against terror in Europe, or to become the soft under-belly of the EU that allowed radical groups an easy point of entry into mainland Europe. It appeared to come as a surprise to many Portuguese leaders just how important the country became in the fight against international terrorism, and also international crime, especially drug-related crime.

Portugal's engagement and commitments towards the outside world were starting to dwindle, despite claims to the contrary by the government. The British noted that they just about managed to keep the Portuguese engaged in Iraq. The previous Portuguese Government had been unable to resist the political temptation of withdrawing most of its paramilitary force from Southern Iraq, just prior to the Portuguese General Election in February 2005.[19]

There appeared little prospect of the Sócrates-led Government increasing Portugal's presence in Iraq. In Afghanistan and Kosovo, the Portuguese conjured with its major commitments to rebuilding and peacekeeping.[20] For most Portuguese, these foreign commit-ments needed to be kept to a minimum for fear of overstretching the country's armed forces, which were in desperate need of invest-ment and modernization.[21]

Lisboetas were, by 2005, able to 'channel-surf', with cable televi-sion offering a multitude of channels. Local broadcasters appeared more interested in running 20 minutes of coverage about the effect of snowfalls on the country, or similar domestic stories, and often overlooked their foreign news. The internet, YouTube, Facebook, all added to a sense of detachment from the harsh realities of the world. This was the post-MTV generation growing up in a country that risked turning in on itself politically and culturally, blindly following the latest trends from the United States.

On 3 November 2005, MTV gave Lisbon its endorsement by staging its MTV Europe Music Awards ceremony in the city. The hosting of the MTV event seemed somehow appropriate for a city, and a country, that was becoming shallow and lazy and in dire need of reform before the money from the EU gravy train came to an end.

On the issue of EU funds, the Portuguese government appeared in a permanent state of anxiety about the EU budget, and this gave their approach to EU issues a very uncharacteristic edge.[22] In short, Portugal was looking for allies within the EU to help ensure that its share of the cake was not reduced by further enlargement or by handing over more of it to the emerging countries of Eastern Europe.

In this respect, despite the presence of the political affinity between two like-minded modernizing left-of-centre governments in Lisbon and London, the British appeared unwilling to do very much to help reassure the Portuguese on budgetary issues.[23] Once again, Britain was only interested in Portugal when it wanted something directly from it. It was no coincidence that the only visit to Portugal by a British Minister during 2005 was from Tessa Jowell (Secretary of State for Culture, Media and Sport and Minister for the Olympics), and came three days before the Olympic Committee vote that chose London to host the 2012 Olympic Games.

So Portugal remained relevant in 2005, but only just. After years, if not decades, of promises to implement reforms to improve the performance of the country, the patience of foreign leaders, international financial institutions and potential foreign investors was fast running out. It wasn't only the case that Portugal was not delivering economically and politically; the outside world was starting to turn its attention to other countries where, just perhaps, investment could make a difference to the development of that country.

There was no dramatic announcement, but Portugal was, little by little, starting to appear like a country at the western edge of Europe, which no longer figured in other Europeans' imaginations except as a holiday destination. Prime Minister Sócrates desperately needed to move the country back up the agenda, and make it appear relevant to the future, and not simply a relic of the past. This would prove to be quite a challenge. In the meantime, Lisbon was treated to a display of freakish weather that lifted some spirits for a few brief hours at the start of 2006.

23

Chasing Cars

In the middle of the afternoon on 29 January 2006, it started to snow in Lisbon for the first time in over 50 years. The snowfall was not dramatic enough to fully settle on the ground, but for a generation of Lisboetas it was the first time that many of them had experienced the magic of a wintry wonderland.[1] The snow covered the city in a white powdering, which masked some of the dark soot that clung to the city's decaying buildings. Lisboetas wandered around as if seeing the city for the first time.

A new beginning, something out of the ordinary, It took minds away from the sense of deep anxiety that characterized the long rainy winter of 2005–6. The Portuguese were looking for a new start and a chance to reassert themselves, to get back on the international map.

There were two opportunities that appeared on the horizon: the football World Cup held in the summer of 2006 in Germany, and the Portuguese presidency of the EU, scheduled to start in the second part of 2007. Before all that, there had been an important Presidential Election in which the candidates of both the main parties in Portugal had sought some kind of redemption from the voters for alleged past sins and mistakes.

On 22 January 2006, the Portuguese were asked to go to the polls again, this time to choose a President. The contest was billed as a heavyweight bout with, in the red corner, Portugal's left eye, Mário Soares, and in the blue corner, its right eye, Cavaco Silva.

Both men were desperate for victory: Soares was seeking a third term as President and Cavaco Silva wanted to make up for the pain of his loss in the Presidential Election a decade earlier. It was meant to be a beauty contest between the most important post-Revolution political leaders in Portugal.

There were many sub-texts to the election. The selection of Soares as the official representative of the Socialist Party had been controversial and split the party. In the end, the contest was not a simple 'stand in the middle of the ring and slug it out' fight between the two candidates, rather a complex threesome with the poet and veteran Socialist, Manuel Alegre, standing as an independent.

In addition, three candidates from the Portuguese far-left were standing. With Cavaco Silva the only centre-right candidate in the race, the election mathematics centred upon whether the ex-Prime Minister would be able to gather enough votes to win in the first round of voting, or whether he would face a second round, and if so, against which of the centre-left candidates.

When all the votes were counted following the election, Cavaco Silva just got over the 50 per cent of the vote needed to win the Presidency in the first round. The final results revealed that Cavaco Silva won 50.54 per cent of the vote, with Manuel Alegre pushing the official Socialist Party candidate into third place by taking 20.74 per cent of the vote to Soares' 14.31 per cent. The voter turnout was 61.53 per cent. The British were very pleased with the result of the election, arguing that cohabitation between the Socialist government and the Social Democrat President underpinned the government reforms.[2]

The election freed Sócrates to concentrate on the programme of reforms, and the government did make some important advances throughout 2006. The promised reforms of the civil service and education were largely implemented, despite the expected strong opposition from the labour unions. There was still much work to be done, as the British wrote: 'Rules and regulations are being simplified. But there is a mountain to climb, and to scale it the Portuguese will have to dump the remaining legislative, institutional and cultural baggage of the dictatorship and subsequent revolution.'[3]

Things did marginally start to look better in some aspects of Portugal's economy during 2006. Growth was forecast to reach 1.4 per cent by the end of the year, and exports were up by 9 per cent. Most important of all, the budget deficit fell to around 4.6 per cent.[4] The bad news, however, was the continued slump in foreign investment, which fell by 3 per cent – despite decisions by IKEA and Volkswagen to make substantial investments in the country. Unemployment remained a constant problem at between 7 and 8 per cent.

And in the World Bank's rankings of labour flexibility and dynamism, Portugal was ranked at 155.[5] It looked for all intents and purposes as if the government's reforms were not having any major impact on the economy. The British felt that it was too soon and adopted a wait-and-see approach, but, in reality, it appeared futile unless the government upped even further the pace of reform.[6]

One area that desperately needed addressing was corruption, which was endemic in all levels of society. The British noted that this was becoming more serious, as the Ambassador wrote to London: 'The Portuguese man in the street thinks that corruption is an increasing problem, with some high-profile cases involving municipal politicians and football plutocrats. Portugal's sclerotic judicial system seems to ensure that none of these corruption cases ever reaches a conclusion.'[7]

The most high profile of these corruption cases was known as the *Apito Dourado* (Golden Whistle Affair). This was arguably the biggest scandal in the history of Portuguese football, which had first come to light in 2004. After a lengthy investigation, the Portuguese police named, among others, several high-profile football plutocrats as suspects in corrupting, or attempting to corrupt, referees – including Jorge Nuno Pinto da Costa, President of FC Porto.

In 2008, FC Porto was docked six championship points (the six points deduction meant that FC Porto still retained the championship title from the 2003/04 season).[8] For its part in the scandal, the second club from the city of Porto, Boavista FC, was sentenced to relegation from the *Primeira Liga*.[9] The Golden Whistle Affair dominated the headlines for months at a time. More importantly, the scandal revealed the seedy underbelly of Portuguese football, which fitted the perception of corruption as an increasing problem in Portuguese society.

Football had traditionally provided a good antidote for the Portuguese trying to forget the economic ills and the problems of corruption in the country. During the early summer of 2006, television sets were once again erected outside the bars in Lisbon in order to watch the 2006 World Cup being hosted in Germany. Once again, it appeared that the Portuguese national team, with Cristiano Ronaldo in full flow, had a decent chance of winning a tournament which was characterized by unseasonably high temperatures in Germany. After beating the old ally, England, in the quarter-finals in a dramatic penalty shoot-out, Portugal came up against their old nemesis in international football, France, in the semi-finals.

Portuguese hearts were broken as France won 1–0, leaving emotional images of weeping Portuguese girls, with red and green face paint, on television screens across the world. So close, and yet so far, but the Portuguese football team had yet again reminded the world that the country remained one of the prominent football nations.[10]

The exploits of the national football team represented Portugal's best overseas success. In foreign and defence policies the Portuguese struggled in 2006, with the gap between their international ambitions and their resources growing larger.[11] The government spent much of the year trying to set up a high-level EU–Africa summit, to be hosted by the Portuguese in Lisbon. Despite the efforts of the Prime Minister to try to talk up Portugal's role in Africa, especially in its ex-colonies, there was a sense that other countries, most notably the Chinese, were eclipsing Portugal.[12]

Portugal's defence budget was measured at just 1.4 per cent of GDP, which was well below the average for member states of NATO. Moreover, with its overseas development budget of just 58 million euros it was not difficult to work out why Portugal's contributions to multilateral deployments were so low.[13] The government had already announced plans to pull the 100 or so Portuguese troops out of Bosnia at the start of 2007, and not to make any greater commitment to Afghanistan.[14]

There was no sign, however, of Portugal losing its attraction to foreign tourists seeking sun, sand and a taste of Portuguese culture. During the first seven months of the year alone, Ryanair flew over half a million passengers to and from Porto, and direct flights started between London and the Azores. The Algarve tourist trade also increased, and with Lisbon firmly established on the city break circuit, you could be forgiven for wondering what all the fuss was about over the woes of the rest of the economy.[15]

To add to the more positive picture, despite the hikes in taxes (direct and indirect), and cutbacks in government expenditure, the Portuguese continued to spend.[16] The trouble was that most were maxing out on their credit cards, which was to lead to further problems later. If there wasn't exactly a feel-good factor present in 2006, most Portuguese did not feel any worse off than they had been in the recent past.

José Sócrates strutted around the international stage, always keen for photo opportunities with EU and world leaders, as if he was rehearsing for a leading role in a major movie production. And little did we know at the time that was exactly what he was doing.

The Portuguese always took the holding of the Presidency of the EU with pride: a chance to bask in the limelight and show off the beauty of Lisbon, and its other cities, as they hosted European meetings and summits. For Sócrates, and President Cavaco Silva, the Presidency of the EU represented an opportunity to shine on the international stage. Furthermore, the Portuguese remained firmly committed to the EU, as noted by the British: 'Their [the Portuguese] experience of EU membership, together with a genuine sense of solidarity, have outweighed their fears of having lost out economically to the new eastern members.'[17]

To some extent, Portugal got lucky with the timing of its presidency, which lasted for the second half of 2007. There were important issues to agree upon, and the presidency culminated in the beautifully choreographed signing ceremony of the appropriately named 'Lisbon Treaty'.

Indeed, for much of 2007, the Sócrates and Cavaco Silva double act was on show for much of the world. On 4 July 2007, the first EU–Brazil Summit took place in Lisbon, which brought Luiz Inácio Lula da Silva, the President of Brazil, to Lisbon. The resulting joint statement from the summit promised much deeper cooperation between the EU and the economic and military regional superpower of South America. As the joint statement put it:

> On the historic occasion of their first summit, the EU and Brazil decided to establish a comprehensive strategic partnership, based on their close historical, cultural and economic ties. Both sides share fundamental values and principles such as democracy, rule of law, promotion of human rights and basic freedoms and a market-based economy.
>
> Both sides agree on the need to identify and promote common strategies to tackle global challenges, including in peace and security issues, democracy and human rights, climate change, biodiversity, energy security and sustainable development, fight against poverty and exclusion.
>
> They also agree on the importance of complying with obligations under existing international disarmament and non-proliferation treaties. The EU and Brazil concur that the best way to deal with global issues is through effective multilateralism, placing the UN system at its centre. Both sides welcome the establishment of an EU–Brazil political dialogue, initiated under the German Presidency of the EU.[18]

The summit represented something of a political coup for the Portuguese government, who were keen to be seen as not merely good Europeans but, through Portugal's historic links with non-European countries, a player on the global political stage as well. The presence of Durão Barroso, President of the European Commission, at the summit made it an even more Portuguese-centric occasion and highlighted the continued importance of the Portuguese-speaking world in the twenty-first century.[19]

At a press conference following the end of the summit, President Lula da Silva emphasized the importance of Portugal: 'I think it is important to say that Portugal has a very great significance for the soul of the Brazilian people. My Silva is not an English or a German Silva, it is a Portuguese Silva. So this relationship with Portugal occupies an important place in European politics.'[20] As part of his visit to Lisbon, the Brazilian President also concluded bilateral business deals between Brazil and Portugal and invited greater Portuguese investment in Brazil.[21]

In addition to the regular and routine arrival of European Union leaders, on 25 October 2007, the Russian leader, President Vladimir Putin, arrived for a two-day visit to Lisbon, including an EU–Russia Summit. At the end of the one-day summit, which had been held in the Mafra area of Lisbon, President Putin addressed the gathered world press:

> We are also pleased with the outcome of the 20th EU–Russia summit. It was conducted in a genuinely constructive environment and a friendly atmosphere. And, in my opinion, it was useful and productive. First I'd like to thank Mr Prime Minister and all our Portuguese friends for taking care of us so well. During the last two days a large number of officials of all sorts and world leaders have descended on Lisbon. We have prowled all over Lisbon, disrupting the normal life of a great city. Please forgive us for this. Now I can say that we haven't gathered in vain. Here in Lisbon we have extensively discussed what we managed to accomplish over the last while.[22]

The summit itself was seen as important. Prior to the summit, as Reuters put it: 'His [Putin's] assertive foreign policy and disagreements on several basic economic issues have alarmed the West and complicated Russian–EU relations.'[23] The summit was seen as a mechanism for preventing any further short-term worsening in EU–Russian relations. To this extent it was probably successful. The summit also put both the Portuguese President and the Prime Minister on the front cover of newspapers across the world and highlighted the apparent importance of Portugal in international diplomatic affairs in 2007.

It was the two major summits held within a week of one another in December 2007, which appeared to be the icing on the cake of Portugal's successful presidency of the EU, and its often less than subtle attempts to remind the world of its importance in the world. The first of these summits, the EU–Africa Summit held in Lisbon from 8 to 9 December 2007, became the most colourful and unpredictable of the two.

As the Libyan leader Muammar Gaddafi set up his tent in the Fort at Carcavelos, near Lisbon, the pre-summit agenda was dominated by the controversial invitation given to President Robert Mugabe of Zimbabwe to this summit of European and African leaders in Lisbon – despite an EU travel ban and sanctions against the 83-year-old dictator and other figures in his regime. The British newspaper, the *Guardian*, summarized the quandary with which Portugal was faced:

> Senior officials in Portugal, which took over the six-month presidency of the EU yesterday, said they were not keen to welcome Mugabe to the December summit, but would do so if that was the price of salvaging a meeting they see as their policy priority while in charge of the EU. 'This is a summit for all African countries at the highest level, heads of government or heads of state. All African countries must be invited a senior Portuguese official was quoted as saying.[24]

In truth the Mugabe issue overshadowed the whole summit, which made little tangible progress in developing any closer ties between the EU and Africa.[25] The leaders of Britain and the Czech Republic chose not to attend, in protest at the presence of Mugabe at the summit.

The presence of the heads of government in Lisbon once again brought the streets of central Lisbon to a near standstill, as black cars with darkened windows zigzagged their way across the city carrying leaders of various nationalities and their large packs of bodyguards. The black Mercedes cars served as a metaphor for Lisbon's position in the world. Portugal was doing its best to chase the fast European cars, while, at the same time, trying to stay ahead of the African ones.

On 13 December 2007, the leaders of the EU – minus Gordon Brown from Britain – gathered in Lisbon to sign the Lisbon Treaty, which would lead to extensive changes in the EU. The last major act of the Portuguese Presidency of the EU took place at the conclusion of the signing ceremony, when the EU leaders took a ride together on a Lisbon tram to emphasize the spirit of unity. It brought to an end a remarkably high-profile Portuguese presidency, which the government hoped would help to reinvigorate an economy that was showing warning signs of heading into another recession.

With two years to go until the next election the government needed to return to concentrating on its domestic agenda and try to get a bump in its popularity from the international and domestic exposure it had enjoyed during the second part of 2007. None of this would prove to be simple, and the challenges of reforming and modernizing the country appeared as great as ever.

PART SEVEN

Cruel World

24

Hometown Glory

'The revolution will not be televised,' sang the legendary American soul and jazz musician, Gil Scott-Heron, who influenced a generation of hip-hop stars with his distinctive politically motivated lyrics. And indeed, that was very much the case in Portugal as the international press packed away their notebooks and cameras and headed on to the next big international news story.

The only journalists that remained in the country did so to cover the continuing mystery of the tragic disappearance of a British child in the Algarve in the spring of 2007. That story continued to haunt Anglo-Portuguese relations with the British tabloid press' enormous thirst for sensationalism and reinforcement of national stereotypes. For once, the old adage that 'any publicity is good publicity' was not true. Portugal's tourist market in the Algarve suffered as British holidaymakers hesitated about booking, awaiting a resolution to the case that never came.

The case left a bad taste in the mouth of the Portuguese authorities, and the police, who were tainted by the tabloid press as being incompetent and somehow to blame for the failure to find the poor little girl. It continued to cast a long shadow over the country as its high-profile Presidency of the EU ended, and Portugal was left to focus on the impending doom of another economic storm that was soon about to make landfall.

As the flags came down and Lisbon returned to its normal winter routine, there was a palpable sense of anti-climax.

Upbeat New Year's Day messages from the Prime Minister and the President, in which they highlighted the successes of the Portuguese presidency of the EU, did little to change the melancholy feeling that hung over the city, like a bad bout of morning pollution. So just as it had been with Expo '98 and Euro 2004, the high-profile presidency of the EU was followed by something akin to a political hangover, and a bad case of anxiety attacks about the future of the country.

Lisbon, which for six brief months appeared the centre of Europe, with Sócrates the ringmaster of the EU circus, saw its fame evaporating into the past tense. With the exception of the heavy media exposure of the city to the outside world, and its name on the title page of one of Europe's least understood treaties of the post-Second World War era, there appeared few palpable gains for the country from the presidency. All of this was reinforced at the start of 2008, when Portugal was relegated from dominating the front-page news to three lines hidden away in the European pages of the international press.

The revolution under Sócrates was not televised, because it never materialized. Throughout 2008, the government's reform agenda ran out of steam as it started to look towards the next General Election, scheduled for 2009. The economy was heading for recession, but as the British Ambassador, Alex Ellis, hoped, 'as there was no boom, the bust doesn't hurt so much'.[1]

In reality, domestic politics became all about the three elections: at local, national and European level. Although the government's popularity fell during 2008, it remained comfortably ahead of the opposition Social Democrats, who appeared more concerned with internal squabbles than taking on the government.[2]

The government was able to point to some success stories: the budget deficit was reduced from 6 per cent of GDP at the time it came into office to around 2.2 per cent in 2008. Sócrates' primary concern appeared to be the potential of leaking votes to the far-left parties in the 2009 General Election. This was seen as damaging the prospects of the government winning another outright majority in the National Assembly.[3]

Externally, with the fizz largely missing from the post-EU Presidency era, Portugal returned to its inward self. Attempts at developing new markets for Portuguese goods with Russia and Venezuela proved not to be wholly successful. So Lisbon was left with its traditional trading partners in Europe, and the EU would be largely judged by the Portuguese for its ability, as Ambassador Ellis put it, 'to help cushion the economic blow' of the recession.[4]

In other areas, the government became more 'isolationist', especially in Afghanistan, where the British believed they had the capacity, but not the will, to deliver more support for the international forces fighting the Taliban.[5] On Africa, the government moved closer to the British position on Zimbabwe: the EU–Africa Summit became increasingly understood in Lisbon to have been an expensive talking shop with few tangible results emerging from it.[6]

Politically within the EU, Portugal quickly resorted to its pre-presidency tactics of not speaking up on issues and generally keeping its head down in Brussels.[7] Put simply, Lisbon rapidly shifted back inwards following the end of the presidency, and in 2008 to 2009, offered very little to the outside world.

In Lisbon, the country appeared to be watching events with a sense of detached indifference. The inauguration of President Barack Obama on 20 January 1999 promised new leadership on international issues from the United States, which would impact upon Lisbon sooner or later. The brutal reality, however, was that the new US President was immediately faced with dealing with the biggest economic crisis that the United States had faced since the era of the Great Depression in the 1930s.

The gathering storm of economic disaster would cross the Atlantic Ocean and its full force would be felt in Portugal in 2010. Prior to that the Portuguese government continued on its way with some progress being made on key infrastructure issues, such as the building of a new airport in the Lisbon area, but by the spring of 2010 these plans would be put on hold due to the economic crisis.

At the end of the August summer break in 2009, Portugal's political elite dusted the sand of the golden beaches of Vilamoura from their feet, and charged up the motorway back to Lisbon. It was once again time to campaign for another General Election. Political sound bites were rehearsed, jackets were put on, ties were carefully straightened, and make-up was applied for the bright lights of the television studios.

It was, as they say in the United States, 'game time', and the Prime Minister was confident that he could win a second overall majority in the National Assembly. Sócrates was a naturally good campaigner, transmitting confidence and a seeming enjoyment of meeting and interacting with the electorate. On television, he had developed a style that was focused on his charm and key ability to transmit a political message in an upbeat manner.

His new opponent from the Social Democrats adopted a very different style and a message that drew heavily from Margaret Thatcher's first election campaign in 1979. Manuela Ferreira Leite had won the contest to lead the Social Democrats in the election. She was measured, happy to discuss substantive issues related to the economy, and robust in her delivery of what she saw as the difficult times ahead for the country.

At the start of the campaign, opinion polls put the two main parties running neck and neck, but during the final part of the campaign the Socialists started to open up a lead. Over the last days of the campaign the key question became whether or not the Socialists would be able to win a second overall majority.

The campaign itself was a largely low-key affair, with the most political noise coming from the parties to the left and to the right of the two main post-Revolution parties. The far-left parties sensed that there was widespread voter dissatisfaction among supporters of the old-style Socialist Party who were opposed to the Prime Minister's Blairite programme of modernization of the economy.

The fact that the Prime Minister had failed to implement much of this programme, and had instead thrown plenty of fillips to such voters, appeared largely overlooked. Instead this group of voters preferred to dance with the parties of the far-left, who offered a variety of tempting dead-ends against globalization.[8]

On the right, Paulo Portas enjoyed a bullish campaign maximizing on the understated style of the Social Democrat leader, and the
fact that a sizeable number of senior figures in her own party did
not think that she would prevail. Portas' message was populist in
tone and substance, focusing on tax cuts and other issues that he
felt would draw support away from the Social Democrats to the
CDS (Centre Democrats).

The General Election was held on 27 September 2009. In the
end, when all the votes had been counted, the Socialists fell short
of achieving an overall majority. Indeed the percentage vote for
the Socialists dropped from 45 per cent in 2005, to 36.6 per cent
in 2009. The Social Democrats were only marginally up, winning
29.1 per cent of the vote compared to 28.8 per cent in 2005.

The major shift in the election was that the small parties from
the far-left and far-right increased their shares of the vote.[9] The
results represented the lack of clear support for either the Prime
Minister's 'spend and tax your way out of economic trouble' or
the Social Democrats' 'cut and save' outlook towards the economy. In political terms the centre had shrunk, and the electorate
was more impressed by parties offering more radical solutions
to Portugal's problems. Voter apathy was a further concern,
with only 59.7 per cent of the electorate casting a ballot. This
was all the more troubling given the apparent closeness of the
contest in published opinion polls up until the final days of
the campaign.

Very soon after the election two problematic developments took
place. The first of these concerned the lack of room for manoeuvre
for the Prime Minister in putting together a ruling coalition. Given
the bad blood between the Socialist Party and many of the far-left
parties there was speculation that Sócrates would try to tempt the
CDS party from the right to formally join a coalition. The CDS
leader, Paulo Portas, reminded its jubilant supporters when the
results were declared that they had gone into double digits in the
election, winning 10.4 per cent of the vote. Eventually this came
to nothing and the government was faced with ruling as a minority
government – something that in the past in Portugal had not gone

well. The second problem concerned the deteriorating state of cohabitation in Portugal with the personal relationship between President Cavaco Silva and Prime Minister Sócrates – with accusations and counter-accusations of political meddling by one side against the other.[10]

The outside world viewed the outcome of the election, and the resulting difficulties during the attempted coalition-forming period, with some concern. At the very moment that the economic storm was about to hit an unsuspecting country, Portugal was left with a minority government, unwilling and unable to try to get any substantive desperately needed reforms to the economy passed in the National Assembly. The preference was for a National Unity or National Emergency government, comprising the two main parties in Portugal.

Instead, with the Social Democrats once more looking inwards and seeking an understanding of how they could reconnect with centre-ground Portuguese voters, there was never really any serious prospect of a unity government. Very soon the party came to the conclusion that its leader had not energized voters beyond the base and, on 26 March 2010, Pedro Passos Coelho replaced Manuela Ferreira Leite and became leader of the opposition.

Lisbon at the end of the first decade of the twenty-first century was a curious mixture of affluence, neglect and increasing poverty. Culturally there was still much to shout about. The city remained firmly established as a location for the international music acts that toured the European continent. Foreign investment in the city, and the country, remained sporadic, with fears continuing over Portugal's tight labour laws and extended periods for planning applications to be approved for changes of status to buildings.

Investors remained intrigued and attracted by the potential of the country, but put off by stories of past difficulties and eventual withdrawals by previous investors. Corruption was also cited as a reason not to invest in the country, as its ranking in the Corruption Perception Index remained far too high for a member state of the EU.[11] As the State Department in Washington put it:

In the past, businesses frequently complained about red tape with regard to registering companies, filing taxes, receiving value-added tax refunds and importing materials. Decision-making tended to be centralized, and obtaining government approvals/permits was often time-consuming and costly. In the past few years, Portugal has undertaken efforts to improve government efficiency.[12]

The efforts of the Portuguese Government to address these issues fell short of solving them, and potential foreign investors looked towards easier and more secure returns in other EU countries, especially in Eastern Europe.

José Sócrates, and the government, were living on borrowed time, but appeared to have no real understanding of the impending tsunami of economic chaos that was just around the corner. Like most political leaders, the Prime Minister was a complex man. Part populist, part traditional tax-and-spend Socialist, part modernizer, and part proponent of an activist foreign policy.

Where Sócrates was fully committed was in his relationship with the EU. He saw the EU as a financier for his big projects such as Lisbon's second airport and high-speed rail links, but also as a safety net for the Portuguese economy during times of financial uncertainty.

Put simply, his viewpoint was from the perspective of a leader who was highly dependent on the goodwill of Brussels. His vision was in direct contrast to that of Portugal's old authoritarian leader, António de Oliveira Salazar, who had viewed the establishment of European institutions, and other large international organizations, as potentially detrimental to Portuguese interests. A simplified version of Salazar's argument was that small states like Portugal have to submit to the will of the larger, more powerful nations in these international organizations, who work to look after their own distinct national interests.

Like Salazar, Sócrates did not come from the established elites of Lisbon and Porto. Rather, his background was from what the British had described as the second of Portugal's 'two nations'. He had grown up in the area of Covilhã, a small city in the interior. His early career had been typical of many young Socialist politicians, as was his election to the National Assembly. His rise to become leader of the party and Prime Minister was more surprising, and he appeared to be never completely embraced by the established political, economic and social elites in Lisbon. He also retained close connections with friends from the area of his original home town.

From early on during his time in office, there were allegations of corruption made against him in the local press, several of which were formally investigated by the police. A number of the cases concerned allegations made about his conduct prior to becoming Prime Minister.

The whiff of corruption that surrounded Sócrates was an unwelcome distraction, not only for the man and the government, but for the country as well. The media, and the legal authorities, investigated a range of allegations, but appeared unable to present enough proof in any one case that would have led to his potential resignation.

On 11 October 2009, only a couple of weeks after the General Election, the Portuguese were asked to vote yet again, this time in Local Elections. The result ended in a near tie between the main parties. The Socialists scored arguably the highest-profile success of the night when the Socialist incumbent Mayor of Lisbon, António Costa, easily defeated the former Mayor and ex-Prime Minister Pedro Santana Lopes from the Social Democrats. The result helped mark António Costa as a national leader in the Socialist Party, and one who would one day challenge for and win the leadership of the party.

For Santana Lopes, who ran a clever campaign attempting to build on traditional areas of support for the Social Democrats, the defeat represented the end of the road as far as active national politics was concerned. He continued to harbour ambitions about a potential run for the Presidency. Coming so soon after the General Election, the Local Elections were largely a vote on issues related to local rather than national politics. Once more, voter apathy was prevalent in this election, with only 59 per cent of the electorate casting a ballot.

Perhaps the key consequence of hosting the General Election together with Local Elections and European Elections (held on 7 June 2009) in the same year was that it took away the opportunity for voters to cast a mid-term verdict on the Government's performance.[13] Although he did not know that at the time, this became significant when the Sócrates-led minority Government hit choppy waters as the economic crisis reached Portugal's shores. In the meantime, without an overall majority, the Government found that opposition parties that were looking to inflict the maximum political damage on it often ambushed its programme of legislation.

The agenda for reforming Portugal's economy, as a result, became further bogged down by petty party politics, often from the newly empowered parties from the far-left and far-right that wanted to be seen to be flexing their new political clout in the National Assembly. For all intents and purposes, at the end of the first decade of the twenty-first century, Portugal resembled a country running on automatic pilot straight into the eye of an impending storm that was to come close to destroying the country's independent sovereignty.

Instead of worrying about the developing financial crisis in Greece, or Portugal's credit downgrading and pressure on the bond markets, the higher concern for most Portuguese in December 2009 was the difficult World Cup draw its national football team was given for the 2010 World Cup competition in South Africa.[14] Drawn against Brazil, Ivory Coast and North Korea, Portugal was said to face the 'group of death' in the first stages of the World Cup.[15]

For those Portuguese looking for a temporary respite from the bad news emerging from the eurozone countries, there was always the comfort of knowing that at least there was still a Portuguese head of the EU. Durão Barroso had been re-elected by the European Parliament for another five years, on 16 September 2009. Although he didn't fully comprehend it at the time, Barroso would face the biggest fight in EU history to keep the European integrationist's vision on track as the economic world collapsed around it.

25

Love the Way You Lie

Portugal was 'a kite dancing in a hurricane', when the full force of the economic storm hit the country during 2010.[1] In layman's terms the economic crisis – or the Great Recession, as it is sometimes known – led to Portugal being unable to repay or refinance its debt without the help of third parties.

Left with no choice, the Portuguese Government requested a bailout in 2011 to prevent the country from defaulting on its debt repayment. This eventually led to the country receiving a €78 billion bailout from the Troika. The definition of the word 'Troika' during the financial crisis was outlined in the *Financial Times*:

> The term Troika, which comes from the Russian meaning
> 'group of three', was increasingly used during the Euro-zone
> crisis to describe the European Commission, International
> Monetary Fund and European Central Bank, who formed a
> group of international lenders that laid down stringent austerity
> measures when they provided bailouts, or promises of bailouts,
> for indebted peripheral European states – such as Ireland,
> Portugal and Greece – in the financial crisis.[2]

The inevitable decision to seek financial aid was viewed collectively as a national shame, and put Portugal, which had struggled so hard to make the euro in the first wave of integration, firmly back in bed with the PIIGS of Europe (Portugal, Ireland, Italy, Greece and

Spain). There was a feeling of bitterness among many political and economic leaders in Lisbon, as to how the country had got into the position of having to take out the begging bowl.

Much of the anger was directed towards the markets, which were blamed for wrongly picking on the Portuguese. There was evidence of a partial improvement in the economy during the first quarter of 2010, and Portugal's recovery rate was estimated at that time as one of the best in Europe. But still the markets, led by the credit rating agencies, targeted Portugal – arguing that the country's high level of rising debt was not sustainable.

Portugal's credit rating was cut, and confidence in the economy from international financial organizations plummeted. Questions of economic rationality were thrown out of the window as panic set in, with the country deemed to be as economically weak as Greece, which had already received a substantial bailout.

Questions remained over the effectiveness of the response to the initial crisis by the Socialist Government in 2009, with critics and political opponents arguing that its response was too slow, muddled and lacking in leadership. The extent to which the impact of the international crisis on Portugal was made worse by the structural problems in the Portuguese economy also needed to be considered.

Put simply, after three and a half decades of poor economic macro-management, especially in the banking sector, the economy could not stand the strain of the international crisis and, effectively, came close to bankruptcy. The immediate impact of the international crisis, and efforts by the EU to manage it, led to a significant shift in the economic policy of the Portuguese government.

During the 2009 General Election, the Socialists had campaigned and won the election on advocating an expansive economic policy. The 'spend our way out of trouble' approach, however, had to be modified when the minority government assumed office. One expert summarized the political problem: 'The political party whose election campaign had been based on the advocacy of the stimulus approach had to immediately draft a budget law shaped by the opposite argument and have it approved in a parliament in which it did not have majority support.'[3]

In other words, a government that was already weak by virtue of not holding an overall majority in the National Assembly was forced to completely modify its economic platform to fit with the austerity-driven measures being demanded by the international financial markets and the EU.

At a time of extreme crisis, the lack of political strength of the government was a key component in the country's failure to deal with the crisis. International markets don't forgive political uncertainty and weakness during times of crisis. José Sócrates tried his best to reassure the nation, appearing on television to explain that everything was under control and that all would be fine in the end, but a happy ending was not on the cards.

Worryingly, he started to resemble a used-car salesman in a shiny suit, who would say whatever it took to keep the nation on board with his sales pitch. Watching the Prime Minister suddenly start to argue the virtues of austerity must have been a galling experience for the opposition Social Democrats, who had run their election campaign in 2009 along those very lines.

At a time of national emergency in 2010, Sócrates started to look, and sound, like a man from a past generation: a time when all things seemed possible, airports and high-speed rail links included. Regardless of what the Portuguese thought of their Prime Minister, and predictably opinions became ever more polarized, the international markets had lost confidence in him, his government, and the country he led.

As the crisis deepened throughout 2010, the government was forced to propose and implement even more draconian austerity measures, the social costs of which could be seen in rising unemployment, particularly in the youth sector.[4] Many educated young Portuguese voted with their feet, and left the country to seek jobs in other European countries, the United States or former Portuguese colonies.

Every week there were sad scenes at Lisbon Airport as parents said goodbye to departing children who were heading for uncertain futures, many of them ending up doing jobs they were massively over-qualified for. The less-educated Portuguese also started to depart the country to take on jobs in traditional destinations for Portuguese émigrés in France, Luxembourg, Germany, and increasingly in Britain.

The loss of the highly educated young Portuguese adults would prove an additional economic complication, with the country largely unable to tempt them to return with the promise of jobs and good salaries. Put simply, a generation of talent was saying goodbye to their motherland, to which they would only return for holidays and family festivities. The full force of their departure on the economy would not be fully felt or understood until much later.

In Lisbon, as Sócrates hustled as well as he could to manage the spiralling crisis, the opposition PSD looked more united and more purposeful than it had been for quite some time. Its new leader, Pedro Passos Coelho, who was elected PSD party leader on 26 March 2010, looked credible Prime Minister material, and his message was that the Socialists were not fit to deal with the economic crisis. Like many Portuguese politicians with lofty aims for high office, he had published his vision and manifesto in good time for the Social Democrats' leadership campaign.

His book was entitled *Mudar* (To Change) and unlike many books in this genre was actually quite readable and forward thinking. Passos Coelho soon emerged as a potential alternative leader of the country. His critics, and some commentators, highlighted his lack of experience in government: in contrast to Sócrates, who had served as a junior Minister prior to his elevation to Prime Minister. Over the course of the spring and summer of 2010, Passos Coelho appeared increasingly like a safe pair of hands, with a good grasp of the economic issues and challenges that the country was facing.

For once, the Social Democrats – by and large – united behind their leader and stopped the internal political strife that had characterized the party since the retirement of Cavaco Silva as party leader over a decade earlier. For Passos Coelho, the key decision centred upon whether the Social Democrats would be willing to bring down the government, with the help of other opposition parties; if so, the timing of such a move was vital given the instability in the financial markets.

In Lisbon, as the winter rains arrived in November 2010, causing people to scurry for cover, and the local metro-based salesmen to change their offerings from fake sunglasses to cheap umbrellas, world leaders gathered in the city once again for an important summit. This was Sócrates' one last walk on the wild side: the big global stage where the leaders of NATO, the United States and the EU arrived in Lisbon for two international summits. Among the cast list was President Obama, whose presence in the city resulted in the barriers going up once again and large sections of the city being closed off.

For Lisboetas who strained to get a glimpse of the President, or any of the other world leaders enjoying a two-day trip to the city, there wasn't much to see. Leaders were once again shunted around the city at high speed with sirens wailing and heavily armed police keeping the crowds well back. For most Portuguese, the two summits that took place in the city appeared something of an unwanted distraction to the economic crisis that steadily worsened over the winter months that straddled 2010 and 2011.

The Prime Minister, however, viewed them as a legitimate opportunity to remind the Portuguese of his statesman-like qualities, and of his apparent popularity among world leaders. The latter point was important for the Prime Minister, as he was probably aware that he might soon be out of a job. It is always good to have friends in high places when seeking employment.

The NATO Summit, which concluded on 20 November 2010, was important not so much for the major changes that it called for in its concluding statement:

> During the two-day meeting, Allies decided to develop new capabilities necessary to defend against modern threats such as ballistic missile and cyber attacks. They made a fresh start in relations with Russia, with the aim of building a true strategic partnership and decided to reach out to partners around the globe. Allies also agreed to streamline the Alliance's military command structure and to make NATO more efficient, so that taxpayers get maximum security for the money they invest in defence.[5]

All of this represented pretty unmemorable waffle and hyperbole from the member states. What the summit will historically be most remembered for was its part in bringing the war in Afghanistan to an end. Or put simply, the West's commitment to fighting the war with the Taliban. As the statement put it:

> Finally, the 28 NATO Allies were joined during the Summit by the 20 partners who are contributing forces to the mission in Afghanistan, as well as representatives of the United Nations, the World Bank and the European Union, and Afghan President Hamid Karzai. Together, they launched the process by which Afghan security forces will increasingly take the lead for security operations across the country, starting early 2011.[6]

This very nice and rounded diplomatic language obscured the brutal truth that the United States was announcing a fairly rapid handover of responsibility for security. President Obama was withdrawing US forces from a war that was increasingly divisive back in the United States.

So the city of Lisbon, as well as being remembered as the name of the EU treaty, will also be seen as the venue where President Obama and NATO marked the beginning of the end of a bitter and entrenched Middle Eastern war. While this might not have seemed hugely important to a Portuguese worker who had just lost his job as a result of the economic crisis, it was hugely significant for the politics of the Middle East and for United States foreign policy.

The second summit that took place in Lisbon at the same time was much less important to the future of mankind. The EU–US Summit of 20 November was heavily criticized in the international press as being irrelevant. Even President Obama was forced to admit: 'This summit was not as exciting as other summits because we basically agree on everything. But nevertheless, I value these meetings for a simple reason: America's relationship with our European allies and partners is the cornerstone of our engagement with the world, and it's a catalyst for global cooperation.'[7]

All of this, along with the rest of the President's speech, was political code for continued EU–US cooperation, especially in the area of dealing with the global economic crisis, which had dominated the summit. Perhaps the most intriguing photographs of the summit were the ones in which Sócrates greeted the world leaders. Smiling, confident, at ease on the world stage, the Prime Minister was keen to 'press the flesh' with as many leaders as possible.

His triumph, however, proved short-lived as once again the international leaders soon departed and the agenda was again dominated by the question of whether Portugal would require a bailout to save its economy. Sócrates thought not, but others disagreed with him. The Prime Minister's view was that an additional package of austerity measures would prove sufficient to regain the confidence of the markets and deal with the question of managing the debt.

At this time, as Sócrates wandered around his office behind the National Assembly in São Bento, it was difficult not to feel some sympathy for him. A leader who believed that Portugal needed to expand its infrastructure, its economy and to spend its way – with other people's money – to a better future, he had seen his dreams go up in the smoke of the global economic crisis. Instead, he was fast having to learn a new language: austerity, in which 'spend, spend and spend' was replaced by a new culture of 'cut, cut and cut'.

By the start of 2011, while Sócrates continued his attempts at reassuring Portugal and the international markets, there was little chance of the crisis ending well. The markets appeared hell-bent on picking off the debt ridden PIIGS one by one, and it was Portugal's time to face their full force.

It was in this context that the Portuguese were asked to go to the polls on 23 January 2011 in the Presidential Election. In the end, President Cavaco Silva was re-elected in a landslide victory over the Socialist Party candidate, Manuel Alegre and the independent, Fernando Nobre. Although Cavaco Silva won each voting district and acquired 53 per cent of the total vote, the key statistic from the election was the new historic low turnout, with only 46.52 per cent of the electorate casting their ballot.

The result meant the continuation, in the short-term, of cohabitation in the Portuguese political system. The traditional ceremonial role of the Presidency that had characterized the era of Soares and Sampaio came to shift a little under Cavaco Silva, as he increasingly intervened in politics, trying to build a consensus for the austerity legislation. From time to time, this caused tensions between the President and the Prime Minister, whose personal relations had not recovered from the post-2009 election era.

The end for Sócrates, and his minority government, came in the spring of 2011, under two years into its four-year mandate. Given the difficulties of attempting to deal with the worst economic crisis in living memory with a minority government in place, the collapse of the government surprised few international observers. The trigger for its demise was an austerity-driven package of measures that it tried to get through the National Assembly, which included significant tax increases and public spending cuts.

The EU had demanded the measures as part of its response to the financial crisis. The government had not consulted with President Cavaco Silva over the austerity measures, and there was widespread anger among the opposition parties about both the legislation itself and the methods the government employed to get it passed.

Tempers were frayed as the country entered arguably its most important month since the 25 April Revolution of 1974. At the back of the minds of key decision-makers in Lisbon, and at the EU, was the fear that democratic Portugal was about to become bankrupt and enter uncharted stormy political waters.

The political developments also took place within a context of an emerging strong anti-austerity movement in Portugal. On 12 March 2011, over a quarter of a million people in Lisbon and Porto took part in an anti-austerity protest, one of the biggest public demonstrations since the 25 April Revolution. Unusually the demonstrations that also took place across the country, and outside Portuguese Embassies, were not organized by the trade unions or political parties, but by a small group of activists who used social media to spread their message and multiply support. Two questions

arose from the start of concerted opposition to austerity: would the
protests be maintained? And how would they impact upon other
EU countries that were facing austerity measures? The answer was
that they were maintained, especially over the long bitter autumn
of 2011, and that they would have some influence on the emerging
Spanish anti-austerity movement.

The primary concern over the summer and autumn of 2011
in Portugal was the fear that the protests would eventually turn
violent and lead to extensive social unrest across the country. There
was some evidence that the anti-austerity movement might have
been infiltrated by groups from overseas anarchist movements with
a history of using violence as a means of protest.

On 23 March 2011, the National Assembly voted on the Stability
and Growth Pact. Inside the Parliament, it was possible to hear
the anti-austerity protestors that had gathered outside amid a large
police presence. All five opposition parties voted against the bill
and this ensured that it was defeated.[8] Later, Sócrates appeared on
television looking ashen-faced, and with a voice that transmitted
both anger and weariness, to announce his resignation. As he put
it: 'Today every opposition party rejected the measures proposed by
the government to prevent Portugal resorting to external aid. The
opposition removed from the government the conditions to govern.
As a result I have tendered my resignation to the president.'[9]

The key to bringing down the government were the votes of the
Social Democrat members, who had previously largely abstained in
votes on austerity, but who in March 2011 chose to vote against.[10]
Given the antipathy between the two main parties, President Cavaco
Silva had little choice but to call for a General Election, which
was scheduled for 5 June 2011. In the meantime, the government
remained in place in a caretaker capacity.[11]

The election campaign began at once and took place under the
full glare and scrutiny of the international press, who wanted to
understand if an incumbent party could survive politically at the
same time as having to try to implement hugely unpopular austerity measures. Before the answer to that question was revealed there
was more drama set to unfold at the start of April 2011.

26

Blame

In a sombre television address to the Portuguese people on 6 April 2011, the caretaker Prime Minister, José Sócrates, after months of personal denial, finally admitted what everybody else in Europe had long regarded as obvious, that Portugal needed a bailout loan.[1] Sócrates tried his very best to look, and sound, reassuring, but the words he uttered came as a shock to many Portuguese, who had failed to understand the severity of the economic turmoil.

'I had always considered outside aid as a last recourse scenario,' he said. 'I say today to the Portuguese that it is in our national inter-est to take this step.'[2] He added, 'I want to inform the Portuguese that the government decided today to ask for financial help, to ensure financing for our country, for our financial system and for our economy . . . This is an especially grave moment for our country . . . Things will only get worse if nothing's done.'[3] In a separate televised address, Passos Coelho, the leader of the Social Democrats, said that he backed the decision to seek outside help to resolve Portugal's economic crisis.[4]

In brutal terms, after nearly four decades of dodging the bullet, the Portuguese were going to have to throw themselves on the mercy of the EU. It was a sad and pitiful day for one of Europe's oldest nations that had been dragged down to virtual bankruptcy by its desire to be part of the 'rich club' of Europe.

Across the sands of time, this was a moment when the rise of Lisbon, its great role in the history of Europe and the New World, turned into the fall, as the city and country descended into a desperate battle for survival and relevance. Writing the day after the request, the *Economist* summed up the extent of the economic woes:

> However painful for its citizens, Portugal's plight will not shock financial markets. The spreads on its debt have been climbing for weeks, particularly since Sócrates's government fell on 23rd March after failing to win support for yet more austerity measures. By 6th April ten-year bond yields had reached almost 9%, and the government had to pay almost 6% to borrow money for just a year. No country with a stagnant economy and a big debt stock can do that for long. Sócrates's decision represents a recognition of the inevitable, not a sudden deterioration of the euro-zone mess.[5]

Following the formal request by Portugal, the European Commission (EC), the European Central Bank (ECB) and the International Monetary Fund (IMF) negotiated an economic adjustment programme. As the European Commission put it, the programme was aimed 'at restoring access to market-based funding, enabling the return of the economy to sustainable growth, and safeguarding financial stability in Portugal, the Euro area and the EU'.[6] The programme was to cover the period May 2011 to June 2014, and comprised a financial package of some €78 billion for potential fiscal financing requirements and support for the Portuguese banking system.

The programme called for comprehensive action in three key areas, as outlined in a European Commission report, which required that:

1   There was a credible and balanced fiscal consolidation strategy, supported by fiscal-structural measures such as better control over public expenditure, Public-Private-Partnerships (PPPs) and state-owned enterprises (SOEs), which aimed at breaking the increase in the gross public debt-to-GDP ratio and putting it on a firm downward path in the medium term.

2 Efforts to safeguard stability in the financial sector through
  market-based mechanisms were supported by ring-fenced
  Programme financing (BSSF); central to these efforts were
  measures to foster a gradual and orderly deleveraging of
  bank balance sheets, reinforced capitalisation of banks and
  improved banking supervision, while ensuring adequate
  financing of the economy.

3 There were deep and frontloaded structural reforms to boost
  potential growth, create jobs, and improve competitiveness; in particular, the Programme contained reforms of the
  labour market, the judicial system, network industries and
  housing and services sectors.[7]

For all the EC's wordy economic jargon, and promises that the
most economically vulnerable in Portugal would be spared the
effects of the fallout from the efforts to reboot the economy, the
bailout would lead to a sustained period of austerity, resulting in
massive social costs to the nation.[8]

Portugal's political parties were warned by the EC to put
forward a consensus on the required tough austerity measures
ahead of electioneering during the General Election campaign.[9]
The European Commission's Economic Affairs Commissioner,
Olli Rehn, warned them to behave in a responsible manner.
'I trust that all political parties, and the government, will realize
their responsibility to overcome the current difficulties for the sake
of all the people of Portugal and for the sake of the financial stability of Europe,' said Rehn.[10] In truth, much of the General Election
campaign focused not on the future, but on the past, and the key
questions of who was most to blame in Portugal for the failure to
deal with the crisis.

When the General Election was held on 5 June 2011, the result
was not unexpected, given the failure of incumbent governments
in other European countries badly affected by the crisis to survive.
The Social Democrats, led by Pedro Passos Coelho, won a comfortable victory over the Socialist Party led by José Sócrates, winning
38.66 per cent of the total vote, to the Socialists' 28.05 per cent.

The Social Democrats, however, fell short of winning an overall majority, but with the support of the right-wing CDS party, which won 11.71 per cent of the vote, it proved possible to put together a relatively stable working coalition and provide a majority in the National Assembly. For Passos Coelho the result represented a personal triumph, which exceeded the support the party had received in most of the opinion polls conducted prior to the day of the election.

The defeat for the Socialists was worse than they had expected, and immediately José Sócrates announced his resignation as leader of the Socialist Party. In doing so, he confirmed that he would be leaving active politics in order to study in Paris. It was a dramatic and swift exit, which was very much in line with his style of leadership. One minute his face dominated TV screens and newspaper headlines, and the next moment he exited stage left, leaving the country to get on with dealing with the effects of austerity. His rapid departure left a bitter taste in the mouth for some Portuguese, but given the daily levels of stress that he had operated under during the final years of his leadership, it is perhaps understandable that he departed so quickly.

The crucial question that surrounds the whole Sócrates era remains: could he have done more to prevent the international economic crisis from escalating in Portugal to unprecedented levels that almost destroyed the country? Linked to this is the additional question of who was most to blame for the crisis: the outside world financial order, or Portugal's failure to develop a modern, dynamic and viable economy to survive in the new global order?

To a large extent, the answers to both questions from an internal perspective have been coloured by the political perspectives of the commentator or politician. It is perhaps too soon to cast a final judgement on the Sócrates era except to say, like his predecessors as Prime Minister, he promised much in the area of economic reform, and when all was said and done, delivered very little.

The era of austerity in Portugal under the leadership of Prime Minister Passos Coelho became akin to a patient who smoked and drank too much alcohol being forced to take vitally needed medicine by the doctor, but still refusing to give up the vices. The medicine of austerity was also long overdue in key parts of the economy, and the far-left fought hard to try to prevent the government from applying austerity to roll back the social and welfare gains that resulted from the 25 April Revolution.

Passos Coelho's retort was simple, in that Portugal had no real choice but to follow the path set out in the terms agreed with the Troika.[11] As a Lisbon-based economist put it:

> The new conservative government took advantage of the situation of limited sovereignty and made a radical political shift. The new policy aims at a fundamental change in socio-economic power relations by deregulation and challenges the institutions of social dialogue created during the past 40 years. The austerity imposed by the Memorandum of Understanding [bailout] launched the country into a deep recession that had devastating impacts on some sectors of the economy . . . More poverty, more unemployed with less benefits, substantial cuts in old age pensions and the national health service . . .[12]

Whether or not the implementation of the austerity measures was partially motivated by the new government's political agenda was hard to measure. The results of austerity, however, were not difficult for all to see. Portugal did not descend into the abyss like the Greeks had done. Thankfully, there were few tales of Portuguese old age pensioners rummaging through rubbish bins looking for medicines, as was the case in Athens.

Social cohesion was largely maintained throughout the period of the bailout, and violence was limited to the usual suspects, and anti-globalization rioters, who were swiftly dealt with by an effective, well-coordinated Portuguese police force. Put simply, Lisbon did not become Athens, but the pain of the cutbacks caused by the austerity programme was still felt right through the country, and in both the public and private sectors of the economy.

Pedro Passos Coelho was very much a Prime Minister for the time, a no-frills, low-cost leader, to follow the 'champagne socialism' of the Sócrates era. He was a leader who sat in economy on airlines, and wanted to be seen to be making cuts in his own government. Some departments were downgraded, such as Culture, and others merged together, with the aim of creating a leaner and cheaper government.

On the European and world stage, Passos Coelho was soon welcomed as one of the strong supporters of austerity. The Troika saw his technocratic Minister of Finance, Vítor Gaspar, as a safe pair of hands, who would implement the rescue plan that was attached to the terms of the bailout.

Almost from day one, European leaders were keen to herald Portugal as an example of good practice in implementing the rescue plan for the economy. Although it was often not actually stated, but merely implied, there was a note of comparison here with Greece, which was not considered to be a model of good practice.

Given the scale of the tax hikes and budget cuts, it came as little surprise to anybody that things did not always go to plan in Lisbon. It became clear that after the initial wave of cuts and tax rises, more would be needed to try to bring the budget deficit under greater control. It was at this point that in 2013 the wheels started to come off the government's wagon, and Portugal entered a period of political crisis that threatened the country's still vulnerable economy.

The crisis, which was seen as the 'theatre of the absurd', made something of a laughing stock of the political elite in Lisbon, and lost the government much of the credibility that it had gained over the previous two years.[13] It all started with the resignation of Vítor Gaspar, which led to a coalition crisis involving the appointment of his successor, and developed into a comical farce, as President Cavaco Silva misread the political temperature of the Social Democrats and the opposition Socialist Party by trying to push them into a joint National Salvation government.

On 1 July 2103, the Minister of Finance Vítor Gaspar resigned, citing the lack of public support for his austerity strategy. A Portuguese newspaper quoted a widely published report that the breaking point for Gaspar had been an irate shopper in a supermarket 'spitting at him and his wife'.[14] On 2 July, the crisis worsened when Paulo Portas resigned as Foreign Minister. He said he objected to the promotion of Gaspar's deputy, Maria Luis Albuquerque, to Minister of Finance.

Portas' resignation came just prior to Albuquerque's swearing-in ceremony. The Troika had warmly welcomed her appointment as a sign of the continuity in Portugal's austerity-driven economic policy. The Prime Minister stood his ground and refused to accept the resignation of Portas, and eventually a deal was agreed whereby Portas was to become Deputy Prime Minister, and would still be senior in rank to Albuquerque.

It was at this point that President Cavaco Silva intervened, dropping a political bombshell by rejecting the coalition solution and calling for negotiations between the Social Democrats and Socialists with the aim of creating a new government that contained both of the main parties.[15] The outside world, and especially the international capital markets, watched with some bewilderment as the President departed Portugal for an overseas trip leaving the two parties to try to hammer out an always implausible coalition deal.

Following six days of fruitless talks between Portugal's two main parties, the talks ended without any potential for an agreement.[16] It became clear that the Socialists sought an end to all policies of austerity, and required that the bailout agreement be effectively ended. At this point, President Cavaco Silva was forced to recognize that the Social Democrat and CDS coalition would have to be accepted, and the government would continue to serve out its full term.[17]

None of the mainstream political elite came out of the crisis smelling of roses. International headlines focused on whether after two years of following the Troika, Portugal was about to become Greece. Amid all the messy personal egos, dirty political games and internal party intrigues that took place during the crisis, it was apparent that several political leaders put their own personal interests above and beyond those of the country.

The crisis revealed the continued lack of maturity of elements of the political elite from all sides of the political spectrum. Arguably, the person most damaged politically from the crisis was President Cavaco Silva. The President badly misread the situation, especially the distance between the two main political parties over the question of economic policy. His motives, however, were largely good; with the government struggling to win votes of confidence, there was the nightmare scenario of a prolonged political crisis, which the financial markets would not have tolerated.

The wild card during the whole crisis was Paulo Portas, who acted like a one-man band intent on maximizing his powerbase. The bad blood between the President and Portas, which dated back to Portas' time as a journalist, also exacerbated an already complicated situation. An additional factor was the deep division within the Socialist Party, which was still coming to terms with its defeat in the 2011 General Election. Opinion polls in 2013 indicated that the party was ahead of the Social Democrats, but not by as much as many people had predicted.

Within the Socialist Party there was a power struggle, which essentially centred upon which leader would have the best opportunity of winning the next election, and returning the party to power with an absolute majority in the National Assembly. Eventually, after much political manoeuvring, it was left to the party members to make this decision in a US-style primary election. The election took place on 28 September 2014, and resulted in a resounding victory for the Mayor of Lisbon, António Costa, over the incumbent leader, António José Seguro – with Costa winning 67.77 per cent of the vote, to Seguro's 31.54 per cent.

Once the crisis was over, the government continued on its course of implementing the economic measure related to the bailout. Portugal stayed the course, and was able to garner some publicity for being in a position to exit the bailout programme earlier than scheduled. On 17 May 2014, the country left the Troika bailout programme without a financial safety net.[18] Portugal, however, was now 'poorer and a long way from recovery'.[19]

Predictions were that it would take between two and three decades of lean times, as the state got rid of its debt burden, before it fully recovered.[20] Estimates as to how successful the bailout programme had been, and how much damage it had done, varied. In assessing the programme both the IMF and the EC appeared relatively happy with its implementation and success in stabilizing the economy.

An IMF delegation visited Lisbon in March 2015, to assess the success of the finished bailout programme. Overall, it concluded:

> Under the economic adjustment program, severe imbalances were corrected, growth was restored and unemployment began to decline. However, long-standing challenges will require sustained structural reforms. A confluence of positive external factors – a more favourable euro exchange rate, a highly supportive monetary policy environment, and low oil prices – provides an excellent window of opportunity to undertake these reforms.[21]

The report, however, went on to warn of three challenges that still needed to be addressed in the Portuguese economy.

1   On present policies, job creation over the next few years would be insufficient to reduce labour slack to acceptable levels, particularly among lower-skilled workers. A more rapid pace of job creation is also needed to reduce poverty and income inequality.
2   Also on present policies, excessive levels of debt in a large section of the corporate sector will continue to act as a brake on investment, lock in misallocation of resources to unproductive firms, and pose a risk to financial stability.
3   Fiscal consolidation needs to continue over the medium term, not only because of the legacy of high public debt, but also to signal that past fiscal policy excesses will not be repeated once the immediate crisis pressures subside.[22]

Writing on a similar theme, the European Commission summarized the success of the programme:

Programme implementation has thus stabilised the economic and financial system and provided the basis for Portugal's return to a path of sustainable growth and job creation. However, the economy remains vulnerable to future negative shocks and further progress is still required in consolidating public finances, safeguarding financial stability and improving the competitiveness, flexibility and resilience of the economy.

To this end, continued effective implementation and a speedy completion of the outstanding budgetary commitments and structural reforms will be crucial to reap the full benefits of the measures already undertaken.

Indeed, the country urgently needs a credible medium-term strategy for sustainable growth, based on a broad political understanding, whose implementation would make the economy more dynamic so as to facilitate economic adjustment, support fiscal consolidation, accelerate financial deleveraging and further reduce the high levels of unemployment and poverty.[23]

Put simply, Portugal gained top marks for effort, but there was still much work to be done. In the meantime, the economy remained vulnerable to major global downturns. The timing of Portugal's withdrawal from the bailout programme came just after the muted celebrations to mark the 40th anniversary of the 25 April Revolution. And what a 40 years it had been.

The democratic state was almost lost on two occasions: in the period following the 25 April Revolution to the totalitarian Communists, and in 2011 to the whims of the international capital markets.

Epilogue

The spring of 2014 was particularly welcomed in Lisbon after an unusually long, cold and wet winter – during which much of the local population had bustled around the city huddled under umbrellas, battered by the winds from the stormy Atlantic Ocean. Spring was different, and brought a new sense of optimism to the city, and to the wider country as well. Portugal's exit from the bailout programme had taken place without a hitch, and in the government there was a sense of relief that the worst of austerity was over, the economy was growing again, albeit slowly, and that better days lay ahead.

Following this return to a semblance of normality, deeper under-standings were sought as to why the country had been pushed so close to bankruptcy, and the impact of this upon the maintenance of Portuguese democracy and the country's place in a world domi-nated by interlinked global economies. In other words, it was a time for quiet stock-taking amid the luxury of being able to look beyond the present towards the future. While it was naturally important to focus on the lessons from the short term, specifically from the economic crisis, it was equally important to look back further to see what could be learnt from the various decades of Portuguese democracy.

In the 40 years since the Revolution, Portuguese democracy had developed in a zigzag manner with the gains outweighing the losses and the setbacks. The country's post-Revolution democratic leaders opted to take the risky path to membership of the European club (the pitfalls of continued isolation were arguably even greater).

Membership of the 'rich club' of Europe was viewed as the route to salvation: the game changer that would transform the country from the periphery of the continent towards the centre. In opening up the country to Europe, Portugal's leaders hoped that this would help underpin Portuguese democracy as the nation, its political and economic institutions, were modernized. By and large, this proved to have been a successful strategy.

What many leaders failed to understand, however, was that with openness came international scrutiny, most notably from international financial institutions, and from the money markets. Portugal's at times pitiful economic modernization has stunted its potential for growth and left large parts of the country – away from the major urban areas of Lisbon and Porto – living in conditions that have improved little since the Estado Novo era.

In this respect, Portugal's leaders (from both the Socialist Party and the Social Democrats) have failed the country. There is a familiar pattern of much initial promise from a new government, followed by some huff and puff, before settling back into the status quo of poor management of the economy. The period of the second government of Cavaco Silva was arguably the only exception to this rule.

During the first 40 years of democracy in Portugal, the outside world has been strong in its praise for the political transformation of the country, but damning over the lack of economic transformation. The two major economic crises the country faced in 1983 and in 2011 had their origins in large-scale global downturns, but their impact on the country was made all the worse by the internal weakness and feeble structure of the Portuguese economy. As a result, it would seem perfectly possible for the dramatic, and potentially devastating, events of 2011 to be repeated in the future.

In the post-Revolution era, Portugal not only had to cope with the rapid shift to democracy and membership of Europe, but was also forced to deal with the thorny issues of rapid decolonization. Portugal lost Africa, but has continued to be a bridge between Europe and parts of the New World.

The notion of a bridge has remained an important feature in its transatlantic relations, with the Azores acting as a strategically important set of islands in the middle of the Atlantic Ocean. The world is changing fast, and in 2015 the United States, which once begged Salazar for access to the Azores during the Second World War, was slowly winding down its air base there.

Portugal simply does not have the financial or military resources to play a significant independent role in global affairs. At various times, it has reminded the world of its importance to world affairs through the hosting of European and international summits. In this respect, Portugal has fought above its diplomatic weight. Here Portugal's mild climate plays a role.

As early winter descends on northern Europe, and the layers of raincoats, boots and gloves come on, leaders must be tempted by a visit to Portugal where they can enjoy the warm autumn sunshine. Portugal has developed this model successfully in the corporate world, and most convention and conference space in the city, and along the coast in Estoril, is booked out by overseas companies during the autumn and spring months.

In truth, Portugal's importance and continued relevance to the world remains in its geographical location, and its links to the other parts of the Portuguese-speaking world. In this area, Lisbon can still contribute much to the world. An advertising campaign for the national airline, TAP, appeared a few years ago in London Underground stations that read, 'Fly to Portugal, to Go to Brazil'. Its sentiment was meant to highlight the successful, and lucrative, TAP routes from Lisbon and Porto to Brazilian cities, but it served as a message for the position of Portugal in the world as a bridge to the Portuguese-speaking world.

The zigzag nature of the development of the Portuguese democratic state was once again illustrated by two dramatic events during the second part of 2014, and resulting financial and legal processes, which culminated in post-bailout Portugal looking back into the abyss. The first of these was the collapse of Banco Espírito Santo (BES), which was officially announced on 3 August 2014, when the Bank of Portugal issued a €4.4 billion bailout of the bank.

The need for the intervention represented a stunning blow to the family-owned bank and to Portugal's improved credibility in the international markets. The question of apportioning blame for the collapse of the bank will not be resolved until the documents relating to it are published in full, and the testimonies of all concerned are given to the inquiry.

The problem for Portugal is that the international markets are impatient, do not wait for inquiries, and often draw their own conclusions. The markets did exactly this and the message that flashed around television screens in Wall Street in New York, and in the rest of the world, was that the Portuguese banks were on shaky ground.

The *Financial Times* summed up the impact of the collapse, arguing that it had shaken confidence in the country's slow economic recovery less than half a year after it had exited the bailout programme.[1] Similar takes on the collapse appeared in the *Wall Street Journal*, Reuters and the *New York Times*. In the blink of an eye, Portugal found itself back on the front pages, and for all the wrong reasons.

The government's response, along with that of the Bank of Portugal, appeared robust as it tried to reassure small investors that their money was safe. The hasty setting up of a new bank, rather unimaginatively given the name Novo Banco (New Bank), for the non-toxic assets of the old bank helped to steady the ship.

On a deeper level, questions remained as to whether the government should have intervened earlier and why it allowed the bank to go under. Prime Minister Passos Coelho tried to reassure the Portuguese that the bank's collapse would not stop the Portuguese economy from growing at 1.5 per cent in 2014, but admitted that it would probably stop it growing any faster.[2]

Whatever the rights and the wrongs in the case, the collapse of the family-run BES shocked many Portuguese and revealed the fragile nature of the Portuguese economy, as the green shoots of recovery were starting to be seen across the country. For those Portuguese who supported the parties of the far-left in 2014 (estimated to be around 18 per cent of the total electorate) the collapse of BES helped fuel their class-war, anti-capitalist hatred of the leaders of BES.

Soon after the collapse, posters started appearing at key road intersections in Lisbon from the parties of the far-left calling for 'prison' for those involved in the collapse, most notably the head of the bank, Ricardo Espírito Santo Silva Salgado. Soon after the collapse, Salgado was arrested, questioned over money laundering and bailed, but placed under house arrest.

The fallout from the collapse continued over the autumn months as it spread to other companies both inside and outside Portugal. Meanwhile, across Novo Banco branches, as signs of the old BES were replaced with a minimum of fuss with new putrid green-coloured logos, the old BES ones were consigned to the history bin. It all represented a terribly sad ending, and served as a reminder that Portugal was by no means out of the financial woods.

As winter arrived in Lisbon, and the days grew shorter and the nights longer, the second important development occurred, which this time rocked not the economy, but the political elite in Lisbon. Late on Friday evening of 21 November 2014, news started to break on local television channels that the former Prime Minister, José Sócrates, had been arrested at Lisbon airport as he returned to the country on a flight from Paris.

Under Portuguese law, the charges only result at the end of an enquiry, but what was known was that he had been arrested on suspicion of corruption, tax fraud and money laundering.[3] The ex-Prime Minister was later remanded in custody, while the police and officials completed their investigation.

Naturally, the arrest of Sócrates caused a great deal of speculation, discussion and analysis among the political chattering classes. The fact that he had been picked up at the airport in front of the press, and not at his private apartment in the city, led some of his supporters to suggest a political motive to his arrest. The government had only recently itself been the subject of an alleged scandal over help in obtaining 'golden visas' for non-EU residents wishing to come to Portugal.

Whatever the eventual outcome of the Sócrates case, much damage was done to Portugal's international standing, all the more as it came only a few months after the collapse of BES. Yet again,

Portugal found itself hitting the headlines for the wrong reasons, and despite the efforts of Prime Minister Passos Coelho to remind everybody that this was a legal case, and not a political one, it created a bad impression about the cleanness of the political elite in the country.[4]

As 2014 ended with the festive season, and downtown Lisbon was lit up by bright white Christmas lights, the country had passed what turned out to be an eventful year for its democracy. With many Portuguese having reached their limits on their credit cards, with the housing market still stuck in the doldrums, and with unemployment still much too high, the after-effects – or after-shocks – of austerity continued to be felt. On the plus side, the country had survived the crisis, and the bad publicity surrounding BES and Sócrates would pass and be replaced by the exploits of individual Portuguese on the world stage. From Cristiano Ronaldo and José Mourinho in football, to Manoel de Oliveira in cinema (who sadly passed away in 2015, at the remarkable age of 106), to Paula Rego in art, and to Álvaro Siza Vieira and Eduardo Souto de Moura in architecture, Portugal continued to produce world-class success stories at an individual level.

The country that went from revolution to stagnation to virtual liquidation needs to continue its long road to a mature and stable democracy. The outside world will continue to watch, with great interest, how this road unfolds over the coming years and decades. It looks set to be an exciting journey into the future, with the country trying to learn the lessons of the past, and understand the mistakes of the present, to provide a secure future for the next generations of Portuguese.

Notes

PROLOGUE

1 The European Cup was the forerunner to the UEFA Champions League.
2 The DGS was formerly known from 1945 until 1969 as PIDE.
3 Kenneth Maxwell (1995), *The Making of Portuguese Democracy*, Cambridge and New York: Cambridge University Press, p. 66.
4 On this read: Neill Lochery (2005), *The View from the Fence: The Arab-Israeli Conflict from Its Origins to the Present Day*, London and New York: Continuum Books.
5 Maxwell, *The Making of Portuguese Democracy*, p. 69.
6 Public Records Office (PRO), PRO/FCO/9/3595, The Leading Personalities in Portugal, p. 76.
7 Ibid.
8 PRO/FCO/9/2275, Annual Review for Portugal for 1974, p. 1.

CHAPTER I REVOLUTION

1 Documentary sources of correspondence between the British Embassy in Lisbon and the Foreign Office in London, and between the American Embassy in Lisbon and the State Department in Washington make little or no reference to the potential for a coup in Portugal in April 1974.
2 Maxwell, *The Making of Portuguese Democracy*, p. 66.
3 PRO/FCO/9/2275, Annual Review for Portugal for 1974, p. 1.
4 Ibid., p. 3.
5 Ibid., p. 1.
6 Ibid., p. 8.
7 Ibid.

 8 Ibid.
 9 Ibid., p. 10.
10 Maxwell, *The Making of Portuguese Democracy*, p. 77.
11 Foreign Relations of the United States (FRUS), FRUS/1969–1976, Volume
    E–15, Part Two, Documents on Western Europe, 1973–1976, p. 518.
12 PRO/FCO/9/2275, Annual Review for Portugal for 1974, p. 11.
13 Ibid., p. 4.
14 Ibid., p. 5.
15 Ibid.
16 Ibid.
17 Ibid.
18 Gerald Ford Presidential Library (GFPL), Memorandum of Con-
    versation between Kissinger and Schlesinger, 22 January 1975.
19 Ibid.
20 FRUS/Memorandum from Denis Clift of the National Security Coun-
    cil Staff to Secretary of State Kissinger, Washington, 3 April 1975.
21 FRUS/Memorandum from the 40 Committee Executive Secretary
    (Ratliff) to Secretary of State Kissinger, Washington, 3 March 1975.
22 GFPL, Briefing Paper for Meeting with Prime Minister Gonçalves
    of Portugal, 29 May 1975, p. 2.
23 Ibid.

CHAPTER 2 WISH YOU WERE HERE

 1 PRO/FCO/9/2416, Annual Review for Portugal for 1975, p. 1.
 2 FRUS/Portugal Memorandum: Contingencies and Recommended
    Courses of Action for the Secretary from Sonnenfeldt, p. 504.
 3 PRO/FCO/9/2416, Annual Review for Portugal for 1975, p. 3.
 4 Ibid., p. 4.
 5 Ibid.
 6 Ibid.
 7 FRUS/Telegram 2395, From the Embassy in Portugal to the
    Department of State, Lisbon, 26 April 1975.
 8 Ibid.
 9 On the background to this relationship see: Bernardino Gomes
    and Tiago Moreira de Sá (2011), *Carlucci Versus Kissinger*,
    Plymouth: Lexington Books.
10 On this see the detailed correspondence between the two men in
    FRUS, 1969–1976, Volume E–15, Part 2.

11 This was a consistent position illustrated in his correspondence with Kissinger. See: FRUS, 1969–1976, Volume E–15, Part 2.

12 PRO/FCO/9/2416, Annual Review for Portugal for 1975, p. 4.

13 Ibid., p. 1.

14 Ibid., p. 7.

15 FRUS/Memorandum from Denis Clift of the National Security Council Staff to Secretary of State Kissinger, Washington, 11 October 1975.

16 Ibid.

17 *Sarasota Herald-Tribune*, 11 April 1976, p. 24.

18 Ibid.

19 Ibid.

20 FRUS/Memorandum from Kissinger to President Ford, Washington, 9 October 1975.

21 Ibid.

22 FRUS/Memorandum from Denis Clift of the National Security Council Staff to Secretary of State Kissinger, Washington, 11 October 1975.

23 Ibid.

24 Ibid.

25 PRO/FCO/9/2416, Annual Review for Portugal for 1975, p. 7.

26 Ibid., p. 8.

27 Ibid.

28 Ibid.

29 Ibid.

CHAPTER 3 SOS

1 PRO/FCO/9/2416, Annual Review for Portugal for 1975, p. 8.

2 Ibid.

3 Ibid., p. 9.

4 Ibid.

5 Ibid.

6 Ibid.

7 Ibid.

8 Ibid.

9 FRUS/Memorandum prepared in the Department of State, Washington, 10 October 1975.

10 Ibid.

11 Memorandum from Denis Clift of the National Security Council Staff to Secretary of State Kissinger, Washington, 11 October 1975.

12 Ibid.

13 Ibid.

14 PRO/FCO/9/2416, Annual Review for Portugal for 1975, p. 6.

15 Telegram 7084 from the Embassy in Portugal to the Department of State, Lisbon, 26 November 1975, p. 1.

16 Ibid.

17 PRO/FCO/9/2416, Annual Review for Portugal for 1975, p. 6.

18 Ibid.

19 Ibid.

20 Telegram 7084 from the Embassy in Portugal to the Department of State, Lisbon, 26 November 1975, p. 1.

21 Ibid.

22 PRO/FCO/9/2416, Annual Review for Portugal for 1975, p. 6.

23 Ibid.

CHAPTER 4 IN THE CITY

1 PRO/FCO/9/2601, Annual Review for Portugal for 1976, p. 1.

2 Ibid.

3 Ibid.

4 PRO/FCO/9/3595, The Leading Personalities in Portugal, p. 72.

5 PRO/FCO/9/2601, Annual Review for Portugal for 1976, p. 4.

6 PRO/FCO/9/3595, The Leading Personalities in Portugal, p. 30.

7 Ibid.

8 Ibid.

9 Ibid.

10 Ibid.

11 Ibid.

12 Ibid., p. 32.

13 Ibid., pp. 32–3.

14 Ibid., p. 32.

15 PRO/FCO/9/2601, Annual Review for Portugal for 1976, p. 2.

16 Ibid.

17 Ibid.

18 Ibid., p. 4.

19 Ibid.

20 Ibid.

CHAPTER 5 TRANS-EUROPE EXPRESS

1   The EEC was also known simply as the European Community
    (EC) long before it was officially renamed as such in 1993.
2   PRO/FCO/9/2754, Annual Review for Portugal for 1977, p. 1.
3   Ibid., p. 2.
4   Ibid.
5   Ibid.
6   Le Centre Virtuel de la Connaissance sur l'Europe (CVCE), Note
    from the General Secretariat of the Council on the visits of Mário
    Soares to the capital cities of the Nine, 9 February 1977.
7   PRO/FCO/9/2754, Annual Review for Portugal for 1977, p. 2.
8   Ibid.
9   Ibid.
10 Ibid.
11 Ibid.
12 Ibid.
13 Ibid., p. 3.
14 Ibid.
15 Ibid.
16 Ibid.
17 Roy Jenkins (1989), *European Diary, 1977–1981*, London: Harper-
    Collins.
18 PRO/FCO/9/2754, Annual Review for Portugal for 1977, p. 4.
19 Ibid.
20 Ibid.

CHAPTER 6 PICTURE THIS

1   *Brandon Sun*, 30 December 1977, p. 25.
2   Ibid.
3   Interview with James Mason by Roger Ebert, *Chicago Sun-Times*,
    12 October 1978.
4   Steve Guttenberg (2012), *The Guttenberg Bible: A Memoir*,
    New York: St Martin's Press, p. 114.
5   Ibid., p. 118.
6   www.imdb.com/title/tt0077269/
7   PRO/FCO/9/2859, Calendar of Events 1978.
8   The price increases took place on 1 April 1978.
9   PRO/FCO/9/2859, Memorandum from Ferguson, 26 January 1979.

10 PRO/FCO/9/2859, Annual Review for Portugal for 1978, p. 1.
11 PRO/FCO/9/2859, from Daunt, Southern European Department to Ferguson, 24 January 1979.
12 PRO/FCO/9/2859, Memorandum from Ferguson, 26 January 1979.
13 Ibid.
14 PRO/FCO/9/2859, Annual Review for Portugal for 1978, p. 1.
15 Ibid.
16 Ibid., p. 2.
17 Ibid.
18 PRO/FCO/9/2859, from Daunt, Southern European Department to Ferguson, 24 January 1979.
19 PRO/FCO/9/3595, The Leading Personalities in Portugal, p. 71.
20 Records of the Central Intelligence Agency, 1894–1992, NARA/263/7283288, Witney W. Schneidman (1989), Diplomacy, Intelligence, and Portugal's Revolution (Summer), p. 20.
21 PRO/FCO/9/2859, Annual Review for Portugal for 1978, p. 3.
22 PRO/FCO/9/2859, Calendar of Events 1978.
23 PRO/FCO/9/2859, Annual Review for Portugal for 1978, p. 3.
24 Ibid.
25 Ibid.
26 PRO/FCO/9/2859, Calendar of Events 1978.
27 PRO/FCO/9/2859, Annual Review for Portugal for 1978, p. 5.
28 PRO/FCO/9/2859, Calendar of Events 1978.
29 PRO/FCO/9/2859, Annual Review for Portugal for 1978, p. 4.
30 Ibid.
31 Ibid.

CHAPTER 7 LONDON CALLING

1 Margaret Thatcher Foundation (MTF), MTF/104149, Winston Churchill Memorial Lecture, 'Europe: The Obligations of Liberty', 18 October 1979.
2 PRO/PMO/19/53/155, Incoming Brief: Cabinet Secretary's Incoming Brief for new PM ('European issues'), 4 May 1979, p. 8.
3 MTF/105668, Interview with ITN, 19 April 1984.
4 Ibid.
5 PRO/PMO/19/53/155, Incoming Brief: Cabinet Secretary's Incoming Brief for new PM ('European issues'), 4 May 1979, p. 8.
6 PRO/FCO/9/3010, Annual Review for Portugal for 1979, p. 1.

7 Ibid., p. 2.

8 Ibid.

9 Ibid.

10 Ibid., p. 3.

11 Ibid.

12 PRO/FCO/9/3010, Calendar of Events for 1979, p. 3.

13 PRO/FCO/9/3010, Annual Review for Portugal for 1979, p. 2.

14 PRO/FCO/9/3595, The Leading Personalities in Portugal, p. 63.

15 Ibid.

16 Ibid.

17 PRO/FCO/9/3010, Annual Review for Portugal for 1979, p. 3.

18 PRO/FCO/9/3010, Calendar of Events for 1979, p. 3.

19 PRO/FCO/9/3010, Annual Review for Portugal for 1979, p. 5.

20 Ibid.

21 Ibid., p. 4.

22 Ibid.

23 Barry Rubin and Judith Colp Rubin (2003), *Yasir Arafat: A Political Biography*, London and New York: Oxford University Press, p. 83.

24 'Arafat Officially Welcomed in Lisbon in What Amounts to a De Facto Recognition of the PLO', *Jewish Telegraphic Agency*, 5 November 1979.

25 Ibid.

26 Rubin and Colp Rubin, *Yasir Arafat*, p. 83.

27 PRO/FCO/9/3010, Annual Review for Portugal for 1979, p. 4.

28 'Arafat Officially Welcomed in Lisbon', *Jewish Telegraphic Agency*, 5 November 1979.

29 Rubin and Colp Rubin, *Yasir Arafat*, p. 83.

30 PRO/FCO/9/3010, Annual Review for Portugal for 1979, p. 4.

31 Ibid., p. 3.

32 Ibid.

33 Ibid.

34 Ibid.

35 Ibid.

36 Ibid.

CHAPTER 8 THE ETERNAL

1 The phrase was used by the Prime Minister, Pedro Passos Coelho, at a ceremony to mark the 31st anniversary of the crash on 4 December 2011.

2 PRO/FCO/9/3233, Annual Review for Portugal for 1980, p. 2.
3 Ibid.
4 Ibid., p. 3.
5 Ibid.
6 Ibid.
7 Ibid., p. 2.
8 Ibid.
9 Ibid.
10 Ibid.
11 Ibid.
12 Ibid.
13 Ibid.
14 PRO/FCO/9/3233, Portugal, 1976 to 1981, p. 1.
15 Ibid.
16 Ibid., p. 2.
17 Ibid.
18 PRO/FCO/9/3233, Chronology of Events in Portugal for 1980.
19 PRO/FCO/9/3233, Annual Review for Portugal for 1980, p. 4.
20 Ibid.
21 Ibid.
22 Ibid.
23 PRO/FCO/9/3233, Portugal, 1976 to 1981, p. 3.
24 Ibid.
25 Ibid.
26 Ibid.
27 Ibid.
28 Ibid., p. 5.
29 Ibid.
30 Ibid.
31 Ibid., p. 4.
32 Extract of speech from www.presidency.ucsb.edu/
   ws/?pid=44664.
33 PRO/FCO/9/3233, Annual Review for Portugal for 1980, p. 3.
34 *Huffington Post*, 8 August 2011.
35 *Independent Television News*, 15 November 1980.
36 PRO/FCO/9/3233, Chronology of Events in Portugal for 1980.
37 Ibid.
38 *Independent Television News*, 15 November 1980.

CHAPTER 9 GHOST TOWN

1 PRO/FCO/9/3595, The Leading Personalities in Portugal, p. 16.
2 Ibid.
3 Ibid.
4 Ibid.
5 Ibid.
6 Ibid., p. 65.
7 Ibid., p. 32.
8 Ibid.
9 PRO/FCO/9/3596, Embassy in Lisbon to Foreign Office,
   22 December 1982, p .1.
10 Ibid.
11 PRO/FCO/9/3596, Embassy in Lisbon to Foreign Office,
   14 December 1982.
12 Ibid.
13 PRO/FCO/9/3596, Local Government Elections, Embassy in
   Lisbon to Foreign Office, 15 December 1982, p. 4.
14 Ibid., p. 8.
15 Ibid.
16 Ibid.
17 PRO/FCO/9/3596, Embassy in Lisbon to Foreign Office,
   22 December 1982, p. 1.
18 Ibid.
19 'Pope John Paul Stabbed by Priest', *Daily Telegraph*, 15 October 2008.
20 Both the *Daily Telegraph* and Reuters news agency give the wrong
   date for the Pope's visit to Fatima, incorrectly stating that it took
   place on 12 May 1982 rather than on 13 May 1982.
21 'John Paul Was Wounded in 1982 Stabbing, Aide Reveals', Reuters, 15 October 2008.
22 www.cbc.ca/news/world/pope-john-paul-injured-in-1982-
   knife-attack-says-aide-1.694776.
23 *Daily Telegraph*, 15 October 2008.
24 www.inters.org/John-Paul-II-university-Coimbra.
25 Ibid.
26 www.w2.vatican.va/content/john-paul-ii/en/speeches/1982/may/
   documents/hf_jp-ii_spe_19820513_corpo-diplomatico.html.
27 Ibid.
28 Author's meeting with Malcolm Allison, Setubal, September 1987.

CHAPTER 10 THIS IS THE DAY

1 Freedom of Information Act (FIA), FIA/NL/FO/DS/6/84, Portugal: Annual Review for 1983, p. 3.
2 Ibid., p. 1.
3 Ibid., p. 2.
4 Ibid.
5 Ibid.
6 Ibid.
7 Ibid.
8 For more on the gold and the Second World War see Neill Lochery (2011), *Lisbon: War in the Shadows of the City of Light, 1939–1945*, New York: PublicAffairs.
9 FIA/NL/FO/DS/6/84, Portugal: Annual Review for 1983, p. 2.
10 Ibid.
11 Ibid.
12 Ibid.
13 Ibid., p. 3.
14 Ibid.
15 Ibid.
16 Ibid.
17 Ibid., p. 4.
18 Ibid., p. 3.
19 Ibid.
20 Ibid.
21 Ibid., p. 1.
22 Ibid.
23 Ibid.
24 Ibid.
25 Ibid., p. 2.
26 Ibid., p. 1.
27 Ibid.
28 Ibid., p. 2.
29 Ibid.
30 Ibid.
31 Ibid., p. 5.
32 Ibid.
33 Ibid.
34 Ibid.
35 Ibid.

CHAPTER 11 WHAT DIFFERENCE DOES IT MAKE?

1 FIA/NL/FO/WSPO/014/4, Portugal: Annual Review for
   1984, p. 1.
2 Ibid.
3 Ibid., p. 2.
4 Ibid.
5 Ibid., pp. 3–4.
6 Ibid., p. 2.
7 Ibid.
8 Ibid.
9 Ibid.
10 Ibid.
11 Ibid., p. 3.
12 Ibid.
13 Ibid., p. 5.
14 Ibid.
15 Ibid.
16 Ibid.
17 Ibid.
18 Ibid., p. 6.
19 Ibid.
20 Ibid.
21 Ibid., p. 7.
22 Ibid.
23 Ibid.
24 Ibid., p. 9.
25 Ibid.
26 Ibid., p. 7.
27 Ibid., p. 6.
28 Ibid.
29 Ibid.
30 Ibid.
31 Ibid.
32 Ibid., p. 7.
33 Ibid.
34 Ibid., p. 9.
35 Ibid.
36 www.uefa.com/uefaeuro/season=1984/matches/round=203/
    match=3461/postmatch/report/index.

37 Ibid.
38 Ibid.
39 www.olympic.org/carlos-lopes.
40 Ibid.
41 observer.theguardian.com/osm/story/0,,803150,00.
42 autosport.pt/lembra-se-da-primeira-vitoria-de-ayrton-senna-no-es-
    toril-a-chuva=f116301.

CHAPTER 12 ROAD TO NOWHERE

 1 FIA/NL/FO/AR1985/, Portugal: Annual Review for 1985, p. 1.
 2 Ibid.
 3 Ibid.
 4 Ibid., p. 2.
 5 Ibid.
 6 Ibid.
 7 Ibid.
 8 Ibid.
 9 'Social Democrats Win in Portugal', *New York Times*, 7 October
    1985.
10 Ibid.
11 FIA/NL/FO/AR1985/, Portugal: Annual Review for 1985, p. 3.
12 'Social Democrats Win in Portugal', *New York Times*, 7 October
    1985.
13 Ibid.
14 FIA/NL/FO/AR1985/, Portugal: Annual Review for 1985, p. 6.
15 Ibid., p. 3.
16 'Spaniards Hail Entry into the Market', *New York Times*, 30 March
    1985.
17 Ibid.
18 Ibid.
19 FIA/NL/FO/AR1985/, Portugal: Annual Review for 1985, p. 3.
20 Ibid., p. 6.
21 Ibid.
22 'Spaniards Hail Entry into the Market', *New York Times*, 30 March
    1985.
23 'Spain and Portugal Hail Market Pact', *New York Times*, 13 June 1985.
24 Ibid.
25 FIA/NL/FO/AR1985/, Portugal: Annual Review for 1985, p. 7.

26 Ibid., p. 6.

27 Ibid.

28 Ibid., p. 7.

29 Ronald Reagan Presidential Library (RRPL), RRPL/Speeches, Address Before the Assembly of the Republic of Portugal in Lisbon, 9 May 1985.

30 Ibid.

31 RRPL/Speeches, 9 May 1985.

32 NATO/Public Diplomacy Division (PDD), Statement by Genscher, 6 June 1985, Lisbon.

33 FIA/NL/FO/AR1985/, Portugal: Annual Review for 1985, p. 4.

CHAPTER 13 HOLDING BACK THE YEARS

1 www.cvce.eu/en/obj/portugal_s_accession_to_the_eec_1_january_1986-en-5dd719fe-909b-41d4-bd3d-962c51fb118d.

2 'Common Market Admits Two Nations', *New York Times*, 2 January 1986.

3 Ibid.

4 Ibid.

5 Ibid.

6 A hardcopy of the treaty is stored and on show for the public in the corridor of the National Archives at Torre do Tombo.

7 Ibid.

8 RRPL/Speeches, 9 May 1985.

9 FIA/NL/FO/AR1986/, Portugal: Annual Review for 1986, p. 3.

10 Ibid.

11 Ibid., p. 1.

12 Ibid., p. 3.

13 Ibid.

14 Ibid.

15 Ibid.

16 Ibid., p. 4.

17 Ibid.

18 The Anglo-Portuguese Treaty was activated during the Second World War and the Falklands War of 1982.

19 FIA/NL/FO/AR1986/, Portugal: Annual Review for 1986, p. 5.

20 Ibid.

21 Ibid.

22 Ibid.
23 Ibid., p. 1.
24 Ibid.
25 Ibid.
26 Ibid.
27 Ibid., p. 2.
28 Ibid.
29 Ibid.
30 Ibid., p. 7.
31 Ibid., p. 6.
32 Ibid., p. 7.
33 Ibid., p. 4.
34 Ibid.
35 Ibid.
36 Ibid.
37 Ibid., p. 5.
38 FIA/NL/FO/AR1987/, Portugal: Annual Review for 1987, p. 3.
39 Ibid.
40 Ibid.
41 Ibid.
42 FIA/NL/FO/AR1986/, Portugal: Annual Review for 1986, p. 7.
43 Ibid.
44 Ibid.

CHAPTER 14 WITH OR WITHOUT YOU

 1 FIA/NL/FO/AR1987/, Portugal: Annual Review for 1987, p. 1.
 2 Ibid.
 3 Ibid.
 4 'Anibal Cavaco Silva: the Runaway Winner in Portugal', *New York Times*, 20 July 1987.
 5 Ibid.
 6 FIA/NL/FO/AR1987/, Portugal: Annual Review for 1987, p. 2.
 7 Ibid.
 8 Ibid.
 9 Ibid.
10 Ibid.
11 Ibid.
12 Ibid.

13 Ibid.
14 Ibid.
15 Ibid., p. 3.
16 Ibid.
17 *Independent Television News*, 11 February 1987.
18 Ibid.
19 Ibid.
20 Ibid.
21 *Independent Television News*, 14 February 1987.
22 *Independent Television News*, 13 February 1987.
23 Ibid.
24 Ibid.
25 *Independent Television News*, 12 February 1987.
26 Ibid.
27 'The Peoples's Princess', *Daily Mirror*, 30 August 2012.
28 FIA/NL/FO/AR1987/, Portugal: Annual Review for 1987, p. 4.
29 Ibid.
30 Ibid., p. 3.
31 Ibid.
32 Ibid.
33 Ibid.
34 Ibid., p. 5.
35 Ibid.
36 Ibid.

CHAPTER 15 ALL AROUND THE WORLD

1 'Lisbon's Chiado Fire Raises Fears for Future', Associated Press,
   29 August 1988. Available at www.news.google.com/newspa-
   pers?nid=1915&dat=19880829&id=0PcgAAAAIBAJ&sjid=nHMF
   AAAAIBAJ&pg=2209,6566513.
2 'Lisbon Shopping Area Burns', *New York Times*, 26 August 1988.
3 'Lisbon's Chiado Fire Raises Fears for Future', Associated Press,
   29 August 1988.
4 www.cm-lisboa.pt/en/city-council/history/lisboa-disasters-histo-
   ry/1988-fire-in-chiado.
5 FIA/NL/FO/AR1988/, Portugal: Annual Review for 1988, p. 1.
6 Ibid.
7 Ibid.

8 Ibid.
9 Ibid.
10 Ibid.
11 Ibid.
12 Ibid.
13 Ibid., p. 2.
14 Ibid.
15 Ibid.
16 Ibid.
17 Ibid.
18 Ibid., p. 3.
19 Ibid.
20 Ibid., p. 5.
21 Ibid., p. 2.
22 Ibid.
23 FIA/NL/FO/AR1989/, Portugal: Annual Review for 1989, p. 1.
24 Ibid.
25 Ibid., p. 3.
26 George Bush Presidential Library (GBPL), GBPL/Memorandum of Conversation between President Bush and President Soares, Tokyo, 23 February 1989.
27 Ibid.
28 FIA/NL/FO/AR1989/, Portugal: Annual Review for 1989, p. 3.
29 GBPL/Memorandum of Conversation between President Bush and President Soares, Tokyo, 23 February 1989.
30 FIA/NL/FO/AR1988/, Portugal: Annual Review for 1988, p. 3.
31 FIA/NL/FO/AR1989/, Portugal: Annual Review for 1989, p. 3.
32 Ibid.
33 Ibid., p. 2.
34 Ibid.
35 Ibid.
36 Ibid.
37 Ibid., p. 4.

CHAPTER 16 WICKED GAME

1 FIA/NL/FO/AR1991/, Portugal: Annual Review for 1991, p. 1.
2 Ibid.
3 Ibid.

4 Ibid.
5 FIA/NL/FO/AR1990/, Portugal: Annual Review for 1990, p. 1.
6 Ibid.
7 Ibid.
8 Ibid.
9 Ibid., p. 2.
10 Ibid.
11 Ibid., p. 1.
12 Ibid., p. 2.
13 Ibid.
14 Ibid.
15 Ibid., p. 3.
16 Ibid.
17 Ibid., p. 2.
18 Ibid.
19 Ibid., p. 3.
20 Ibid.
21 Ibid.
22 FIA/NL/FO/AR1991/, Portugal: Annual Review for 1991, p. 2.
23 Ibid., p. 3.
24 Ibid.
25 Ibid., p. 2
26 Ibid.
27 Ibid.
28 Ibid.
29 Ibid., p. 3.
30 Ibid., p. 2.
31 Ibid., p. 1.
32 Ibid., p. 4.
33 GBPL, Record of Conversation between President Bush and Prime
    Minister Cavaco Silva, 11 October 1991.
34 FIA/NL/FO/AR1991/, Portugal: Annual Review for 1991, p. 6.

CHAPTER 17 UNDER THE BRIDGE

1 FIA/NL/FO/AR1992/, Portugal: Annual Review for 1992, p. 1.
2 Ibid.
3 Ibid.
4 Ibid., p. 2.

5 Ibid.
6 Ibid.
7 Ibid.
8 Ibid.
9 Ibid.
10 Ibid., p. 3.
11 Ibid.
12 Ibid.
13 Ibid.
14 Ibid.
15 Ibid.
16 Ibid.
17 www.nycaviation.com/2011/02/dutch-authorities-covered-up-
cause-of-1992-martinair-dc-10-crash-in-portugal-report.
18 FIA/NL/FO/AR1994/, Portugal: Annual Review for 1994, p. 2.
19 Ibid.
20 Ibid., p. 1.
21 Ibid.
22 Ibid., p. 2.
23 Ibid., p. 5.

CHAPTER 18 FAKE PLASTIC TREES

1 Kimberely DaCosta Holton, 'Dressing for Success: Lisbon as
European Cultural Capital', *The Journal of American Folklore*, 111
(440): 173–96, p. 173.
2 FIA/NL/FO/AR1995/, Portugal: Annual Review for 1995, p. 4.
3 FIA/NL/FO/AR1994/, Portugal: Annual Review for 1994, p. 1.
4 Ibid.
5 Ibid., p. 4.
6 Ibid.
7 Ibid.
8 Ibid.
9 FIA/NL/FO/AR1995/, Portugal: Annual Review for 1995, p. 2.
10 Ibid., p. 1.
11 Ibid., p. 2.
12 Ibid., p. 3.
13 Ibid.
14 Ibid.

15 Ibid.
16 Ibid.
17 Ibid.
18 Ibid., p. 2.
19 Ibid.
20 Ibid., p. 4.
21 Ibid.
22 Ibid.
23 Ibid., p. 5.

CHAPTER 19 DON'T LOOK BACK IN ANGER

1 FIA/NL/FO/AR1996/, Portugal: Annual Review for 1996, p. 2.
2 Ibid.
3 Ibid.
4 Ibid.
5 Ibid., p. 4.
6 Ibid.
7 Ibid.
8 Ibid.
9 Ibid., p. 3.
10 Ibid.
11 FIA/NL/FO/AR1995/, Portugal: Annual Review for 1995, p. 5.
12 Ibid.
13 FIA/NL/FO/AR1997/, Portugal: Annual Review for 1997, p. 1.
14 Ibid.
15 Ibid.
16 Ibid.
17 Ibid., p. 2.
18 Ibid., p. 3.
19 Ibid.
20 Ibid., p. 1.
21 Ibid.
22 Ibid., p. 2.

CHAPTER 20 OVERLOAD

1 'Nobel Writer: A Communist Defends Work', *New York Times*,
   12 October 1998.

2 www.nobelprize.org/nobel_prizes/literature/laureates/1998/sarama-
    go-bio.
3 Public Papers of the Presidents of the United States: William J.
    Clinton, p. 1048.
4 Ibid., p. 1050.
5 FIA/NL/FO/AR2001/, Portugal: Annual Review for 2001, p. 1.
6 Ibid., p. 2.
7 Ibid., p. 1.
8 Ibid.
9 'Portuguese PM under Attack for Bridge Collapse', *Guardian*,
    5 March 2001.
10 Ibid.
11 FIA/NL/FO/AR2001/, Portugal: Annual Review for 2001, p. 1.
12 Ibid., p. 2.
13 Ibid.
14 Ibid.
15 Ibid., p. 1.
16 FIA/NL/FO/AR2002/, Portugal: Annual Review for 2002, p. 1.
17 Ibid.
18 Ibid.
19 Ibid.
20 Ibid., p. 2.
21 Ibid.
22 Ibid.
23 Ibid.
24 Ibid.
25 Ibid.

CHAPTER 21 HURT

1 www.metoffice.gov.uk/learning/learn-about-the-weather/
    weather-phenomena/case-studies/heatwave.
2 Ibid.
3 www.fire.uni-freiburg.de/iffn/iffn_34/02-IFFN-34-Portugal-Coun-
    try-Report-1.pdf.
4 FIA/NL/FO/AR2003/, Portugal: Annual Review for 2003, p. 1.
5 Ibid., p. 2.
6 Ibid.
7 Ibid.

8 Ibid.
9 Ibid.
10 Ibid.
11 Ibid., p. 1.
12 Ibid.
13 Ibid., p. 2.
14 Ibid., p. 3.
15 Ibid.
16 Ibid.
17 www.dezeen.com/2011/03/29/key-projects-by-eduardo-souto-de-moura/.
18 www.uefa.com/uefaeuro/season=2004/.
19 FIA/NL/FO/AR2004/, Portugal: Annual Review for 2004, p. 2.
20 Ibid.
21 Ibid.
22 Ibid., p. 1.
23 Ibid., p. 2.
24 Ibid.
25 Ibid.
26 Ibid.

CHAPTER 22 FIX YOU

1 news.bbc.co.uk/2/hi/europe/6350651.stm.
2 'Low Turnout Undercuts Portugal Vote on Abortion', *New York Times*, 12 February 2007.
3 Ibid.
4 FIA/NL/FO/AR2005/, Portugal: Annual Review for 2005, p. 2.
5 Ibid.
6 Ibid.
7 Ibid.
8 Ibid., p. 1.
9 Ibid., p. 2.
10 Ibid.
11 Ibid.
12 Ibid., p. 3.
13 Ibid.
14 Ibid.
15 Ibid.

16 Ibid.
17 Ibid., p. 4.
18 Ibid.
19 Ibid.
20 Ibid., p. 5.
21 Ibid.
22 Ibid.
23 Ibid.

CHAPTER 23 CHASING CARS

1 'E a Neve Caiu Sobre Lisboa, 50 Anos Depois', Diário de Notícias, 30 January 2006.
2 FIA/NL/FO/AR2006/, Portugal: Annual Review for 2006, p. 1.
3 Ibid., p. 2.
4 Ibid.
5 Ibid.
6 Ibid.
7 Ibid., p. 3.
8 www.uefa.com/memberassociations/association=por/news/news-id=693942.
9 Ibid.
10 www.fifa.com/worldcup/archive/germany2006/groups/index.
11 FIA/NL/FO/AR2006/, Portugal: Annual Review for 2006, p. 2.
12 Ibid.
13 Ibid., p. 3.
14 Ibid.
15 Ibid., p. 4.
16 Ibid., p. 3.
17 Ibid., p. 2.
18 www.consilium.europa.eu/uedocs/cms_data/docs/pressdata/en/er/95167.pdf.
19 noticias.uol.com.br/ultnot/efe/2007/07/04/ult1808u96384.jhtm.
20 Press conference given by President Luiz Inacio Lula da Silva, after Plenary Session of the European Union–Brazil Summit in Lisbon, Portugal, 4 July 2007.
21 Ibid.
22 Kremlin Archive (KA), KA/Speeches, 26 October 2007.
23 'Putin Sticks to Guns Ahead of EU-Russia Summit', Reuters, 25 October 2007.

24 'Mugabe Invited to Lisbon Summit Despite Ban', *Guardian*, 2 July 2007.
25 www.dw.de/eu-africa-summit-ends-with-meager-results/a-2996175.

CHAPTER 24   HOMETOWN GLORY

1 FIA/NL/FO/AR2008/, Portugal: Annual Review for 2008, p. 3.
2 Ibid.
3 Ibid.
4 Ibid.
5 Ibid.
6 Ibid., p. 2.
7 Ibid.
8 Ibid., p. 3.
9 'Portugal's Socialists Lose Overall Majority', *Financial Times*, 28 September 2009.
10 'Tension Follows Portugal Election', *Financial Times*, 1 October 2009.
11 www.state.gov/e/eb/rls/othr/ics/2013/204717.
12 Ibid.
13 FIA/NL/FO/AR2008/, Portugal: Annual Review for 2008, p. 3.
14 'Greek Bond Signal to Eurozone', *Financial Times*, 10 December 2009.
15 'English Hopes Rise after World Cup Draw', *Financial Times*, 4 December 2009.

CHAPTER 25   LOVE THE WAY YOU LIE

1 Paraphrased from the James Bond film, *SPECTRE*, 2015.
2 'Definition of Troika', *Financial Times*, Lexicon, no date provided.
3 'Portugal and the Global Crisis: The Impact of Austerity on the Economy, the Social Model and the Performance of the State', library.fes.de/pdf-files/id/10722.pdf.
4 Ibid.
5 www.nato.int/cps/en/natohq/news_68877.
6 Ibid.
7 www.whitehouse.gov/the-press-office/2010/11/20/statement-president-end-eu-us-summit.

8 www.dw.de/portuguese-prime-minister-resigns-over-rejected-austerity-plan/a-14939779.
9 'Portugal's Government Falls on Budget Dispute, Stocks Rise', *Wall Street Journal*, 24 March 2011.
10 'Portugal in Crisis after Prime Minister Resigns over Austerity Measures', *Guardian*, 24 March 2011.
11 'Portugal PM Resigns as Parliament Rejects Austerity', Reuters, 23 March 2011.

CHAPTER 26 BLAME

1 'Portugal: The Third Bail Out', *The Economist*, 7 April 2011.
2 'Portugal Asks for European Bail Out', *New York Times*, 6 April 2011.
3 'Portugal's PM Calls for EU Bail Out', *Guardian*, 7 April 2011.
4 'Portugal Asks for European Bail Out', *New York Times*, 6 April 2011.
5 'Portugal: The Third Bail Out', *The Economist*, 7 April 2011.
6 'The Economic Adjustment Programme for Portugal, 2011 to 2014', *European Economy Occasional Papers*, 202, European Commission, p. 3.
7 Ibid.
8 Ibid.
9 www.dw.de/europe-offers-bailout-to-portugal-with-strings-attached/a-14975240.
10 Ibid.
11 'Portugal and the Global Crisis: The Impact of Austerity on the Economy, the Social Model and the Performance of the State', library.fes.de/pdf-files/id/10722.pdf., p. 2.
12 Ibid., p. 1.
13 'Portugal Political Crisis a Catalogue of Missteps', Reuters, 24 July 2013.
14 Ibid.
15 Ibid.
16 'Portugal Political Crisis Talks Break Down', *BBC News*, 20 July 2013.
17 Ibid.
18 'Portugal Laden With $293 Billion Debt Exits Bailout Plan', Bloomberg, 16 May 2014.

19 'Portugal Exits Bailout Poorer and Long Way from Recovery',
    Reuters, 16 May 2014.
20 'Portugal Laden With $293 Billion Debt Exits Bailout Plan',
    Bloomberg, 16 May 2014.
21 www.imf.org/external/np/ms/2015/031715.
22 Ibid.
23 'The Economic Adjustment Programme for Portugal, 2011 to
    2014', *European Economy Occasional Papers*, 202, European
    Commission, p. 6.

EPILOGUE

1   'Banco Espírito Santo: Family Fortunes', *Financial Times*,
    11 September 2014.
2   'Portugal Will Reach 1.5 Per Cent Growth in 2015 Despite BES
    Collapse, PM Says', Reuters, 30 October 2014.
3   'Portugal ex-PM Jose Socrates to Be Held Amid Corruption
    Probe', *BBC News*, 25 November 2014.
4   edition.cnn.com/2014/11/22/world/europe/portugal-socrates-arrest/.

Note on Sources

In preparation for the writing of this book, I felt that it was wise to first read all the documents and secondary sources relating to the period of the Estado Novo. This helped me re-familiarize myself with the period that preceded the 25 April Revolution of 1974, and the subsequent 40 years of democracy that followed the Revolution. While the intention of this book was not to directly compare the authoritarian era with the democratic one, I believed it important to understand what changed in Portugal after the Revolution, and equally importantly what remained the same.

As I soon discovered, I could not have written this book on 1974 to the present day without having a deep understanding of the Estado Novo, and the protests against it. This all proved useful in helping to shape the section of the book that outlines the political instability that dominated Portuguese politics in the years immediately following the Revolution.

The book would not have been possible in its present form without securing the release of the British papers under the Freedom of Information Act. In this respect, I remain extremely grateful to the Foreign Office in London for the efficient and polite manner in which they handled my requests. Receiving newly declassified documents is always exciting for a historian, and these documents led me to change many of my initial thoughts about the book.

In the United States, I am grateful for the help of the National Archives in providing me with documents relating to Henry

Kissinger and his thought process towards Lisbon. I had also been fascinated by Kissinger's complex attitude towards Portugal both before and after the Revolution. Much of my initial thinking on Kissinger focused on why he didn't simply press the 'reset button' on Portugal following the Revolution, when the United States believed that Lisbon might be lost from the Western Alliance.

The Americans did just this in Chile and launched a major covert campaign leading to a regime change in that country. The US papers, however, highlight that on Portugal, the Nixon administration was more split on the best course of action, and the communication between the US Embassy in Lisbon and Kissinger made for colourful and insightful reading.

In this area, the CIA papers, while far from complete – as many are yet to be declassified – highlight the compromise that was eventually agreed upon within the Nixon administration for limited action in Lisbon. The movement of US funds through Europe and into Lisbon was well documented, but there remain gaps in the records of the amounts of money transferred to the democratic parties in Portugal, and how it was spent by those that received the funds. The release of documents by WikiLeaks related to this transaction still does not give us the complete picture as to what exactly went on in this area.

As I have written earlier in this book, I chose not to conduct formal interviews with key political leaders and government officials for this book. I have done this in some of my previous books, which were more political science-based, and have always felt that such interviews, while producing some useful information, can distract the historian with too many micro points and not enough macro ones.

A final useful source was the media. I must confess to being a little surprised at the quality of some of the journalism (both Portuguese and international) that has covered the period since 1974. My previous two books on Lisbon were both written about the period of the Estado Novo when the local press was heavily censored, and the international press operating in Portugal also had to be careful about what it said.

For me personally, as I read the secondary source material, and went through the primary source documents, this project has been an interesting learning curve. Many of my own thoughts and views about the country have changed as a result of writing this book.

As with my other projects on Portugal, this book has thrown up new subject matter and avenues that I would like to investigate further in the future. The deep divisions in Portugal over the past 40 years cannot obscure the important point that Portuguese democracy is not all grey, but is colourful and full of life. As more documents are declassified relating to the country (including documents from the Portuguese National Archives at Torre do Tombo), I very much look forward to developing new projects based on these releases.

Finally, it is important to remember that officials who write the diplomatic and political documents are human beings, and they sometimes get things wrong. There are many causes for this: lack of quality intelligence information, rapid changes in political situations, unforeseen developments. The historian enjoys the benefit of hindsight, while the authors of the documents do not.

Bibliography

Freedom of Information Documents: Foreign Office, London
The Annual Review for Portugal for 1983–97
The Annual Review for Portugal for 2000–9
In the two years that are not included above, the documents were
   not produced by the Embassy in Lisbon and the Foreign Office in
   London.

Unpublished Documents and Photographs
National Archives (Public Records Office) Kew, London
ADM –   Records of the Admiralty, Naval Forces, Royal Marines,
         Coastguard and related bodies, 1939–1945
AIR –   Records created or inherited by the Air Ministry, the Royal
         Air Force and related bodies, 1939–1945
BT –   Records of the British Board of Trade and of successor and
         related bodies
BW –   Records of the British Council, 1938–1974
CAB –   Records of the British Cabinet Office, 1933–1974
CO –   Records of the Colonial Office, Commonwealth, Foreign
         and Commonwealth Offices, Empire Marketing Board and
         related bodies
DEFE –   Records of the Ministry of Defence
DO –   Records created or inherited by the Dominions Office,
         and of the Commonwealth Relations and Foreign and
         Commonwealth Offices, 1933–1968
FO –   Records created and inherited by the Foreign Office,
         1933–1968

FCO –   Records created and inherited by the Foreign and
          Commonwealth Office, 1968–1974
GFM –   Copies of captured records of the German, Italian and
          Japanese Governments
HO –   Records created or inherited by the Home Office, Ministry of
          Home Security and related bodies, 1933–1974
HS –   Records of the Special Operations Executive, 1939–1945
HW –   Records created and inherited by British Government
          Communications Headquarters (GCHQ), 1939–1945
KV –   Records of the Security Service, 1939–1945
PREM –   Records of the British Prime Minister's Office, 1933–1974
T –   Records created and inherited by HM Treasury, 1933–1974
WO –   Records created or inherited by the War Office, Armed
          Forces, Judge Advocate General and related bodies,
          1939–1945

Arquivo Nacional Torre do Tombo, Lisbon, Portugal
AOS – Arquivo Salazar
Diários 1936–1968
Comissão do Livro Branco do Ministério dos Negócios Estrangeiros
Correspondência Diplomática, 1935–1968
Correspondência Oficial, 1928–1968
Correspondência Oficial Especial, 1934–1968
Correspondência Particular, 1928–1968
Papéis Pessoais, 1936–1968
PIDE (Secret Police)

Arquivo Geral
Direcção dos Serviços de Estrangeiro
Gabinete do Director
Propaganda Apreendida, 1936–1946
SPD Subdelegação de Ponta Delgada, 1942–1945

Arquivo Municipal de Lisboa, Lisbon, Portugal
Photographs of Lisbon, 1933–1974

Arquivo Histórico Municipal de Cascais, Cascais, Portugal
AFTG – Arquivos Fotográficos

CAM – Colecção Antiga do Município
CAP – Colecção António Passaporte
CCGC – Colecção César Guilherme Cardoso
CFCB – Colecção Família Castelo Branco
CSAG – Colecção Sérgio Álvares da Guerra

The Wiener Library, London
Mf Doc 2 – International Committee of the Red Cross: G59 Israélites, 1939–1961
Mf Doc 56 – World Jewish Congress: Central Files, 1919–1976
548 – Wilfrid Israel Papers, 1940s
585 – Documents concerning Nazis in Spain, 1933–1936
660 – Thomas Cook & Son Ltd: Storage Record Book, 1914–1969
683 – Jewish Refugees in Portugal: various papers, 1930s
1072 – Reports and Correspondence concerning Gurs and other French Concentration Camps, 1940s
1100 – NSDAP Auswärtiges Amt: Papers on Jews in Spain and Portugal, 1930s
1206 – Hepner and Cahn: Family Papers, 1874–1950s
1514 – Wilfrid Israel: Correspondence, 1937–1943
1579 – Frank Family: Copy Red Cross Telegrams

US Presidential Libraries
President Richard Nixon Presidential Library
President Gerald Ford Presidential Library
President Jimmy Carter Presidential Library
President Ronald Reagan Presidential Library
President George Bush Presidential Library
President William Clinton Presidential Library
President George W. Bush Presidential Library

CIA Archives
Documents Relating to Portugal
Documents Relating to Spain
Documents Relating to Western Europe

US Holocaust Memorial Museum (USHMM), Washington, DC
General Correspondence between Jewish Refugees in Lisbon and Officials and Relatives

Series RG-60: Video footage of Jewish refugees in Lisbon and Caldas
    da Rainha, the port of Lisbon, the Pan Am Clipper arriving and
    António Oliveira de Salazar holding political meetings
Steven Spielberg Film and Video Archive at USHMM

US Holocaust Memorial Museum Photograph Archive,
    Washington, DC
W/S/59581–86458: Photographs of Jewish Refugees in [and departing
    from] Lisbon during World War II

US National Archives, College Park, Maryland
Foreign Relations of the United States – Relevant parts of volumes on
    Portugal, 1939–1948. Also available online at www.digicoll.library.
    wisc.edu.
RG 84 Entry 3126 – General Records of the US Embassy in Lisbon
    Portugal, 1936–1946
RG 84 Entry 3127 – Classified General Records of the US Embassy in
    Lisbon Portugal, 1941–1949
RG 84 Entry 3128 – Top Secret General Records of the US Embassy in
    Lisbon, 1945–1949
RG 84 Entry 3129A – Top Secret Subject Files related to Operation
    Safehaven, 1947–1948, and German external Assets, 1950–1952
RG 84 Entry 3130 – General Records Relating to War Refugees, 1942
RG 84 Entry 3131 – Files Relating to War Refugees, 1944–1945
RG 84 Entry 3138 – Records Relating to German External Assets in
    Portugal, 1947–1956
RG 84 Entry 3139 – Files of the Financial Attachés, James E. Wood,
    1942–1945
RG 84 – Classified Records of the US Embassy in Madrid,
    1940–1963
RG 84 – Classified Records of the US Embassy in Paris, 1944–1963
RG 226 – Records of the Office of Strategic Services, relevant files to
    Portugal and Operation Safehaven

Centro de Historia BES, Banco Espírito Santo, Lisboa, Portugal
Documentation about the Second World War
Photographic archive of the family
Transcripts of excerpts of the Diary of Salazar, 1933–1946

Published Documents

Correspondência de Pedro Teotónio Pereira para Oliveira Salazar,
    Volume 1, 1931–1939
Mira e Sintra, Presidência do Conselho de Ministros, Comissão do
    Livro Negro Sobre o Regime Fascista, 1987
Correspondência de Pedro Teotónio Pereira para Oliveira Salazar,
    Volume 2, 1940–1941
Mira e Sintra: Presidência do Conselho de Ministros, Comissão do
    Livro Negro Sobre o Regime Fascista, 1989
Grande Hotel e Hotel Atlântico, Boletins de Alojamento de
    Estrangeiros. Cascais: Câmara Municipal de Cascais, 2005
Hotel Palácio, Boletins de Alojamento de Estrangeiros. Cascais: Câmara
    Municipal de Cascais, 2004

Media – Magazines, News Agencies, Newspapers and Television

Associated Press
BBC News
Bloomberg
British Pathé News
Daily Express
Daily Mail
Daily Telegraph
Diário da Manha
Diário de Lisboa
Diário de Noticias
Diário Popular
El Pais
Expresso
Financial Times
Grande Reportagem
Guardian
Harper's
Independent Television News
Jornal do Comercio
Life
The Met Office (UK)
New York Times
Novidades
O Sábado

O Século
O Século Ilustrado
O Voz
Primeiro de Janeiro
Republica
Reuters
RTP News
San Francisco Chronicle
The Atlantic
The Economist
The Tablet
The Times (London)
Time
Visão
United Press
Wall Street Journal
Washington Post

Fiction – Books and Film
Beauvoir, Simone de (1982), *The Mandarins*. London: Flamingo.
Fleming, Ian (2006), *Casino Royale*. London: Penguin.
Gabbay, Tom (2007), *The Lisbon Crossing: A Novel*. New York: William
    Morrow.
Koestler, Arthur (1971), *Arrival and Departure*. London: Penguin.
Lisbon (1956). USA: Republic Pictures Corporation.
Mercier, Pascal (2008), *Night Train to Lisbon*. London: Atlantic.
Pessoa, Fernando (2000), *Poesia Inglesa 1*. Lisbon: Assírio e Alvim.
Pessoa, Fernando (2000), *Poesia Inglesa 2*. Lisbon: Assírio e Alvim.
Saramago, José (2004), *Blindness*. Austin, New York, San Diego, and
    London: Harcourt.
— (1995), *The Stone Raft: A Novel*. New York, San Diego, and London:
    Harcourt Brace.
— (1992), *The Year of the Death of Ricardo Reis*. London: Harvell.
Wilson, Robert (2002), *A Small Death in Lisbon*. New York: Berkley Books.
— (2002), *The Company of Strangers*. London: HarperCollins.

Non-Fiction – Books and Articles
Afonso, Rui (2009), *Um Homem Bom: Aristides de Sousa Mendes*.
    Alfragide: Texto.

Agarossi, Elena (2006), *A Nation Collapses: The Italian Surrender of September 1943*. Cambridge: Cambridge University Press.

Agudo, Manuel Rós (2009), *A Grande Tentacao: Os Planos de Franco para Invadir Portugal*. Alfragide: Casa das Letras.

Allen, Martin (2000), *Hidden Agenda: How the Duke of Windsor Betrayed the Allies*. London: Macmillan.

— (2003), *The Hitler/Hess Deception: British Intelligence's Best-Kept Secret of the Second World War*. London: HarperCollins.

Allen, Peter (1983), *The Crown and the Swastika: Hitler, Hess and the Duke of Windsor*. London: Robert Hale.

Anderson, James M. (2000), *The History of Portugal*. Westport, CT, and London: Greenwood.

Andrew, Christopher (2009), *The Defence of the Realm: The Authorized History of MI5*. London: Allen Lane.

Araújo, Rui (2008), *O Diário Secreto que Salazar Não Leu*. Cruz Quebrada: Oficina do Livro.

Asprey, Robert (2000), *The Rise and Fall of Napoleon Bonaparte*, Vol. 1, *The Rise*. London: Little, Brown.

— (2001), *The Rise and Fall of Napoleon Bonaparte*, Vol. 2, *The Fall*. London: Little, Brown.

Assor, Miriam (2009), *Aristides de Sousa Mendes: Um Justo Contra a Corrente*. Lisbon: Guerra e Paz.

Babo, Maria João and Maria João Gago (2014), *O Último Banqueiro: Ricardo Salgado*. Alfragide: Lua de Pape.

Bachrach, Fabian (1948), *The Memoirs of Cordell Hull*, Vol. 1. London: Hodder & Stoughton.

— (1948), *The Memoirs of Cordell Hull*, Vol. 2. London: Hodder & Stoughton.

Baecque, Antoine de and Serge Toubiana (2000), *Truffaut: A Biography*. Berkeley and Los Angeles: University of California Press.

Baigent, Michael and Richard Leigh (2000), *The Inquisition*. London: Penguin.

Bailey, Rosemary (2008), *Love and War in the Pyrenees: A Story of Courage, Fear, and Hope, 1939–1944*. London: Weidenfeld and Nicolson.

Barroso, Durão (2002), *Mudar de Modelo*. Lisbon: Gradiva.

Bassett, Richard (2011), *Hitler's Spy Chief: The Wilhelm Canaris Mystery*. London: Phoenix.

Beauvoir, Simone de (ed.) (1995), *Quiet Moments in a War: The Letters of Jean-Paul Sartre to Simone de Beauvoir, 1940–1963*. London: Penguin.

Beevor, Anthony and Artemis Cooper (2007), *Paris: After the Liberation, 1944–1949*. London: Penguin.

Beevor, Antony (2009), *D-Day: The Battle for Normandy*. London: Viking.

— (1999), *Stalingrad*. London: Penguin.

— (2006), *The Battle for Spain: The Spanish Civil War, 1936–1939*. London: Weidenfeld and Nicolson.

Beevor, J. G (1981), *SOE: Recollections and Reflections, 1940–1945*. London: Bodley Head.

Benoliel, Joshua (2005), *1873–1932: Repórter Fotográfico*. Lisbon: Câmara Municipal de Lisboa.

Bercuson, David J. and Holder H. Herwig (2006), *One Christmas in Washington: Churchill and Roosevelt Forge the Grand Alliance*. London: Phoenix.

Berlin, Isaiah (2004), *Isaiah Berlin*, Vol. 1, *Letters, 1928–1946*. Cambridge: Cambridge University Press.

Bermeo, Nancy Gina (1986), *The Revolution within the Revolution: Workers' Control in Rural Portugal*. Princeton, NJ: Princeton University Press.

Bethencourt, Francisco and Diogo Ramada Curto (eds) (2007), *Portuguese Oceanic Expansion, 1440–1800*. New York: Cambridge University Press.

Birmingham, David (2007), *A Concise History of Portugal*. Cambridge: Cambridge University Press.

— (1999), *Portugal and Africa*. Athens, OH: Ohio University Press.

Bloch, Michael (1986), *Operation Willi: The Plot to Kidnap the Duke of Windsor, July 1940*. London: Weidenfeld and Nicolson.

— (1996), *The Duchess of Windsor*. London: Weidenfeld and Nicolson.

— (1982), *The Duke of Windsor's War*. London: Weidenfeld and Nicolson.

— (1989), *The Secret File of the Duke of Windsor*. London: Corgi Books.

Bower, Tom (1997), *Nazi Gold: The Full Story of the Fifty-Year Swiss–Nazi Conspiracy to Steal Billions from Europe's Jews and Holocaust Survivors*. New York: HarperCollins.

Brandão, F. Norton (1960), 'Epidemiology of Venereal Disease in Portugal during the Second World War'. *British Journal of Venereal Diseases*, 36, no. 2, 136–8.

Brandão, Fernando de Castro (2011), *António de Oliveira Salazar: Uma Cronologia*. Lisbon: Prefacio.

Breitman, Richard (1995), 'A Deal with the Nazi Dictatorship: Himmler's Alleged Peace Emissaries in Autumn 1943'. *Journal of Contemporary History*, 30, 411–30.

Briggs, Asa (2000), *History of England: England in the Age of Improvement*. London: Folio Society.

Buck, Paul (2002), *Lisbon: A Cultural and Literary Companion*. Oxford: Signal Books.

Burleigh, Michael (2006), *Sacred Causes: Religion and Politics from the European Dictators to Al Qaeda*. London: HarperPerennial.

— (2001), *The Third Reich: A New History*. London: Pan.

Burman, Edward (2004), *The Inquisition: The Hammer of Heresy*. Stroud: Sutton.

Burns, Jimmy (2009), *Papa Spy: Love, Faith and Betrayal in Wartime Spain*. London: Bloomsbury.

Caetano, Marcello (1977), *Minhas Memorias de Salazar*. Lisbon: Verbo.

Caldwell, Robert (1942), 'The Anglo-Portuguese Alliance Today'. *Foreign Affairs*, 21, no. 1 (October), 149, 157.

Cannadine, David (2003), *In Churchill's Shadow: Confronting the Past in Modern Britain*. London: Penguin.

Cantwell, John (1998), *The Second World War: A Guide to Documents in the Public Record Office*. London: The National Archives.

Caron, Vicki (1999), *Uneasy Asylum: France and the Jewish Refugee Crisis, 1933–1942*. Stanford, CA: Stanford University Press.

Carpozi, George J. R. (1999), *Nazi Gold: The Real Story of How the World Plundered Jewish Treasures*. Far Hills: New Horizon Press.

Carr, Raymond (1986), *Modern Spain, 1875–1980*. Oxford, Oxford University Press.

Carrilho, M. et al. (eds) (1989), *Portugal Na Segunda Guerra Mundial*. Lisbon: Dom Quixote.

Carter, Miranda (2002), *Anthony Blunt: His Lives*. London: Pan Books.

Caruana, Leonard and Hugh Rockoff (2003), 'A Wolfram in Sheep's Clothing: Economic Warfare in Spain, 1940–1944'. *The Journal of Economic History*, 63, no. 1 (March), 100–26.

Carvalho, Manuel de Abreu Ferreira (2003), *Relatório dos Acontecimentos de Timor, 1942–45*. Lisbon: Instituto da Defesa Nacional.

Castanheira, José Pedro (2012), *Jorge Sampaio: Uma Biografia*. Porto: Porto Editora.

Castaño, David (2013), *Mário Soares e a Revolução*. Lisbon: Dom Quixote.

Castro, Pedro Jorge (2009), *Salazar e os Milionários*. Lisbon: Quetzal.

Cavaco Silva, Anibal (2002), *Autobiografia Política I: O Percurso até à Maioria Absoluta e a Primeira Fase da Coabitação*. Lisbon: Temas e Debates.

— (2004), *Autobiografia Política II: O Percurso até à Maioria Absoluta e a Primeira Fase da Coabitação*, Lisbon: Temas e Debates.

Cave Brown, Anthony (1987), *'C': The Secret Life of Sir Stewart Menzies, Spymaster to Winston Churchill*. New York: Collier Books.

Céu e Silva, João (2013), *1975 – O ano do Furacão Revolucionário*. Porto: Porto Editora.

— (2013), *Uma Longa Viagem com Manuel Alegre*. Porto: Porto Editora.

Chandler, David G. (2002), *The Campaigns of Napoleon*, Vol. 2: *The Zenith, September 1805–September 1812*. London: Folio Society.

Chaves, Miguel de Mattos (2005), *Portugal e a Construção Europeia: Mitos e Realidades*. Lisbon: Sete Caminhos.

Churchill, Winston S. (ed.) (2003), *Never Give In: The Best of Winston Churchill's Speeches*. London: Pimlico.

Churchill, Winston (2002), *The Second World War* (Abridged Version). London: Pimlico.

— (2000 edn), *The Second World War*, Vol. 1, *The Gathering Storm*. London: Folio Society.

— (2000 edn), *The Second World War*, Vol. 2, *The Finest Hour*. London: Folio Society.

— (2000 edn), *The Second World War*, Vol. 3, *The Grand Alliance*. London: Folio Society.

— (2000 edn), *The Second World War*, Vol. 4, *The Hinge of Fate*. London: Folio Society.

— (2000 edn), *The Second World War*, Vol. 5, *Closing the Ring*. London: Folio Society.

— (2000 edn), *The Second World War*, Vol. 6, *Triumph and Tragedy*. London: Folio Society.

Clair, Jean (1999), *Henri Cartier-Bresson: Europeans*. London: Thames & Hudson.

Clausewitz, Carl von (1993), *On War*. London: Everyman's Library.

Coelho, Pedro Passos (2010), *Mudar*. Lisbon: Bertrand Editora.

Colvin, Ian (2013), *Flight 777: The Mystery of Leslie Howard*. Barnsley: Pen & Sword Aviation.

Corkill, David and José Carlos Pina Almeida (2009), 'Commemoration and Propaganda in Salazar's Portugal: the Mundo Portuguese Exposition of 1940'. *Journal of Contemporary History*, 44, no. 3, 381–99.

Costa, António, (2012) *Caminho Aberto: Textos de Intervenção Política*. Lisbon: Quentzal Editores.

Costa, Fernando (1998), *Portugal e a Guerra Anglo-Boer*. Lisbon: Edições Cosmos.

Costa, Ricardo (2013), *Portugal – Manual de Instruções*. Alfragide: Livros d'Hoje.

Coward, Noël (2004), *Future Indefinite*. London: Methuen Drama.

Crosswell, D. K. R. (2010), *Beetle: The Life of General Walter Bedell Smith*. Lexington: The University Press of Kentucky.

Cunha, Adelino (2013), *António Guterres: Os Segredos do Poder*. Lisbon: Alêtheia Editores.

Cunhal, Álvaro (2014), *Obras Escolhidas*, Vol. 5 (1974–1975). Lisbon: Edições Avante.

Dacosta, Fernando (2007), *Máscaras de Salazar*. Cruz Quebrada: Casa das Letras.

— (2013), *Os Retornados Mudaram Portugal*. Lisbon: Parsifal.

Dallek, Robert (2004), *John F. Kennedy: An Unfinished Life, 1917–1963*. London: Penguin.

— (2007), *Nixon and Kissinger: Partners in Power*. London: Penguin.

Damas, Carlos Alberto and Augusto De Ataíde (2004), *O Banco Espírito Santo: Uma Dinastia Financeira Portuguesa, 1886–1973*. Lisbon: Banco Espírito Santo.

Damas, Carlos Alberto (2002), 'Espírito Santo e Os Windsor em 1940'. *Grande Reportagem*, 96–101.

— (2008), *Hotel Tivoli Lisboa, 1933–2008*. Lisbon: Centro de Historia do Grupo Banco Espírito Santo.

— (2008), *Manuel Ribeiro Espírito Santo Silva: Fotobiografia, 1908–1973*. Lisbon: Centro de Historia do Grupo Banco Espírito Santo.

— (2003), 'Ricardo Espírito Santo e o Duque de Windsor'. *Historia*, no. 62, 46–51.

Day, Barry (ed.) (2007), *The Letters of Noël Coward*. London: Methuen.

De Sousa, Maria Leonor Machado (2008), *A Guerra Peninsular em Portugal: Relatos Britânicos*. Casal de Cambra: Calei dos Copio.

Deakin, F. W. (1962), *The Brutal Friendship: Mussolini, Hitler, and the Fall of Italian Fascism*. London: Penguin.

Dearborn, Mary (2008), *Peggy Guggenheim: Mistress of Modernism*. London: Virago Press.

Delgado, Humberto (1964), *The Memoirs of General Delgado*. London: Cassell.

Diamond, Hanna (2007), *Fleeing Hitler: France 1940*. Oxford: Oxford University Press.

Dias, Marina Tavares (2005), *Lisboa nos Anos 40: Longe da Guerra*. Lisbon: Quimera Editores.

Dilks, David (ed.) (1971), *The Diaries of Sir Alexander Cadogan, 1938–1945*. London: Cassell.

Disney, A. R. (2009), *A History of Portugal and the Portuguese Empire*, Vol. 1. Cambridge: Cambridge University Press.

— (2009), *A History of Portugal and the Portuguese Empire*, Vol. 2. Cambridge: Cambridge University Press.

Doerries, Reinhard (2003), *Hitler's Last Chief of Foreign Intelligence: Allied Interrogations of Walter Schellenberg*. London and Portland: Frank Cass.

Duggan, Christopher (1997), *A Concise History of Italy*. Cambridge: Cambridge University Press.

Eccles, David (1983), *By Safe Hand: The Letters of Sybil and David Eccles, 1939–42*. London: Bodley Head.

Eden, Anthony (1960), *Full Circle: The Memoirs of Sir Anthony Eden*. London: Cassell.

Edmondson, John (1993), *France: A Traveller's Literary Companion*. London: In Print.

Eilade, Mircea (2010), *The Portugal Journal*. Albany: State University of New York Press.

Eisenhower, Dwight D. (1948), *Crusade in Europe*. London: Heinemann.

Eizenstat, Stuart E. (2003), *Imperfect Justice: Looted Assets, Slave Labour and the Unfinished Business of World War II*. New York: PublicAffairs.

Esdaile, Charles (2007), *Napoleon's Wars: An International History, 1803–1815*. London: Allen Lane.

Evans, Richard E. (2009), *The Third Reich at War: How the Nazis Led Germany from Conquest to Disaster*. London: Penguin.

Faria, Miguel Figueira de (2009), *Alfredo da Silva e Salazar*. Lisbon: Bertrand Editora.

Ferguson, Niall (2004), *Empire: How Britain Made the Modern World*. London: Penguin.

— (2007), *The Ascent of Money: A Financial History of the World*. London: Penguin.

— (1998), *The House of Rothschild: Money's Prophets, 1798–1848*. New York: Penguin.

— (1998), *The House of Rothschild: The World's Banker, 1849–1999*. New York: Penguin.

— (1999), *The Pity of War*. London: Penguin.

— (2007), *The War of the World*. London: Penguin.

Ferro, António (1939), *Salazar: Portugal and Her Leader*. London: Faber and Faber.

Figueiredo, António de (1975), *Portugal: Fifty Years of Dictatorship*. London: Penguin.

Foot, M. R. D and J. M. Langley (2011), *MI9: Escape and Evasion 1939–1945*. London: Biteback Publishing.

Foot, M. R. D. (1999), *SOE: The Special Operations Executive, 1940–1946*. London: Pimlico.

Fralon, José-Alain (2001), *A Good Man in Evil Times: The Story of Aristides de Sousa Mendes, the Man Who Saved the Lives of Countless Refugees in World War II*. New York: Carroll and Graf.

Freire, Leonor Costa, Susana Munch Miranda and Pedro Lains (2011), *História Económica de Portugal*. Lisbon, A Esfera dos Livros.

Fry, Varian (1997), *Surrender on Demand*. Boulder: Johnson Books.

Gaddis, John Lewis (2011), *George F. Kennan: An American Life*. London and New York: Penguin.

Garcia, Maria Madalena (1992), *Arquivo Salazar: Inventario e Índices*. Lisbon: Editorial Estampa.

Garland, Albert N. and Howard McGaw Smyth (1965), *The Mediterranean Theater of Operations: Sicily and the Surrender of Italy*. Washington: Library of Congress.

Garnier, Christine (1952), *Férias com Salazar*. Lisbon: Parceria A. M. Pereira e Grasset e Fasquelle.

— (1954), *Salazar in Portugal: An Intimate Portrait*. New York: Farrar, Straus, and Young.

Gilbert, Martin (1997), *A History of the Twentieth Century*, Vol. 1, 1900–1933. London: HarperCollins.

— (2004), *Churchill: A Life*, Vol. 2. London: Folio Society.

— (2005), *Churchill and America*. New York: Free Press.

— (2004), *D-Day*. Hoboken, NJ: Wiley.

Ginsburg, Paul (1990), *A History of Contemporary Italy: Society and Politics, 1943–1988*. London: Penguin.

Glancey, Jonathan (2007), *Spitfire: The Biography*. London: Atlantic Books.

Glass, Charles (2009), *Americans in Paris: Life and Death under German Occupation, 1940–1944*. London: Harpers Press.

Greene, Richard (ed.) (2007), *Graham Greene: A Life in Letters*. London: Little, Brown.

Guggenheim, Peggy (2005), *Out of This Century: Confessions of an Art Addict*. London: Andre Deutsch.

Gulbenkian, Nubar (1965), *Pantaraxia: The Autobiography of Nubar Gulbenkian*. London: Hutchinson.

Gurriarán, José António (2001), *Um Rei no Estoril: Dom Juan Carlos e a Família Real Espanhola no Exílio Português*. Lisbon: Dom Quixote.

Hayward, James (2007), *Mitos e Lendas da Segunda Guerra Mundial*. Lisbon: A Esfera dos Livros.

Henriques, João, Miguel and Olga Bettencourt and Teresa Ramirez (eds) (2007), *The History of Sailing in Cascais: From the First Regatta to the Internationalisation of Sailing*. Lisbon: Edicoes Inapa.

Henriques, Mendo Castro and Gonçalo De Sampaio e Mello (eds) (2010), *Salazar, António, De Oliveira: Pensamento e Doutrina Politica*. Lisbon: Verbo.

Herz, Norman (2004), *Operation Alacrity: The Azores and the War in the Atlantic*. Annapolis, MD: Naval Institute Press.

Higham, Charles (2004), *Mrs Simpson: Secret Lives of the Duchess of Windsor*. London: Pan Books.

Hildebrand, Klaus (1973), *The Foreign Policy of the Third Reich*. Berkeley and Los Angeles: University of California Press.

— (1985), *The Third Reich*. London: George Allen and Unwin.

Hinsley, F. H. (1993), *British Intelligence in the Second World War* (abridged version). London: Her Majesty's Stationery Office.

Hoare, Samuel (1946), *Ambassador on Special Mission*. London: Collins.

— (1954), *Nine Troubled Years*. London: Collins.

Hoffmann, Peter (2001), *History of the German Resistance, 1933–1945*. Quebec: McGill-Queen's University Press.

Holland, James (2004), *Fortress Malta: An Island under Siege, 1940–1943*. London: Phoenix.

Holt, Thaddeus (2005), *The Deceivers: Allied Military Deception in the Second World War*. London: Phoenix.

Howard, Ronald (1981), *In Search of my Father: A Portrait of Leslie Howard*. London: William Kimber.

Hyland, Paul (1996), *Backwards Out of the Big World*. London: HarperCollins.

Hynes, Samuel, Anne Matthews, Nancy Caldwell Sorel and Roger J. Spiller (eds), *Reporting World War II: Part One: American Journalism, 1938–1940*. New York: Library of America.

Ingrams, Richard (1995), *Muggeridge: The Biography*. London: HarperCollins.

Jack, Malcolm (2007), *Lisbon: City of the Sea, a History*. New York: I. B. Tauris.

Janeiro, Helena Pinto (1998), *Salazar e Pétain: Relações Luso-Francesas durante a II Guerra Mundial, 1940–44*. Lisbon: Edições Cosmos.

Jeffery, Keith (2010), *MI6: The History of the Secret Intelligence Service, 1909–1949*. London: Bloomsbury.

John, Otto (1974), *Twice Through the Lines: Autobiography of a Super-Spy*. London, Futura.

Johnson, Paul (2002), *Napoleon*. London: Phoenix.

Justino, Ana Clara (ed.) (2002), *O Século XX em Revista*. Lisbon: Câmara Municipal de Cascais.

Kaplan, Marion (2006), *The Portuguese: The Land and Its People*. Manchester: Carcanet.

Kassow, Samuel D. (2009), *Who Will Write Our History? Rediscovering a Hidden Archive from the Warsaw Ghetto*. London: Allen Lane.

Kaufman, Sanford B. (1995), *Pan Am Pioneer: A Manager's Memoir from Seaplane Clippers to Jumbo Jets*. Lubbock: Texas Tech University Press.

Kay, Hugh (1970), *Salazar and Modern Portugal*. New York: Hawthorn Books.

Kennan, George F. (1967), *Memoirs 1925–1950*. Boston and Toronto: Little, Brown.

Koestler, Arthur (2006), *Scum of the Earth*. London: Eland Publishing.

Laqueur, Walter (2001), *Generation Exodus: The Fate of the Young Jewish Refugees from Nazi Germany*. Hanover and London: Brandeis University Press.

Leal, Ernesto Castro (1994), *António Ferro: Espaço Político e Imaginário Social, 1918–32*. Lisbon: Edições Cosmos.

Lee, Laurie (1993), *Red Sky at Sunrise: An Autobiographical Trilogy*. London: Penguin.

Leitz, Christian (2000), *Nazi Germany and Neutral Europe during the Second World War*. Manchester: Manchester University Press.

— (2003), 'Nazi Germany and the Luso-Hispanic World'. *Contemporary European History*, 12, no. 2 (May), 183–96.

Lewis, Paul H. (1978), 'Salazar's Ministerial Elite, 1932–1968'. *Journal of Politics*, 40, no. 3 (August), 622–47.

Lima, Mário João and José Soares Neves (2005), *Cascais e a Memória dos Exílios*. Lisbon, Câmara Municipal de Cascais.

Livermore, H. V. (1966), *A New History of Portugal*. Cambridge: Cambridge University Press.

Lob, Ladislaus (2008), *Dealing with Satan: Rezso Kasztner's Daring Rescue Mission*. London: Jonathan Cape.

Lodwick, John with D. H. Young (1958), *Gulbenkian: An Interpretation of Calouste Sarkis Gulbenkian*. London, Melbourne and Toronto: Heinemann.

Louça, António and Ansgar Schafer (no publication date), 'Portugal and the Nazi Gold: The Lisbon Connection in the Sales of Looted Gold by the Third Reich'. Yad Vashem, Jerusalem.

Louça, António and Isabelle Paccaud (2007), *O Segredo da Rua O Século Ligações Perigosas de um Dirigente Judeu com a Alemanha Nazi, 1935–1939*. Lisbon, Fim de Século.

Louça, António (2000), *Hitler e Salazar: Comercio em Tempos de Guerra, 1940–1944*. Lisbon: Terramar.

Loureiro, Vítor Gonçalves (2005), *A Agenda de Cavaco Silva*. Lisbon: Oficina do Livro.

Lourenço, Camilo (2012), *Basta! O que fazer para tirar a crise de Portugal*. Porto: Matéria Prima.

Louro, Sónia (2009), *O Cônsul Desobediente*. Parede: Saída de Emergência.

Lycett, Andrew (1996), *Ian Fleming*. London: Phoenix.

MacDonagh, S. J. (1940), 'A Professor in Politics: Salazar and the Regeneration of Portugal'. *Irish Monthly*, 417–27.

Macintyre, Ben (2007), *Agent Zigzag: The True Wartime Story of Eddie Chapman: Lover, Betrayer, Hero, Spy*. London: Bloomsbury.

— (2010), *Operation Mincemeat: The True Spy Story that Changed the Course of World War II*. London: Bloomsbury.

Macmillan, Margaret (2002), *Peacemakers: Six Months That Changed the World*. London: John Murray.

McNeese, Tim (2006), *Salvador Dali: The Great Hispanic Heritage*. New York: Chelsea House.

Makovsky, Michael (2007), *Churchill's Promised Land: Zionism and Statecraft*. New Haven and London: Yale University Press.

Manchester, William (1988), *The Last Lion: Winston Spenser Churchill, Alone 1932–1940*. Boston, New York and London: Little, Brown.

Marinho, António Luís and Mário Carneiro (2014), *1974: O Ano Que Começou em Abril*. Lisbon: Temas e Debates.

Marques, Viriato Soromenho (2014), *Portugal na Queda da Europa*. Lisbon: Temas e Debates.

Martins, Luís Almeida (2015), *História Não Oficial de Portugal: Uma Maneira Diferente de Contar como Tudo Aconteceu*. Lisbon: A Esfera dos Livros.

Mather, Philippe (2013), *Stanley Kubrick at* Look *Magazine: Authorship and Genre in Photojournalism and Film*. Bristol and Chicago: Intellect.

Matos, Helena (2010), *Salazar: A Construção do Mito, 1928–1933*. Lisbon: Circulo de Leitores.

— (2010), *Salazar: A Propaganda, 1934–1938*. Lisbon: Circulo de Leitores.

Matos, Vitor (2012), *Marcelo Rebelo de Sousa*. Lisbon: A Esfera dos Livros.

Mattoso José and Fernando Rosas (1998), *Historia de Portugal*, Vol. 7, *O Estado Novo, 1926–1974*. Lisbon: Editorial Estampa.

Maxwell, Kenneth (1995), *The Making of Portuguese Democracy*. Cambridge: Cambridge University Press.

Mayson, Richard (2004), *Port and the Douro*. London: Octopus.

Meneses, Filipe Ribeiro de (2009), *Salazar: A Political Biography*. New York: Enigma Books.

— (2000), *União Sagrada e Sidonismo: Portugal em Guerra, 1916–18*. Lisbon: Edições Cosmos.

Milgram, Avraham (1999), 'Portugal: the Consuls, and the Jewish Refugees, 1938–1941'. *Yad Vashem Studies*, 27 (Jerusalem), 123–56.

— (2010), *Portugal, Salazar e os Judeus*. Lisbon: Gradiva.

Mitchell, Alex (2011), *Come the Revolution: A Memoir*. Sydney: NewSouth Publishing.

Mocatta, Frederic David (1933), *The Jews of Spain and Portugal and the Inquisition*. Longmans Green, London.

Monteiro, Armindo (1939), 'Portugal in Africa'. *Journal of the Royal African Society*, 38, no. 151 (April), 259–72.

Moran, Lord (2002), *Churchill at War, 1940–45*. London: Robinson.

Moreira de Sá, Tiago and Bernardino Gomes (2008), *Carlucci vs Kissinger: Os EUA e a Revolução Portuguesa*. Lisbon: Dom Quixote.

Moreira de Sá, Tiago (2011), *Os Estados Unidos e a Descolonização de Angola*. Lisbon: Dom Quixote.

Morison, Samuel Eliot (2002), *History of the United States Naval Operations in World War II: Sicily-Salerno-Anzio*. Champaign: University of Illinois Press.

Mueller, Michael (2007), *Canaris: The Life and Death of Hitler's Spymaster*. London: Chatham Publishing.

Muggeridge, Malcolm (ed.) (2006), *Chronicles of Wasted Time: An Autobiography*. Vancouver: Regent College Publishing.

— (1947), *Ciano's Diary, 1939–1943*. London: Heinemann.

— (1981), *Like It Was: A Selection from the Diaries of Malcolm Muggeridge*. London: Collins.

Neillands, Robin (2003), *Wellington and Napoleon: Clash of Armies, 1807–1815*. Barnsley: Pen and Sword.

Newitt, Malyn (2012), *Portugal na História da Europa e do Mundo*. Alfragide: Texto Editores.

Nicholas, Lynn (1996), *Europa Saqueada: O Destino dos Tesouros Artisticos Europeus no Terceiro Reich e na Segunda Munidal*. Sao Paulo: Compania Das Letras.

Nogueira Pinto, Jaime (2014), *Portugal – Os Anos do Fim*. Lisbon: Dom Quixote.

Nogueira, Franco (2000), *Salazar*, Vol. 1, *A Mocidade e os Princípios, 1889–1928*. Porto: Civilização Editora.

— (2000), *Salazar*, Vol. 2, *Os Tempos Áureos, 1928–1936*. Porto: Civilização Editora.

— (2000), *Salazar*, Vol. 3, *As Grandes Crises, 1936–1945*. Porto: Civilização Editora.

— (2000), *Salazar*, Vol. 4, *O Ataque, 1945–1958*. Porto: Civilização Editora.

— (2000), *Salazar*, Vol. 5, *A Resistência, 1958–1964*. Porto: Civilização Editora.

— (2000), *Salazar*, Vol. 6, *O Ultimo Combate, 1964–1970*. Porto: Civilização Editora.

Norwich, John Julius (2007), *The Middle Sea: A History of the Mediterranean*. London: Vintage.

Nunes, João Paulo Avelãs (2010), *O Estado Novo e o Volfrâmio, 1933–1947*. Coimbra: Imprensa da Universidade de Coimbra.

O'Hara, Maureen with John Nicoletti (2004), *'Tis Herself: A Memoir*. London: Simon and Schuster.

Oliveira, Pedro Aires (2000), *Armindo Monteiro: Uma Biografia Politica*. Lisbon: Bertrand Editora.

Oliveira, Raquel, Orlando Leite and Sónia Trigueirão (2012), *A Vida Louca dos Presidentes de Portugal*. Lisbon: Marcador.

Overy, Richard (2005), *The Dictators: Hitler's Germany, Stalin's Russia*. London: Penguin.

Page, Martin (2002), *The First Global Village: How Portugal Changed the World*. Cruz Quebrada: Casa das Letras.

Paice, Edward (2008), *Wrath of God: The Great Lisbon Earthquake of 1755*. London: Quercus.

Paxton, Robert O. (2005), *The Anatomy of Fascism*. London: Penguin.

Payne, Stanley G. (2001), *A History of Fascism, 1914–45*. London: Routledge.

— (1973), *A History of Spain and Portugal*, Vol. 1. Madison and London: University of Wisconsin Press.

— (1973), *A History of Spain and Portugal*, Vol. 2. Madison and London: University of Wisconsin Press.

— (2008), *Franco and Hitler: Spain, Germany, and World War II*. Yale: Yale University Press.

Pélissier, René and Douglas L. Wheeler (2011), *História de Angola*. Lisbon: Tinta da China.

Pena, Paulo (2014), *Jogos de Poder*. Lisbon: A Esfera dos Livros.

Petropoulos, Jonathan (2006), *Royals and the Reich: The Princes von Hessen in Nazi Germany*. New York: Oxford University Press.

Philby, Kim (2002), *My Silent War: The Autobiography of a Spy*. New York: Modern Library.

Picaper, Jean-Paul (1998), *No Rasto Dos Tesouros Nazis*. Lisbon: Edicoes 70.

Pignatelli, Marina (2008), *Interioridades e Exterioridades dos Judeus de Lisboa*. Lisbon: Instituto Superior de Ciências Sociais e Políticas.

Pimentel, Irene Flunser (2010), *Cardeal Cerejeira: O Príncipe da Igreja*. Lisbon: A Esfera dos Livros.

— (2006), *Judeus em Portugal durante a II Guerra Mundial: Em Fuga de Hitler e do Holocausto*. Lisbon: A Esfera dos Livros.

Pinheiro, Magda (2011), *Biografia de Lisboa*. Lisbon: A Esfera dos Livros.

Pinheiro, Miguel (2010), *Sá Carneiro*. Lisbon: A Esfera dos Livros.

Pinto, António Costa and Nuno Severiano Teixeira (2005), *A Europa do Sul e a Construção da União Europeia, 1945–2000*. Lisbon: Imprensa de Ciências Sociais.

Pinto, António Costa (2013), *História Contemporânea de Portugal*, Vol. 1. Lisboa: Âncora Editora, 2014; Vol. 3 *A Crise do Liberalismo*. Carnaxide: Objectiva, 2014.

Pinto, Jaime Nogueira (2008), *António de Oliveira Salazar: O Outro Retrato*. Lisbon: A Esfera dos Livros.

— (1995), *O Fim do Estado Novo e os Origens do 25 de Abril*. Algés, Lisbon: Difel.

Pinto, M. Vieira (2014), *O General Ramalho Eanes e a História Recente de Portugal*. Vol. 1. Lisboa: Âncora Editora, 2014.

Pires de Lima, Bernardo (2013), *A Cimeira das Lajes: Portugal, Espanha e a Guerra do Iraque*. Lisbon: Tinta da China.

Preston, Paul (2006), *Comrades: Portraits from the Spanish Civil War*. London: HarperPerennial.

— (1994), *Franco*. London: Basic Books.

— (2005), *Juan Carlos: Steering Spain from Dictatorship to Democracy*. London: Harper Perennial.

— (1986), *The Spanish Civil War, 1936–39*. London: Weidenfeld and Nicolson.

— (2006), *The Spanish Civil War: Reaction, Revolution and Revenge*. London: HarperPerennial.

— (2012), *The Spanish Holocaust: Inquisition and Extermination in Twentieth-Century Spain*. London: HarperPress.

Raby, Dawn Linda (1990), 'The Portuguese Presidential Election of 1949: A Successful Governmental Maneuver?'. *Luso-Brazilian Review*, 27, no. 1 (Summer), 63–77.

Ramalho, Miguel Nunes (2001), *Sidónia Pais: Diplomata e Conspirador, 1912–1917*. Lisbon: Cosmos.

Rankin, Nicholas (2008), *Churchill's Wizards: The British Genius for Deception, 1914–1945*. London: Faber and Faber.

Redondo, Juan Carlos Jiménez (1996), *Franco e Salazar: As Relações Luso-Espanholas durante a Guerra Frio*. Lisbon: Assírio e Alvim.

Reynolds, David (2004), *In Command of History: Churchill Fighting and Writing the Second World War*. London: Allen Lane.

Rezola, Maria Inácia (2008), *25 de Abril: Mitos de uma Revolução*. Lisbon: A Esfera dos Livros.

Roberg, Kurt W. (2009), *A Visa Or Your Life!: A Boy's Life and the Odyssey of His Escape From Nazi Germany*. Bloomington: Author House.

Roberts, Andrew (2006), *A History of the English-Speaking Peoples Since 1900*. London: Weidenfeld and Nicolson.

— (2003), *Churchill and Hitler: Secrets of Leadership*. London: Phoenix.

— (2009), *Masters and Commanders: The Military Geniuses Who Led the West to Victory in World War II*. London: Penguin.

— (2001), *Napoleon and Wellington*. London: Phoenix.

— (1991), *The Holy Fox: The Life of Lord Halifax*. London: Phoenix.

— (2010), *The Storm of War: A New History of the Second World War*. London: Penguin.

Rodrigues, Luís Nuno (ed.) (2008), *Franklin Roosevelt and the Azores during the Two World Wars*. Lisbon: Fundacao Luso-Americana.

Rodrigues, Luís Nuno (2002), *Salazar e Kennedy: A Crise de uma Aliança*. Lisbon: Casa das Letras.

— (2010), *Spínola*. Lisboa: A Esfera dos Livros.

Rodrigues, Teresa Ferreira and Rafael Garcia Perez (2011), *Portugal e Espanha: Crise e Convergência na União Europeia*. Lisbon: Tribuna da História.

Rohr, Isabelle (2008), *The Spanish Right and the Jews, 1898–1945*. Brighton and Portland: Sussex Academic Press.

Rosas, Fernando and Francisco Louçá (2010), *Os Donos de Portugal*. Porto: Edições Afrontamento.

Rosas, Fernando, Júlia Leitão de Barros and Pedro de Oliveira (1996), *Armindo Monteiro e Oliveira Salazar: Correspondência Politica, 1926–1955*. Lisbon: Editorial Estampa.

Rosas, Fernando (2007), *Lisboa Revolucionaria: Roteiro dos Confrontos Armados no Século XX*. Lisbon: Tinta da China.

— (1995), *Portugal entre a Paz e a Guerra, 1939–1945*. Lisbon: Editorial Estampa.

— (2002), 'Portuguese Neutrality in the Second World War', in Neville Wylie (ed.), *European Neutrals and Non-Belligerents during the Second World War*, 268–82. Cambridge: Cambridge University Press.

Russell-Wood, A. J. R. (1998), *The Portuguese Empire, 1415–1808: A World on the Move*. Baltimore and London: Johns Hopkins University Press.

Ryan, John (1946), 'Election in Portugal'. *Irish Monthly*, 52–8.

Santana Lopes, Pedro (2006), *Percepções e Realidade*. Lisbon: Alêtheia Editores.

Saraiva, António José (2007), *Politica à Portuguesa: Ideias, Pessoas e Factos*. Cruz Quebrada: Oficina do Livro.

Saraiva, José Hermano (1997), *Portugal: A Companion History*. Manchester: Carcanet.

Saramago, José (2000), *Journey to Portugal: In Pursuit of Portugal's History and Culture*. San Diego, New York and London: Harvest.

— (2009), *Small Memories: A Memoir*. London: Harvill Secker.

— (2010), *The Notebook*. London and New York: Verso.

Scammell, Michael (2009), *Koestler: The Indispensable Intellectual*. London: Faber and Faber.

Schellenberg, Walter (2006), *The Memoirs of Hitler's Spymaster*. London: Andre Deutsch.

Schwarz, Reinhard (2006), *Os Alemães em Portugal, 1933–1945: A Colónia Alemã Através das Suas Instituições*. Porto: Antilia Editora.

Sedgwick, Ellery (1954), 'Something New in Dictators: Salazar of Portugal'. *The Atlantic* (January), 40–5.

Selby, Walford (1953), *Diplomatic Twilight: 1930–1940*. London: John Murray.

Serrado, Ricardo (2010), *História do Futebol Português: Das Origens ao 25 de Abril: Uma Análise Social e Cultural*, 2 Vols. Estoril: Prime Books.

Shepherd, Naomi (1984), *A Refuge from Darkness: Wilfrid Israel and the Rescue of the Jews*. New York: Pantheon Books.

Shirer, William L. (1995), *The Rise and Fall of the Third Reich: A History of Nazi Germany*, Vol. 3. London: Folio Society.

— (1999), *This is Berlin: Reporting from Nazi Germany 1938–40*. London: Hutchinson.

Shrady, Nicholas (2008), *The Last Day: Wrath, Ruin and Reason in the Great Lisbon Earthquake of 1755*. New York: Penguin.

Smith, Alfred (2001), *Rudolf Hess: And Germany's Reluctant War, 1939–41*. Lewes: The Book Guild Limited.

Smith, Amanda (ed.) (2001), *Hostage to Fortune: The Letters of Joseph P. Kennedy*. New York: Viking.

Smith, Michael (2011), *The Secrets of Station X: How the Bletchley Park Codebreakers Helped Win the War*. London: Biteback Publishing.

Soares, Mário (2012), *Crónica de um Tempo Difícil*. Lisbon: Temas e Debates.

Soutar, Ian (ed.) (rev. edn January 1997), 'History Notes: Nazi Gold: Information from the British Archives'. Historians LRD, Foreign and Commonwealth Office.

— (May 1997), 'History Notes: Nazi Gold: Information from the British Archives: Part II, Monetary Gold, Non Monetary Gold and the Tripartite Gold Commission'. Historians LRD, No. 12, Foreign and Commonwealth Office.

Spoto, Donald (2010), *High Society: Grace Kelly and Hollywood*. London: Arrow.

Steury, Donald (2007), 'CSI: The OSS and Project Safehaven'. Available at www.cia.gov.library.

Stevens, Edmund (1952), 'Portugal Under Salazar'. *Harper's* 205, no. 1227 (August), 62–8.

Stewart, Jules (2012), *Madrid: The History*. London and New York: I. B.Tauris.

Stone, Glyn A. (2005), *Spain, Portugal and the Great Powers, 1931–1941*. New York: Palgrave Macmillan.

— (1975), 'The Official British Attitude to the Anglo-Portuguese Alliance, 1910–1945'. *Journal of Contemporary History* 10, no. 4 (October), 729–46.

— (1994), *The Oldest Ally: Britain and the Portuguese Connection, 1936–1941*. Woodbridge, Suffolk: Boydell Press.

Strachan, Hew (ed.) (1998), *The Oxford Illustrated History of the First World War*. Oxford: Oxford University Press.

Streeter, Michael (2005), *Franco*. London: Haus Publishing.

Sullivan, Rosemary (2006), *Villa Air-Bel: The Second World War, Escape and a House in France*. London: John Murray.

Sweeney, J. K. (1974), 'The Portuguese Wolfram Embargo: A Case Study in Economic Warfare'. *Military Affairs* 38, no. 1 (February), 23–6.

Tarling, Nicholas (1996), 'Britain, Portugal and East Timor in 1941'. *Journal of Southeast Asian Studies* 27, no. 1 (March), 132–8.

Taylor, A. J. P. (1991), *A History of England, 1914–1945*. London: Folio Society.

— (1991), *The Origins of the Second World War*. London: Penguin.

Teixeira, Nuno Severiano (1992), 'From Neutrality to Alignment: Portugal in the Foundation of the Atlantic Pact'. *Luso-Brazilian Review* 29, no. 2 (Winter), 113–26.

— (1996), *O Poder e O Guerra, 1914–1918: Objectivos Nacionais e Estratégias na Grande Guerra*. Lisbon, Editorial Estampa.

Telo, António Jose (2000), *A Neutralidade Portuguesa e o Ouro Nazi*. Lisbon: Quetzal Editores.

— (2011), *História Contemporânea de Portugal: Do 25 de Abril à Actualidade*, Vol. 1. Lisbon: Editorial Presença.

— (1991), *Portugal na Segunda Guerra, 1941–1945*. 2 vols. Lisbon: Vega.

Thomas, Hugh (1990), *The Spanish Civil War*. London: Penguin.

Trabulo, António (2008), *O Diário de Salazar*. Lisbon: Parceira e A. M. Pereira.

Tremlett, Giles (2006), *Ghosts of Spain: Travels Through a Country's Hidden Past*. London: Faber and Faber.

Trevor-Roper, Hugh (1995), *The Last Days of Hitler*. London: Macmillan.

Truffaut, François (1994), *The Films In My Life*. New York: Da Capa Press.

Unger, Irwin and Debi Unger (2006), *The Guggenheims: A Family History*. New York: HarperPerennial.

Vail, Karole (ed.) (2009), *The Museum of Non-Objective Painting: Hila Rebay and the Origins of the Solomon R. Guggenheim Museum*. New York: Guggenheim Museum Publications.

Varela, Raquel (2014), *História do Povo na Revolução Portuguesa, 1974–75*. Lisbon: Bertrand Editora.

Vicente, Ana (1992), *Portugal Visto pela Espanha: Correspondência Diplomática, 1939–1960*. Lisbon: Assírio e Alvim.

Vieira, Joaquim (2013), *Álvaro Cunhal – O Homem e o Mito*. Carnaxide: Objectiva.

Walters, Guy (2010), *Hunting Evil*. London: Bantam Books.

Waugh, Evelyn (1985), *Labels: A Mediterranean Journal*. London: Penguin.

West, Nigel (1985), *MI6: British Secret Intelligence Service, 1909–45*. London: Panther.

West, Nigel and Juan Pujol Garcia (2011), *Operation Garbo: The Personal Story of the Most Successful Spy of World War II*. London: Biteback Publishing.

West, Nigel (ed.) (2005), *The Guy Liddell Diaries, Vols 1 and 2: 1939–1942*. London and New York: Routledge.

Wheeler, Douglas L. (1989), 'And Who Is My Neighbour? A World War II Hero of Conscience for Portugal'. *Luso-Brazilian Review* 26, no. 1 (Summer), 119–39.

— (1997), 'Fifty Years of Dictatorship by António Figueiredo' (review article). *The International Journal of African Historical Studies* 10, no. 3, 486–92.

— (1993), *Historical Dictionary of Portugal*. Metuchen, NJ, and London: Scarecrow Press.

— (1983), 'In the Service of Order: The Portuguese Secret Police and the British, German and Spanish Intelligence, 1932–1945'. *Journal of Contemporary History* 18, no. 1 (January), 107–27.

— (1978), *Republican Portugal: A Political History, 1910–1926*. Madison, WI: University of Wisconsin Press.

— (1986), 'The Price of Neutrality: Portugal and the Wolfram Question and World War II'. *Luso-Brazilian Review* 23, no. 1 (Summer), 107–27.

Wiarda, Howard J. and Margaret MacLeish Mott (2001), *Catholic Roots and Democratic Flowers: Political Systems in Spain and Portugal*. Westport and London: Praeger.

Wigg, Richard (2008), *Churchill and Spain: The Survival of the Franco Regime, 1940–1945*. Brighton and Portland: Sussex Academic Press.

Wilcken, Patrick (2004), *Empire Adrift: The Portuguese Court in Rio de Janeiro, 1808–1821*. London: Bloomsbury.

Wills, Clair (2007), *That Neutral Island: A Cultural History of Ireland during the Second World War*. London: Faber and Faber.

Wise, James E. Jr and Scott Baron (2002), *International Stars at War*. Annapolis: Naval Institute Press.

Woodward, Llewellyn (1962), *British Foreign Policy in the Second World War*. London: Her Majesty's Stationery Office.

Wriggins, William Howard (2004), *Picking Up the Pieces from Portugal to Palestine: Quaker Refugee Relief in World War II*. Lanham: University Press of America.

Wullschlager, Jackie (2010), *Chagall: Love and Exile*. London: Penguin.

Wylie, Neville (2001), 'An Amateur Learns His Job? Special Operations Executive in Portugal, 1940–1942'. *Journal of Contemporary History* 36, no. 3 (July), 441–57.

Ziegler, Philip (1990), *King Edward VIII: The Official Biography*. London: Collins.

Acknowledgements

The researching and writing of a non-fiction book is a long and, at times, a frustrating experience. Archival searches take time, patience and most importantly the help of dedicated staff. I was extremely fortunate to be able to spend a great deal of time in Lisbon in order to conduct the research for this book, as well as in London, Washington DC and New York. The book would not exist in its present form without the kind help and support that a number of individuals and archives gave me during the process of the research and writing of the book.

This book covers a more contemporary timeframe than my other recent books. As a result, I must start by thanking the relevant members of staff of the Foreign Office in London for dealing so professionally and promptly with my endless requests for documents to be released under the Freedom of Information Act. This book would not have been possible without the release of these documents, and I am extremely grateful to have received them.

I was able to visit several archives in Lisbon, some for the first time. As always, I would like to thank the staff at Torre do Tombo. The Portuguese National Archives remains one of my favourite archives in the world: it is full of hidden treasures of documents and photographs. The organization of the archive is world class and the staff dedicated to helping professional, and not so professional, researchers discover what they are looking for. At the Portuguese

Foreign Ministry Archives I am grateful to the staff for their guidance in this other great hidden treasure trove of an archive.

Discovering new archives is one of the great pleasures of my job. At the outset of this project João Céu e Silva was kind enough to extend to me an introduction to the archives of the Diário de Notícias in central Lisbon. The archive is outstanding and it was a great pleasure to conduct research in it. I particularly enjoyed looking at the original editions of *O Século*, which are kept in the archive. I would like to express my thanks to the head of the archive, Simões Dias and his staff for all their help.

Antonio Pina Falcau at the Arquivo Histórico da Presidencia da Republica, Patricia Diniz, Susana Rodrigues and all the team at the archive were extremely helpful in providing me with photographic material of the visits to Lisbon of overseas leaders. I would also like to thank Manuela Magalhaes and her staff at the Arquivo Histórico Parlamentar at the Assembleia da Republica, with special note of thanks for the kind assistance of Helena Medeiros. In Porto, at the Arquivo Histórico Municipal do Porto I would like to extend my grateful appreciation to Paula Cunha and her team. These archives hold important information and many great photographs of the period covered in this book.

I would also like to thank the British Council in Portugal for their help in identifying and providing a number of photographs of the British Royals and political leaders during their visits to Lisbon. And a special note of thanks to Carlos Alberto Damas at the Centro de História at Novo Banco for his continued support.

At the archives of Portugal's national airline TAP, I am once again extremely grateful for the generous assistance of Adelina Arezes and her staff, who were kind enough to provide me with some rarely seen photographs of the arrival and departure of many of the personalities who are featured in the book. It is a shame that the position of an official photographer at airports no longer exists. In this world of smartphones, selfies and Instagram the art of formal 'arrival and departure' photography has seemingly vanished for ever.

In Estoril, along the Lisbon coast, I must thank Francisco Corrêa de Barros, Manuel Guedes de Sousa and the staff at the

Hotel Palacio. The archive, while in need of formal cataloguing to preserve it for the future, has proven to be a great source of information on the Royals and international celebrities who stayed in Lisbon during the period. The Hotel Palacio remains today one of the great luxury hotel icons of the Lisbon coast, retaining many of its original features.

In London, the staff at the Public Records Office (National Archives) in Kew were, as ever, very helpful and enthusiastic in directing me to the huge wealth of documentary material on Portugal between 1974 and 1984. The 30-year rule meant that I could get no further in my research than the first ten years covered in this book, and I look forward to returning to the files when new documents on Portugal are released each January.

In the United States, at the US National Archives at College Park in Maryland, I am extremely grateful to the staff who assisted me in locating the files I needed in order to write this book. The continued lack of a good centralized computer system in the archive made the help provided by the team there absolutely invaluable. There is much valuable material on Portugal located across the various series of civilian and military records held in the archive. And over on the west coast of the United States, in Hollywood, I must give a special note of thanks to Kevin Cleary at Pooka Entertainment for his support and enthusiasm for my books on Portugal and Brazil.

It has been an enormous pleasure working with my editor Robin Baird-Smith, Jamie Birkett and the team at Bloomsbury in both London and New York. It has been a pleasure dealing with such a professional publisher.

Thanks must also go to Matt Freeman, who continues to do a fantastic job of helping to develop and evolve my website.

At University College London, I would like to thank my colleague Michael Berkowitz for his endless enthusiasm for all things photographic and Portuguese. Sacha Stern, Helen Beer, François Guesnet, Lily Kahn, Tsila Ratner, Willem Smelik, Belinda Stojanovic and Lia Kahn-Zejtmann are all wonderfully supportive colleagues.

I am lucky enough to work in a department of different disciplines, and one that has ancient and modern historians. There is a great deal that we learn from one another. University College London continues to allow us to follow our research interests. As always, I am extremely grateful to David Lewis for continuing to financially support my position at the college.

On a personal note, I would like to thank my friends for their support, and for understanding why I disappeared for long periods of time during the various stages of the book. And finally, but most important of all, I owe a huge debt of gratitude to my family for their continued support: to my mother, and my parents-in-law Patrick and Gillian Castle-Stewart. A big debt of gratitude must also go to my wife, Emma, and my children, Benjamin and Hélèna. Emma, as well as being my wife and mother to my children, is my agent, conducts photographic research, curates my exhibitions, reads my manuscripts, manages my website and books, and organizes my talks. This book would not have been possible without her. My children were fantastic in knowing when to let Daddy get on with his writing tasks.

Many of these people have helped me not only on this book, but also on my first two books about Lisbon. It has been a great pleasure working with my Portuguese friends in Lisbon and its surroundings, and during 2014–15 I have found enormous satisfaction in conducting the research for this book. Portuguese archives are some of the friendliest that I have come across in my travels around the world. Portugal is a country with a rich history and it is vital that the story of this nation is preserved and that the public uses these wonderful archives to learn more about the country.

Index

About the Author

Neill Lochery is a world-renowned source on the politics and modern history of Europe, Israel and the Mediterranean Middle East. He is the Catherine Lewis Professor of Middle Eastern and Mediterranean Studies at University College London, where he has been based since 1997.

Coupled with his ongoing research and teaching at UCL, over the past decade Neill has served as an advisor to several political leaders and heads of state, giving expert insight on Europe and the Mediterranean Middle East. He also provides consultancy to major international companies on a broad range of topics, from risk assessments on the Middle East to more bespoke consultancy pieces.

As well as giving a number of private and public seminars each year, Neill is a frequent contributor to newspapers. He has had op-ed and commentary articles published in the *Wall Street Journal*, the *National Post* (Canada), *Chicago Sun-Times*, *Jerusalem Post*, *Scotsman*, *New York Sun*, *Washington Post* and *United Press International*.

Neill is married with two children, and divides his time between London, Portugal, the Middle East and the United States.

www.neill-lochery.com.

Twitter: @NeillLochery

A Note on the Type

The text of this book is set in Adobe Garamond. It is one of several versions of Garamond based on the designs of Claude Garamond. It is thought that Garamond based his font on Bembo, cut in 1495 by Francesco Griffo in collaboration with the Italian printer Aldus Manutius. Garamond types were first used in books printed in Paris around 1532. Many of the present-day versions of this type are based on the *Typi Academiae* of Jean Jannon cut in Sedan in 1615.

Claude Garamond was born in Paris in 1480. He learned how to cut type from his father and by the age of fifteen he was able to fashion steel punches the size of a pica with great precision. At the age of sixty he was commissioned by King Francis I to design a Greek alphabet, and for this he was given the honourable title of royal type founder. He died in 1561.